TOWARD FAIR EMPLOYMENT

TOWARD
FAIR EMPLOYMENT

by PAUL H. NORGREN

and SAMUEL E. HILL

with the assistance of F. RAY MARSHALL

COLUMBIA UNIVERSITY PRESS
New York and London 1964

A PROJECT OF THE INDUSTRIAL RELATIONS SECTION
PRINCETON UNIVERSITY

PAUL H. NORGREN is Project Director and SAM-
UEL E. HILL is Associate in Research of the Research Project on Minority Group Employment
of the Industrial Relations Section.

FOREWORD

The study *Toward Fair Employment* was undertaken by the Industrial Relations Section of Princeton University with a grant from the Taconic Foundation of New York. The authors, Paul H. Norgren and Samuel E. Hill, carried out the research with the assistance of a Project Advisory Committee composed of the undersigned.

We feel that this book is an important contribution to knowledge on the problems of providing equal employment opportunities in the United States. In the years ahead, when this country will be engaged in what we hope will be a final national effort to grant the Negro his full political and civil rights, the administrative arm of government at the local, state, and Federal levels will surely have a vital role to play. This study should help those who will be responsible for structuring and implementing government administrative actions at all levels.

When the manpower stringencies of World War II brought the issue of equal employment opportunity to the fore, President Roosevelt, making use of his war powers, established the Committee on Fair Employment Practice to assist in opening jobs, training, and promotion opportunities to members of minority groups. At the end of the War, Congress refused to make the Committee permanent and passed the Russell Amendment, which prohibited the President from allocating funds to executive agencies whose budgets had not been previously approved by Congress, thus setting a framework within which the Executive Branch was thenceforth constrained in seeking changes.

The question may properly be asked whether the modest accomplishments of the several Presidential committees are to be ascribed solely to the hamstringing conditions set up by Congressional restraint. The authors of this book, in their critical appraisal

of fifteen years of these committees, provide a basis for answering
this question. While the Russell Amendment has much to answer
for, the limited effectiveness of these administrative efforts cannot
be explained solely by Congressional restrictions.

On the surface, the authors' account of the experience of state
and local fair employment and human rights commissions tells a
different story. These commissions, without exception, were established through legislative action. There is no apparent, and
surely no continuing, conflict between the legislative and the administrative branches of government in these areas. And yet if we
follow carefully what the authors have to report, we find a dis-
turbing parallel. In all too many instances, the state and local commissions have been given broad responsibility but have not been
provided with the resources in money or manpower which would
make it possible for them to show solid accomplishment. Once
again, the authors' review of what these commissions have been
able to do—as well as of their failures—can provide a balanced
judgment of the strengths and weaknesses of the administrative
framework within which these agencies operate.

While the study is principally concerned with appraising governmental fair employment agencies at the Federal, state, and local
levels, it does more than this. The earlier chapters include an in-
cisive account of the major trends in the larger economy that affect the demand for minority manpower and consider the role of
managements and unions in this process. A subsequent chapter examines the significant progress made by Negroes in Federal government employment in recent years, both in the armed forces and
in the civilian agencies.

Viewing the main analysis in the setting of these supporting
chapters, it might appear that the authors have focused on one of
the less important facets of their subject. We learn that while governmental fair employment measures can expedite the process, the
essential key to full employment equality for racial minorities is to

be found in changing labor market behavior and in equalization of educational opportunities.

However, it is the virtue of a good study that it clarifies the significance of the factors and forces which it assesses. The Norgren-Hill study shows that the administrative approach to equal employment opportunity as developed during the post–World War II period has severe limitations. It none the less concludes from the state and local commission experience that this approach, if backed by proper legislation and with adequate financing and a major reorientation of administrative policy and practice, can yield substantial positive results. In the search for successful strategies, new knowledge that differentiates promising from unpromising alternatives can prove profoundly important.

The authors have set out the prerequisites for an effective legislative and administrative attack on the problem. Of course, even the best-structured commission, with adequate resources, cannot alone transform the employment and economic position of a minority group. But it can contribute to such a change. And the ways in which it can do so are clearly delineated in the present study.

It is always risky to prognosticate how the history of one's own period will appear in the perspective of time, but there is little risk in stipulating that President Kennedy's Second Civil Rights Message of June, 1963, marked a turning point in race relations in the United States. Surely it set the stage for a marked change in the role of the Federal government. Against the changes that are to come—and that must come if the United States is to stop wasting the manpower resources of the Negro community and thereby jeopardizing its democratic commitment to itself and to the other nations of the free world—the present study points to the many powerful instruments and instrumentalities that will have to be employed.

A democratic society can progress only as it learns to make more effective use of all its instruments, public and private, in every domain. The authors have summed up in a clear and concise fashion the experience that our nation has had with one such instrument—administrative action by government—during the two post–World War II decades.

Dr. Norgren has been working in the area of minority manpower ever since he assisted Gunnar Myrdal in preparing his classic study, *An American Dilemma*, in the early 1940s. With others, he was an author of a volume on *Employing the Negro in American Industry* in the late 1950s. Throughout two decades he has maintained a continuing interest and concern with these issues. Dr. Hill, a former member of the staff of the Industrial Relations Section, is a labor economist who has had extensive experience in the government service and is the coauthor of *Manpower and Innovation in American Industry*, which was published by the Industrial Relations Section in 1959. Both have been actively concerned for many years with the movement to develop and insure fair employment practices.

We join in expressing appreciation for the substantial help and active encouragement of those persons mentioned specifically by the authors in their acknowledgments.

ELI GINZBERG
Director, Conservation of Human Resources Project,
Columbia University

FREDERICK HARBISON
Director, Industrial Relations Section,
Princeton University

RICHARD A. LESTER
Chairman, Department of Economics
Princeton University

Princeton, New Jersey
February 15, 1964

ACKNOWLEDGMENTS

We wish to thank all those whose support and cooperation have enabled us to carry this study to completion. We are especially indebted to Stephen R. Currier, Jane Lee Eddy, and Lloyd K. Garrison of the Taconic Foundation for making the project possible, and for valued counsel and encouragement throughout its course. We are also deeply grateful to the members of the Project Advisory Committee for helpful guidance and advice at every stage of the preparation.

Our principal collaborator was F. Ray Marshall of the University of Texas, who prepared a comprehensive research memorandum on the racial practices of labor organizations, based on his studies in this area over an extended period of years. Dr. Marshall's memorandum formed the factual basis for Chapter 3 ("Union Racial Practices") and Chapter 9 ("Alternatives to Fair Employment Legislation").

Two other scholars in the field of minority group employment, Herman B. Bloch of Cornell University and Emory F. Via of the University of Wisconsin, prepared research memoranda on particular problem areas of the study. Professor Bloch's report dealt with racial practices of building trades unions in New York City. Professor Via reported on current racial practices in a wide range of industrial and commercial establishments in Atlanta.

The following individuals read the manuscript in its original form and made helpful comments and suggestions, either verbally at a conference held in New York on May 2, 1963, or in the form of written memoranda: Carl Auerbach, University of Minnesota; John A. Davis, City College of New York; Walter G. Davis, AFL-CIO; John Feild, Potomac Institute; Harold Fleming, Potomac Institute; Herbert Hill, National Association for the Advancement of Colored People; Adolph Holmes, National Urban League; Arthur Levin, Potomac Institute; Will Maslow, American Jewish Congress; George Schermer, Philadelphia Commission on Human Relations; Shirley Adelson Siegel, New York State Department of Law; Michael Sovern, Columbia University; William Taylor, United States Commission on Civil Rights.

We take this opportunity to acknowledge the cooperation extended to us by various government agencies and private organizations during the research stage of the study. The following Federal agencies were especially helpful: the President's Committee on Government Contracts, the President's Committee on Equal Employment Opportunity, the Department of Defense, the General Services Administration, the Atomic Energy Commission, the Bureau of the Census, and the Bureau of Labor Statistics. The state and municipal agencies that also merit special mention are the Baltimore Equal Employment Opportunity Commission, the California Fair Employment Practice Commission, the Connecticut Commission on Civil Rights, the Massachusetts Commission Against Discrimination, the Michigan Fair Employment Practices Commission, the New Jersey State Department of Education, the New York State Commission for Human Rights, the Ohio Civil Rights Commission, the Oregon State Bureau of Labor, the Pennsylvania Commission on Human Relations, the Philadelphia Commission on Human Relations, and the Washington State Board Against Discrimination. Of the private organizations that furnished valuable information, special acknowledgment is due the National Association for the Advancement of Colored People; the National Urban League and its affiliated local branches in Baltimore, Louisville, New Orleans, St. Louis, and Washington, D.C.; the American Jewish Congress; the Board of Home Missions of the Congregational Christian Churches; the Jewish Labor Committee; and the Southern Regional Council.

While it would be impractical to cite all of the individuals who contributed from their knowledge and experience during the research phase of the project, we wish to express our special appreciation to John Bushnell, New York State Commission for Human Rights; John Hope, II, and David Mann, President's Committee on Equal Employment Opportunity; David Kaplan, U.S. Bureau of the Census; Frederick Routh, National Association of Intergroup Relations Officials; Oscar Smith, U.S. Atomic Energy Commission; and the Reverend Jerome Toner, St. Martin's College.

Finally, we wish to thank Nellie Offutt, Administrative Assistant in the Section, for her efficient management of the accounts and finances of the study; and Barbara Clarke and Selma Weitz for typing the manuscript through its several drafts.

While gratefully acknowledging our debt to all those mentioned and to many others, we of course assume sole responsibility for any errors of fact or interpretation in this volume.

PAUL H. NORGREN
SAMUEL E. HILL

Stamford, Connecticut
February 15, 1964

CONTENTS

*Part Three. A Program for Public Fair Employment
Policy and Action*

TOWARD FAIR EMPLOYMENT

1

INTRODUCTION

The disadvantages suffered by racial, religious, and ethnic minorities in the competition for jobs and steady work have been a subject of increasing public concern in this country over the past twenty-five years. During this period numerous Federal, state, and local government agencies have been established for the purpose of combating job discrimination and promoting equal employment opportunity for all persons and groups. The efforts of these agencies have been directed principally toward ending discrimination against Negroes, by long odds the nation's largest and most disadvantaged minority.

Despite the proliferation of such agencies, however, and despite the significant results achieved by a few of the longer-established state and local bodies, racial inequality in employment over the country as a whole has not been substantially reduced. Moreover, the Negro's discontent with the treatment accorded him in the job market, far from diminishing, has steadily increased throughout the period.

With the recent rise of a massive protest movement among the nation's Negroes, the spread of the revolt against job discrimination has reached an all-time high. This movement, which actually began with several sporadic group actions in the middle 1950s but did not take on the character of a mass uprising until five years later, is unique in American social history. Taking their cue from four Negro students occupying stools at a "whites only" lunch counter in Greensboro, North Carolina, in February, 1960, Negro groups in hundreds of Southern and Northern communities have engaged in sit-ins, picketings, marches, boycotts, and other demonstrations of passive rebellion against the inequities and indignities under which they are forced to live. It is a truly spontaneous movement, stemming from a deep-rooted sense of injustice in the hearts of millions of deprived citizens. From all present indications it will not abate until these millions can see tangible evidence of a fairer deal at hand and a better day in store.

The mass protests have been directed against discriminatory treatment in all phases of daily life—in education, in voting, in housing, in public accommodations and recreational facilities, and elsewhere. Discrimination in employment, however, has been the predominant target from the outset. It has been a major motivating factor, even when the declared objective of the demonstrations has been the removal of racial barriers in other areas.

It is not difficult to understand why revolt against job inequality is the principal driving force behind the Negro protest movement. Negro workers, when employed, commonly occupy the heaviest, dirtiest, most menial, lowest-paid, and generally least desirable jobs. They are unemployed more than twice as often as white workers and for longer periods of time. As the combined consequence of low-paid employment and frequent joblessness, the average Negro family's income is barely more than half that of the average white family. Thus, of all the forms of inequality to which the Negro group is subjected, job discrimination is more widely experienced, and its impact more constantly and acutely felt, than any other.

The wide geographical dispersion of the Negro protest activities points up the fact that employment discrimination exists in all sections of the country, despite efforts in some sections, by a variety of governmental fair employment practice (FEP) agencies, to combat discrimination. More than two decades after the creation of the first Federal and state antibias agencies, the movement to assure equal job opportunities to minority groups is still a woefully inadequate and regionally limited attempt to deal with a problem manifestly national in scope and importance. The current Federal effort, like its predecessors, is based on a Presidential executive order and is handicapped both by limited coverage and by a lack of effective means of implementation and enforcement. While twenty-two states have fully enforceable FEP laws, very few of the administering commissions are supplied with adequate funds and staff to deal effectively with the problem. In the states lacking such laws, discrimination continues unimpeded, except for the scattered Federal contract situations that come to the attention of the Presidential committee.

Yet, despite the inadequacy of the current measures, the fact that a beginning attempt has been made to deal with the problem of employment discrimination is of considerable significance. In addition to the successive Federal executive orders, ten of the enforceable state laws have been in effect for a decade or more; and the agencies charged with administering these orders and laws have accumulated a substantial body of experience over the past twenty years.

The prospect that exploration and analysis of this experience might prove useful for more effective policy and action in the future provided the primary impetus for undertaking the study reported upon in this book. The decision to proceed with the study was made following a preliminary review of existing literature and available statistical data relating to the problem. This review yielded considerable evidence indicating that enforceable governmental measures are necessary if meaningful reduction in job discrimination is to be achieved. An examination of the decennial Census statistics on employment showed that Negroes have failed to make appreciable occupational progress over the past fifty years, except during periods of stringent labor shortage. Published accounts of experience under various non-enforceable state and municipal FEP laws and voluntary local programs indicated that these measures had uniformly failed to bring any significant improvement. Records of legal actions seeking to halt discriminatory practices of unions by invoking existing Federal labor laws revealed that these efforts had likewise ended in failure.

Several published monographs and articles dealing with enforceable state FEP laws were available, but only one of these attempted any appraisal of experience under this type of legislation. This study, published in 1952 and confined to the New York State Law Against Discrimination, concluded that the law had reduced the amount of discrimination and had opened new job opportunities to members of minority groups in the state.[1] This finding could hardly be considered conclusive evidence of the effectiveness of FEP legislation, since it was based on only six years of experience under a single state law. An assessment of all available relevant information revealed, however, that many progressive leaders in business and organized labor, as well as in government, considered public measures, based on voluntary compliance but with ultimate recourse to enforcement sanctions, to be the most practicable means of promoting equal treatment for minorities in the job market and the work place. The only important source of disagreement among these leaders was on the question of whether legislation as such is necessary or whether the objective can be achieved equally well through mandates from the executive arm of government.

Conduct of the Study

It was decided at the outset to confine the study of the results of fair employment measures to their effect on Negroes, rather than attempt to assess their impact on all disadvantaged minorities. This was done with full realization that a number of other minorities, including Mexican-Americans, Puerto Ricans, Orientals, Indians, Jews, and various southern and eastern European ethnic groups are also subject to considerable discrimination in employment. The decision to focus on the Negro group was based on two main considerations: it was by far the largest minority subject to pervasive employment discrimination, and it was the only

[1] Berger, *Equality by Statute*, p. 164.

group for which relevant factual information on a significant scale was obtainable. The experience records and other data available from state and municipal FEP commissions were confined largely to activities involving Negro workers; and the same was true of the several successive Federal agencies established to combat employment discrimination. Furthermore, the only minority group classifications in the Federal Census statistics on employment are racial and color classifications, which do not include such groups as Mexican-Americans and Puerto Ricans; and much of this information is confined to the "nonwhite" classification, which can be given meaningful interpretation only if it is equated with "Negro." Focusing on the Negro group, therefore, was the only feasible procedure.

In view of the strong presumption that governmental policy and action is a prerequisite to effective promotion of racial equality in employment, it was further decided to focus the study on the question of what kind of public measures and agencies will best meet the need. For purposes of conducting research into the accumulated experience under Federal orders and state and municipal laws, the question was reformulated as a pair of interrelated objectives. We attempted, first, to gauge the effect—if any—that each of the measures and agencies studied has had in abating racial discrimination in employment and, second, to determine whether the indicated differences in effectiveness among them could be attributed to particular features of particular measures or to the organization and functioning of particular administering agencies.

In the course of the field research, we examined in detail the mandates, practices, and experience of twenty FEP agencies, including the seven former and currently functioning Federal committees, the ten longest established state commissions, and three of the major municipal commissions.[2] The exploratory work was

2 The state laws and commissions studied in detail were those of New York, New Jersey, Massachusetts, Connecticut, Pennsylvania, Ohio, Michigan, California, Oregon, and Washington. The cities included in the detailed survey were Philadelphia, Cleveland, and Baltimore.

conducted largely through interviews with committee and commission members and staff officials and with other knowledgeable
persons in the several states and cities as well as in Washington
and through examination of both published and unpublished records of the agencies studied. The state information was supplemented by annual reports and other publications issued by the
commissions in most of the remaining states with FEP laws. Information concerning racial employment practices of managements
was available from an earlier survey conducted by one of the
authors and from other published studies. Another member of the
study team prepared a comprehensive report on racial practices of
labor unions, based on his extensive research in this area over the
past several years, for use as a source document in the preparation
of this volume. The results of the field research were analyzed in
the light of the aforementioned information on prevalent management and union racial practices and of recent trends in the occupational status of Negroes as revealed by the Federal Census statistics
on employment.

Plan of the Book

In sequence of presentation, the book follows the course pursued in developing the study. The three ensuing chapters deal
with the institutional nature of employment discrimination and
its adverse effects on the Negro group. The principal types of
employment discrimination, as manifested in the practices of managements that maintain racial distinctions in their work forces, are
described in Chapter 2, as are also the procedures of employment
agencies that collaborate with discriminatory managements. The
management practices are confined mainly to four functional areas:
recruitment, hiring and placement, training, and promotion. Chapter 2 also examines the experience of a number of firms, both in
the North and the South, in introducing and implementing a policy
of racial equality and establishing integrated work forces.

The discriminatory practices engaged in by some labor unions and the adverse effects of these practices on employment opportunities for Negroes are dealt with in Chapter 3. The two most prevalent practices are exclusion of Negroes from membership by local unions in certain skilled crafts and discrimination in referring Negro members for employment by locals in certain other craft and various noncraft occupations.

Chapter 4 traces the long-term and recent trends in the employment of Negroes and gives an overview of their employment and occupational status at the present time, relative to the white majority. The analysis of trends shows that, while the Negro group has made appreciable occupational progress during wartime periods of stringent labor shortage, in other periods it has made little or no progress. The overview of the Negro's present employment status provides a basis for assessing the current extent and nature of employment discrimination over the country as a whole and of certain significant differences between the North and the South in this regard. In concluding this first phase of the presentation, we point out that the widespread racial practices of managements and unions and the motivations on which they are based are the main causal factors behind the Negro group's failure to make significant occupational progress under the normal operation of the labor market.

The next five chapters present the results of the intensive study of governmental antidiscrimination measures and agencies which constituted the major phase of the project. Chapters 5 and 6 are concerned with the FEP laws now operative in two-fifths of the states and in several major cities. The essential substantive provisions of these laws and the powers, duties, and procedures of the commissions charged with their enforcement are set forth in Chapter 5. Chapter 6 examines the experience of the longest-established commissions in administering the respective statutes over periods of twelve to fifteen years. The successful compliance efforts of the New York State commission and certain other state agencies in a number of "all-white" industries and the subsequent growth of Negro employment in these industries are reviewed and assessed. These agencies' efforts—considerably less successful—in dealing with noncomplying employment agencies and labor unions are also discussed in some detail. Finally, the causal relationships between the notable results achieved by the New York Commission in dealing with employers and the Commission's unique approach and procedures in conducting employer-related compliance activities are examined and appraised.

The experience under the five successive Presidential committees charged with enforcing the nondiscrimination clause in Federal procurement contracts is recounted and analyzed in Chapter 7. The analysis indicates that the earlier committees did not effect any significant abatement of employment discrimination. The currently functioning committee, however, has a somewhat better record of accomplishment. The counterpart experience under the executive orders barring discrimination in the armed services and in Federal civilian employment is dealt with in Chapter 8. Substantially greater racial integration has been achieved in these two areas than in government contract employment, largely because the President has direct executive authority over both the armed services and the civilian agencies of the Federal government.

Chapter 9 discusses the pros and cons of the Federal labor relations laws and certain other measures as possible alternatives to FEP legislation. The analysis of experience under the National Labor Relations Act and the Railway Labor Act shows that neither of these laws affords Negroes any meaningful remedies against discriminatory treatment by labor unions or by employers. The discussion of proposals for various types of indirect legal sanctions as antidiscrimination enforcement devices indicates that these measures would be more cumbersome and less effective than those provided for in existing FEP laws. A similar conclusion is reached regarding certain proposals for encouraging fair employment through government subsidies. Finally, it is concluded that boycotts aimed at obtaining more and better jobs for Negroes are very limited in scope and are a highly uncertain substitute for enforceable FEP legislation.

The major findings adduced in the detailed presentation are brought together and coordinated in Chapter 10, and their implications for improving existing fair employment measures and for developing new and more effective approaches to the problem are discussed. Finally, in Chapters 11 and 12, the conclusions and implications emanating from the study are translated into a proposed program for public policy and action, designed to aid leaders at all levels of government in formulating and administering legislation that will foster affirmative efforts by employers, unions, and employment agencies to bring about genuine racial equality in the allocation of jobs.

Major Conclusions

The principal conclusions on which the recommendations for public policy and action are based can be summarized as follows:

Enforceable legislation along the lines of existing state FEP laws, but with appropriate revision of certain substantive and procedural features, constitutes the most effective approach to combating racial discrimination in employment.

A comprehensive Federal law, designed along these lines and applicable to all employment affecting interstate commerce, would provide the most effective specific instrument for dealing with the problem. State laws would still be needed, however, in all states having sizable racial minorities to deal with discrimination in intrastate employment. With appropriate cooperative arrangements between the Federal administering commission and the counterpart state agencies, the respective jurisdictions could be readily delineated. It appears likely that extension of enforceable FEP legislation to certain cities in the South may be feasible before it becomes politically practicable in any Southern state.

To make existing and future state laws as well as the proposed Federal law more effective, the statutory powers of the administering commissions should be extended to enable them (1) to deal with complaints of discriminatory practices filed by organizations (as well as complaints by aggrieved individuals), (2) to initiate and deal with complaints on their own motion, and (3) under either of these types of complaint, to deal with general patterns of discriminatory practices on the part of employers, employment agencies, or labor unions (as well as with discrimination against specific individuals).

The makeup of existing state commissions should be strengthened (1) by providing that commission members serve on a full-time basis, (2) by appointing as commission members the most highly qualified persons obtainable, particularly in terms of talent and experience in the crucially important function of promoting compliance through conciliation, (3) by providing for salaries for commission members commensurate with these qualifications, and (4) by providing for sufficient professional, administrative, and clerical staffs to enable the commissions to function in an effective manner. To make these improvements possible, it will be necessary to appropriate for the respective commissions substantially larger operating funds than they are currently receiving. These criteria should also be followed in establishing future state commissions as well as the proposed Federal commission.

To abate the anomalous racial discrimination that persists in the functioning of public employment offices in all sections of the country, the U.S. Employment Service (USES) should establish a mandatory policy prohibiting discrimination in the staffing and operation of these offices and prescribing as the penalty for violation the forfeiture of Federal operating funds. The USES should also discard its present formula for allocating these funds to local offices and adopt a formula that will encourage nondiscriminatory referrals. The local offices in turn should cooperate with FEP commissions (if any) in their states by reporting all discriminatory employer requests for workers to the commissions.

Existing and future commissions should direct their efforts to the greatest extent possible toward eliminating over-all patterns of discriminatory practices pervading entire firms, employment agencies, or labor unions and should plan and program these pattern-centered compliance efforts over a period of years. In conducting these efforts, they should pursue a policy of seeking commitments from noncomplying employers to take affirmative compliance action by employing Negroes in jobs from which they have previously been excluded and should conduct periodic follow-up surveys of racial employment patterns in all employing establishments and unions involved in compliance actions. In dealing with unusually resistant firms, employment agencies, or unions, the commissions should avoid prolonged conciliation efforts and proceed instead to hold public hearings at an early stage and, where warranted, issue orders requiring the recalcitrant organizations to comply affirmatively with the fair employment statute.

Finally, it is necessary to note that the benefits that would accrue to Negroes and other minorities if the above suggestions were adopted would be rather limited in scope and degree, at least over the near future. The potentialities for improving the employment status of Negroes through well-designed and effectively administered FEP legislation are essentially short-run in character and limited mainly to lower- and middle-level occupations. There is little prospect that extension and improvement of FEP laws would bring more than minor gains in managerial, professional, and other upper-level jobs, since very few Negro workers currently in, or soon to enter, the labor force possess the educational qualifications required for these occupations. Substantial progress in the higher echelons will not be possible until equal educational opportunities at all levels are accessible to Negroes and even then cannot be realized unless and until Negro children in significant numbers avail themselves of these opportunities. In short, the practical possibilities of achieving equal educational status lie considerably farther in the future than the prospects for extending and improving FEP legislation.

This long-range problem area is largely, though not entirely, outside the scope of the present study. The decision to concentrate attention on the nearer and more limited potentialities for improvement was made with full cognizance of the importance of the longer-range issue. Since, however, the available time and resources did not permit dealing with both, the logical choice lay with the more urgent short-run problem.

There is, nevertheless, an undeniable need for a comprehensive study of the problems involved in establishing equal educational opportunities for the Negro minority, since this eventuation is clearly necessary to the ultimate attainment of full occupational and economic equality. It is our hope that such a study can be undertaken in the near future.

PART ONE

Employment Discrimination and Racial Inequality

2

MANAGEMENT RACIAL PRACTICES

The economic progress of Negroes has been affected by employer attitudes and practices on racial matters, which in turn have been determined largely by prevailing attitudes toward Negroes in the dominant white community. The racial practices of public and private employment agencies frequently reflect employer practices. In this chapter we summarize some of the more common management and employment agency practices which impede the economic progress of Negroes. The chapter also summarizes certain management efforts to improve the occupational status of Negroes and indicates under what circumstances such programs are apt to be adopted and their probable success.

Discrimination by Management

Though discrimination in employment is now somewhat less frequent and certainly less overt than it was ten or twenty years ago, it still persists. At one extreme are the employers who do not hire Negroes in any capacity and take few pains to hide the fact that they do not intend to do so. At the opposite extreme are the employers who have gone to some lengths to encourage Negroes to apply for employment and make certain that they are accorded equal opportunity once they have been employed. The great bulk of employers fall between such extremes and display a mixture of discriminatory and nondiscriminatory behavior. Examination of establishment employment patterns, by race and occupation, gives the clearest indications of the results of employer practices. The existence of discrimination can frequently be inferred from such data, though such data alone are not acceptable as proof of discrimination under any of the existing FEP laws.

Company employment practices are usually more important than formal company policies in determining Negro access to desirable jobs. Discrimination can occur at any stage in the employment process, but is most common in the areas of recruitment, hiring, assignment, promotion, and training.

RECRUITMENT

Recruitment practices that result in exclusion of Negroes from employment are common. Some are intended to exclude Negroes altogether or to maintain a given racial quota or distribution by occupation. Others not in themselves discriminatory lead just as surely to Negro exclusion. Among the common deliberately discriminatory devices are understandings with personnel of private or public employment agencies to refer prospective employees from specified racial groups, identification of race on pre-employment application forms, and coding of such forms to indicate race of applicants. Southern employers frequently restrict their recruitment efforts to segregated white schools or colleges, while Northern employers may try to draw employees from schools located in predominantly white neighborhoods or from colleges where few Negroes are enrolled. Recruitment of new employees from the ranks of relatives and friends of present employees is a very common practice that tends to perpetuate existing racial employment patterns. Use of union hiring halls or referral systems results in discrimination if Negroes encounter difficulty in securing admission to the union or in securing referral to jobs once they have become members.

The state FEP commissions that possess enforcement powers have had some success in compelling employers and employment agencies to abandon such overtly discriminatory practices as the specification of race in "Help Wanted" newspaper advertisements and the coding of pre-employment application forms. They have been much less successful in dealing with informal understandings between employment agencies and employer personnel offices. Only in two states—New York and Wisconsin—are public employment offices required to report discriminatory requests for workers to the state's FEP commission. In the remaining FEP-law states, the employment service officials have refused to cooperate with the FEP agencies, with the result that the acceptance and honoring of discriminatory job orders is still a common occurrence in these states, as well as in states having no FEP laws.

The effect of recruiting new employees from friends of present employees can be illustrated by an example from the steel industry. A number of Negroes complained to a state FEP commission that a certain Northern steel mill would not hire them as laborers because of their race. The company denied that it practiced discrimination and sought to show that the qualifications of the rejected Negro applicants were inferior to those of white applicants hired for work as laborers during the same period. The commission's investigation revealed, however, that nearly all the white persons hired as laborers had been recommended by relatives, friends, or labor union officials, most of whom were past or present company employees, whereas no recommendations appeared opposite the names of any of the rejected Negro applicants. The case files of state commissions indicate that giving preference in hiring to applicants referred by present employees is a common practice in many areas of employment. Obviously, such practices tend to perpetuate existing racial employment patterns.

HIRING AND WORK ASSIGNMENT

Complaints of refusals to hire because of race are far more common than any other type of complaint received by fair employment commissions. Two considerations indicate why this has been the case. The rejected applicant has nothing to lose by filing a complaint, but those who have employment of some kind may hesitate to file complaints for fear of reprisals. Furthermore, persons who suffer discrimination in the recruitment process are usually unaware of the discrimination they have in fact encountered.

Refusal to employ Negroes for *any* type of work is rare, but restriction of newly hired Negroes to a range of unskilled or semi-skilled jobs traditionally regarded as suitable for them is still common practice. For example, it was long a practice in Southern petroleum refineries to hire Negroes only for work in departments composed of laborers. Promotion from these departments was all but impossible for Negroes. Some years ago a number of refineries agreed to change their practices and permit Negroes in their labor departments who had finished high school to bid for jobs in operating and maintenance departments. Very few Negroes could qualify for promotion under the new policy because they had been hired in the expectation that they would never be promoted from the labor departments, and for this reason few of them were high school graduates. At the same time, companies began to insist on a high school certificate from Negroes seeking entrance to their labor departments, but hired whites who had not completed high school for employment in operating and maintenance departments. Under such arrangements almost no change in racial employment patterns could occur. Such hiring practices can be preserved in countless ways ranging from the overtly discriminatory to covert use of double standards.

Foremen and other supervisors who reflect racial prejudices in their day-to-day employment decisions frequently engage in discriminatory practices and perpetuate existing racial employment patterns. Such actions can be quite successful in excluding Negroes from employment unless there is careful review of foreman decisions by representatives of management or by FEP commissions. In the steel plant mentioned above, for example, more than one-third of the departments had no Negro employees and about two-thirds of all Negroes employed by the firm were found in two departments where the work was particularly arduous and disagreeable.

PROMOTION

Negroes frequently encounter even greater difficulty in securing promotions on the job than in obtaining initial employment. In many firms Negroes are employed only in unskilled occupations or in departments where such positions predominate. Once employed in such capacities, they are likely to be overlooked when promotions are made unless a rigorously fair system governs bidding for promotions. The problem is illustrated by another complaint filed against a Northern steel mill. A group of Negroes employed in the labor department of the mill complained to a state fair employment commission that they were seldom loaned out to other departments and therefore had no opportunity to acquire skills that would qualify them for promotions when permanent openings occurred in these departments. Upon investigation it was found that the allegations were substantially correct and that discrimination by the turn foreman, who selected employees to be loaned to other departments, was responsible for the condition. It had become customary to loan Negroes from the labor department only to certain departments where Negroes predominated or to fill certain jobs that were looked upon as "Negro jobs" in departments otherwise dominated by whites.

In most Southern plants Negroes are employed in segregated labor and "service" departments. Where the plants are unionized, they are frequently debarred by the terms of the labor agreements from transferring to production or maintenance departments. In the rare instances where such transfers are permitted, the Negro employees can do so only at the cost of forfeiting all their accumulated seniority. Yet transfers provide the only avenue of escape from employment in unskilled and menial jobs.

ADMISSION TO TRAINING PROGRAMS

Employers engage in a wide variety of training programs, and participation in them is an increasingly important determinant of employee prospects for promotion. Negroes frequently encounter difficulty in securing admission to such programs. For example, much publicity has been given to the exclusion of Negroes from apprenticeship programs jointly sponsored by unions and managements. In 1950, only 1.7 percent of all apprentices were Negro, and Negro apprentices tended to be concentrated in occupations such as bricklaying, where Negroes have been employed in significant numbers for many years. Less than 1 percent of all apprentices in the electrical, plumbing, and pipefitting occupations, where discrimination has been particularly common, were Negro.[1] In 1960, about 2.2 percent of all apprentices were Negro.[2]

Racial apprenticeship practices of employers and unions are frequently reflected in enrollments by race in vocational education programs of public schools. If there is reason to believe that it will be difficult to place Negro graduates in certain occupations, teachers of vocational subjects frequently advise their Negro students to avoid courses in these skills in favor of others traditionally open to Negroes. Graduates of apprenticeship programs seem certain to form a decreasing fraction of the supply of skilled manpower in future years, though apprenticeship will continue to play an important role in certain parts of the construction, metalworking, and printing trades, where it has a long tradition as the preferred means of training skilled workers. Because it seems destined to decline in importance as a training technique, discrimination in apprenticeship is probably less important to the future occupational status of Negroes than practices in other employer-sponsored training programs. Such programs have grown very rapidly during

[1] U.S. Bureau of the Census, *U.S. Census of Population, 1950: Occupational Characteristics*, Special Report P–E No. 1B, 32.

[2] U.S. Bureau of the Census, *U.S. Census of Population, 1960: Detailed Characteristics, United States Summary*, Final Report PC(1)–1D, Table 205.

recent decades and now cover a wide range of instructional procedures from relatively simple on-the-job training programs, on
the one hand, to advanced training at the postgraduate level for
junior and senior professional and management personnel on the
other. There is little direct evidence concerning practice in these
areas, but it is virtually certain that Negroes are grossly underrepresented in advanced training programs because of their absence
from the professional, executive, and administrative occupations
from which trainees are selected. The absence of Negroes from
these programs tends to widen still further the existing disparity
between Negro and white educational attainment levels.

EXTENT OF DISCRIMINATORY PRACTICES

The practices summarized above can be observed in all parts of
the country, but tend to take different forms in the South from the
remainder of the nation. In the South, exclusion of Negroes from
certain occupations, maintenance of work groups segregated on a
racial basis, and perpetuation of racial occupational employment
patterns through discriminatory promotion procedures are practiced more openly than in the North and frequently defended as
necessary or even desirable. Differences between Southern and
Northern practice are so great that they almost constitute a difference in kind of practice rather than degree. The less overt practices common in the remainder of the country can be used to
exclude Negroes from employment opportunities almost as effectively as Southern practices. Abatement of discriminatory practices
can be observed, however, in several Northern states that have
enforced their fair employment laws fairly effectively.

The North. The authors of a 1953 study of the employment
practices of 1,200 firms in Pennsylvania concluded that nine-tenths
of the surveyed firms showed some degree of discrimination in
hiring, apprenticing, and promoting workers. Discrimination was
more common in skilled and white-collar occupations than in un-

skilled or semiskilled work.[3] A review of employment practices in Ohio in 1958 reached somewhat similar conclusions.[4] A 1958 review of minority group employment practices in San Francisco led to the general conclusion that "employment opportunities in private industry in San Francisco are still widely restricted according to race. These restrictions are experienced most acutely by Negro members of the labor force." [5] Each of these studies was undertaken at a time when no enforceable FEP laws were in effect in the respective states. While the subsequent enactment of FEP laws in these three states has unquestionably resulted in some improvement, discrimination in employment is still practiced in many establishments in these states.

The South, as Typified by Atlanta. That Negroes are still almost completely excluded from any but traditionally "Negro jobs" in Southern cities is shown by racial employment patterns in Atlanta, Georgia, in the winter of 1962.[6] One of the automobile assembly plants in the Atlanta metropolitan area employed 1,700 to 1,800 persons, of whom about seventy were Negroes. Only eight Negroes were employed on the assembly line, four having been put on the line in October, 1961, and four in January, 1962. All other Negro employees of the plant worked in the service department as janitors, sweepers, truck drivers, and power sweepers. No Negroes were employed in white-collar occupations.

Other automotive and farm equipment plants in the Atlanta area presented about the same picture of Negro employment in traditional jobs, with a few token placements of very recent date

[3] Report of the Governor's Commission on Industrial Race Relations, *Employment Practices in Pennsylvania* (Harrisburg, Commonwealth of Pennsylvania, 1953).

[4] Report of the Governor's Advisory Commission on Civil Rights, *Part V, Employment Study* (Columbus, State of Ohio, 1958).

[5] Babow and Howden, *Civil Rights Inventory: Part I, Employment*, p. 304.

[6] The description of racial employment practices in Atlanta is based on interviews in the winter of 1962 with management representatives, union staff members, Negro workers, and persons connected with race relations agencies. Emory F. Via, a member of the faculty of the School for Workers, University of Wisconsin, Madison, conducted the interviews.

in production work. Several Atlanta firms have recently changed from departmental to plant-wide seniority arrangements, and it is possible that Negroes will be able to secure promotion more readily under such arrangements than under the departmental arrangements previously in effect. A steel mill in the city employed about 1,250 persons, of whom about one-third were Negro. There were thirty-two job classes in the plant with pay rates ranging from $2.02 to $4.12 per hour. The highest rank held by a Negro was a Class 11 job that paid $2.65 per hour. Negroes were concentrated in the lower job classes. A union representative stated that "no really skilled jobs" were held by Negroes. Under a labor agreement concluded in 1961, Negroes may bid for jobs throughout the plant. Seniority is based on occupational and departmental lines of progression and, under unspecified circumstances, may be calculated on a plant-wide basis as well. Prior to this agreement, there was a more rigid separation of lines of progression, and no provision was made for computing occupational seniority on unskilled and semiskilled jobs. Under earlier contracts and practices, Negroes were virtually limited to particular lines of progression which did not lead to qualification for or employment in skilled occupations.

In the construction industry of Atlanta, there were few departures from usual Southern practices. There were about 1,800 carpenters in separate white and Negro local unions. The white local bargained for the Negro local, which had only seventeen members, according to a report filed by the latter with the area office of the Bureau of Labor and Management Reports of the U.S. Department of Labor. In 1960, according to Census reports, there were about 350 Negro carpenters in the Atlanta area. Apparently very few of them belonged to a union, and most of them were engaged almost exclusively in residential work on a nonunion basis. Union membership among construction electricians totaled about 1,200, of whom none were Negro. Two Negro licensed electrical contractors employed about fifteen journeymen. In the plumbing trade, the situation was the same; no Negroes belonged to the local union, but six licensed Negro plumbing contractors employed about twenty-five journeymen. Negroes were almost entirely absent from local unions of sheet-metal workers, operating engineers, and ironworkers, but dominated the lathing, plastering, and cement-finishing trades. The segregated local unions of bricklayers had about 1,000 members, of whom around 15 percent were Negro. Membership in the Negro local was said to have declined in recent years, perhaps because Negroes could obtain employment with only two general contractors in the city on commercial work where union scales are paid. Other Negro bricklayers worked most frequently as independent "subcontractors" on residential work, where the union scale is seldom observed. The Negro brick-layers' local was reported to be composed primarily of older men —only three members were under thirty years of age. This local has been unable to maintain an apprenticeship program.

In such activities as trucking, warehousing, and lumberyards, Negroes were well represented and held jobs in most classifications. In Atlanta, as elsewhere in the South, Negro penetration has been noticeable in truck-driving and in automobile maintenance and repair, perhaps because the nature of the work permits persons so employed to accommodate themselves to segregated employment practices. Negroes have not, however, obtained employment in substantial numbers as milk deliverymen, beer and soft drink drivers, and the like, although they have been employed to some extent as helpers on such trucks. The few Negroes who have broken this pattern usually serve Negro customers only. In the local transit system, two Negroes were employed as bus drivers and there were reported to be two other Negroes in training for such jobs. All were recent additions to what had been an all-white force.

The local telecommunications company, which employed between 4,000 and 5,000 persons, had one Negro auto mechanic and one Negro house mechanic. All other Negroes employed by the company were engaged in custodial or culinary occupations. With the possible exception of one or two persons, no Negroes were employed in banking and insurance establishments except in traditionally Negro jobs, save for those employed in the Negro banking and insurance institutions of the city. In retail trade there were virtually no departures from traditional practices, although a few local outlets of a national chain store were reported to have hired one or two Negro clerks. With this exception, Negro employment in large retail establishments was confined to menial jobs, shipping, and delivery. A similar situation existed in the hotel and restaurant industry of the city, where racial segregation, by occupation, has long been common practice. Atlanta's racial employment practices prevail throughout the South, with minor local variations. Additional studies of racial employment practices in the South are cited below.[7]

EMPLOYER EXPERIENCE WITH RACIAL EQUALITY

The racial employment practices summarized above stem from a variety of attitudes and beliefs as to the kinds of work appropriate for Negroes. Management personnel frequently state that fear of hostile reaction from white customers, white employees, labor unions, or the community at large prevents them from departing from established racial employment patterns. Resistance to employment of Negroes may also be based on the belief that it is impossible to find Negroes with suitable qualifications for work in occupations outside of those traditionally regarded in the establishment as suitable for them. Almost as important as these factors is simple inertia. Traditional racial employment patterns tend to persist for long periods of time unless there is a conscious decision on the part of top management to move in the direction of an integrated work force and unless management takes specific steps to

[7] Among the more recent published studies of Negro employment practices in the South, the following are especially noteworthy: Dewey, *Four Studies*, and "Negro Employment in Southern Industry," *Journal of Political Economy*, LXXX (1952), 279–93; Gallaher, *Houston*; Hawley, *The Birmingham Area*; Hope, *International Harvester*; Jones, *Chattanooga*.

implement the decision. A sizable number of managements in the North and in the border area and a much smaller number in the South have made and implemented such decisions.

Northern Establishments. The following summary of the experience of employers located in the North is based on information furnished by thirty-five establishments, each of which had had at least three years of experience with expanded employment of Negroes in 1958. Firms that employed Negroes only in unskilled jobs were not included.[8]

In the majority of these firms, the employment of Negroes in nontraditional jobs did not occur spontaneously but came about as a response to a management decision. The decision was reached most frequently because of legal obligations under fair employment laws. Manpower shortages, moral considerations, good community relations, and appeals from Negro groups were also cited as reasons for changes in company policy. Firms that announced their new racial employment policies to supervisors and employees in a firm and forthright manner met less resistance in giving effect to them than did firms that vacillated or temporized on the matter. Distribution to supervisors and employees of clear and unequivocal statements of company policy, in writing, was found to be helpful when followed up by well-planned measures for implementation. Company experience also showed, however, that such measures were not absolutely essential to success, because a number of firms increased their use of Negro employees in a widening group of occupations without circulating such statements. Mere changes in purely formal company policy had no real effect on racial employment patterns unless management acted promptly to hire Negroes or to promote them to positions not previously held by Negroes. In cases where such measures were not taken, announced policy changes were apt to be disregarded in practice.

In the initial stages of recruitment and selection of Negroes,

[8] The material in this section is based on Norgren, *et al., Employing the Negro,* and on information collected for that study.

these firms took great care to make certain that their usual hiring standards were met by Negro applicants. After traditional employment patterns had been broken, companies tried to move as rapidly as possible to a situation in which both Negro and white applicants for employment or promotion were treated on a routine basis. Companies found it necessary to make certain that their new employment policies were made known to employment agencies and other sources of Negro applicants. If they did not do so, a reasonable supply of Negro applicants frequently did not materialize. Careful explanation to such agencies of company job requirements and selection standards was found to be necessary to assure referral of qualified applicants and to avoid misunderstandings concerning employer needs. No adjustment upward or downward of usual selection standards was found to be required. Some firms deemed it advisable, however, at least initially, to exercise extra care in screening Negro applicants for employment in order to hire Negroes of unusual maturity who could tolerate displays of racial prejudice among white employees.

About two-thirds of the establishments adopted no special placement or orientation procedures for new Negro employees or for Negroes promoted to skilled jobs for the first time. These firms found that their usual procedures worked just as well with Negroes as with whites if soundly conceived and well administered. A number of firms that developed special placement and orientation procedures for Negroes abandoned them when it was realized that they were unnecessary. These firms had frequently developed special procedures in anticipation of open resistance from white employees, which did not occur. In the remaining firms, it was felt that departures from usual practices were necessary if friction was to be avoided during a period of transition. These companies felt it necessary to take into account in special induction procedures such factors as local traditions concerning the employment of Negroes, the views of white employees, and the characteristics of Negroes in local labor markets. As a group, these latter firms tended to favor gradualism in the induction of Negroes into new occupations rather than a sudden change to a completely nondiscriminatory employment policy at all occupational levels. Several company representatives stated that objections from white employees to the use of Negroes in nontraditional jobs could be effectively countered by citing state FEP laws as a reason for changes in company policy.

In this small but widely diversified sample of firms, the occupational status of Negroes was quite similar to that described in Chapter 4, though significant Negro employment gains were noted in about one-third of the companies. Negro penetration was most pronounced in unskilled and semiskilled production jobs in industrial establishments, but was seldom noted in skilled craft jobs, because of difficulties in securing admission to certain trade unions, inadequate preparation for skilled work, and the frequent preference of Negroes for unskilled jobs that paid the highest possible entrance wage. Negroes had made substantial progress in a variety of white-collar occupations in a few predominantly white-collar firms, but had made little progress in white-collar employment in industrial establishments. Negro supervisors were extremely few in number and had seldom progressed beyond the position of first-line supervisor.

Managements were asked to compare the performance of Negro and white employees selected under the same standards and engaged in similar work under the same supervision. The replies indicated that Negroes and whites performed in about the same manner when judged by such criteria as quantity and quality of work, job attitudes, absenteeism, tardiness, turnover, industrial accidents, and illnesses. Managements usually anticipated that unpleasant racial incidents would occur when Negroes were hired or promoted. Such problems were encountered, but reached the stage of work stoppages, or threats thereof, in only a few cases. Undesirable behavior on the part of white or Negro employees usually disappeared quite rapidly if newly hired Negroes were competent and if management took prompt and equitable disciplinary measures. In some instances, it became necessary to let protesting white employees know that they must accept the new situation or quit their jobs. In all but a very few cases, protesting white employees chose to remain on the job when given such alternatives. In the few cases where Negroes were appointed to supervise racially mixed work groups, there sometimes were initial difficulties; but, if the Negro demonstrated competence on the job, objections disappeared quite quickly.

Southern Establishments. Because of the greater prevalence and persistence of discriminatory practices in the South than in the North, it was difficult to secure information as to the experience of Southern firms that had departed from traditional segregated patterns of employment. However, ten establishments located in Southern and border states provided comparable information on their experience. Four plants were located in border states and six in states of the middle or deep South. Eight of the ten were local plants of multiestablishment companies with headquarters offices in the North, one was locally owned and managed, and one was a Federal establishment. Southern establishments encountered in more acute form the same problems met by their Northern counterparts when introducing nondiscriminatory employment policies. They also encountered additional problems, such as segregated facilities, separate seniority rosters based on race, and restrictive action by such racist organizations as White Citizens' Councils and the Ku Klux Klan.

Southern plant managements were more fearful of difficulty and approached the problems of transition much more cautiously than Northern managements. Southern managements paid much greater attention to planning and preparation for changes in employment policy and practice. Special announcements or publicity specifically covering changes in policy were avoided by most of the companies, but the management decision was made known to the local communities in various ways. Certain managements, for example, informed local union leaders in advance of any significant extension of Negro employment, with the result that the decision quickly became known to all employees. One company, in planning the opening of a new plant under a merit employment policy, informed the local Chamber of Commerce, state and city officials, clergymen, school heads, and Negro organizations of its intentions. All groups in the community, whatever their relations to the new plant, were fully informed as to company policy before the plant opened. Most persons accepted the policy, although many of them must have had deep-rooted personal feelings to the contrary. Apparently, community leaders did not find acceptance of an employment policy alien to Southern traditions too high a price to pay for the additional business the plant would bring to the town, nor was there a lack of white job applicants.

In existing plants, policy changes were more difficult because they required action to disturb the status quo in a way contrary to regional practices. Plants that undertook such changes felt it necessary to educate and persuade supervisors and foremen as to the necessity for changes in company policy and tried to show them how to deal with employee protests. Supervisors were sometimes asked to help management select the jobs on which Negroes were to be employed for the first time, but were *not* asked whether a fair employment policy should be adopted. Such companies tended to introduce carefully selected Negroes into a few nontraditional jobs and gradually expand the classes of jobs open to Negroes only after Negroes had been accepted in the first group of jobs. Companies tended to be opportunistic and take advantage of unforeseen developments to advance their fair employment programs rather than adhere rigidly to preconceived plans.

For the most part, Southern firms followed the same practices in recruitment and selection of Negro employees used in the North. The following differences, however, between Northern and Southern recruitment practices were noted. In Southern plants the first Negroes selected for placement in nontraditional jobs were recruited from company Negro work forces, usually from common labor pools and from janitorial and other service groups. Managements looked primarily for Negro employees with good work records and with even and cooperative dispositions, on the ground that such Negroes would be more readily accepted by white employees and would be best able to withstand any slights received from hostile whites. One company which adopted such a procedure discontinued its long-established practice of hiring whites for direct placement in skilled jobs. All new employees were required to begin work as laborers. The expected objections of whites to working with Negroes in this lowest-level occupation—hitherto staffed exclusively by Negroes—did not materialize. Several companies that recruited Negroes from outside the plant work force tried to confine their recruitment to the local labor market on the ground that such Negroes would be accustomed to local community practices and would not have to make an adjustment to both plant and community practices. When recruitment outside of the locality was undertaken, companies usually took some pains to avoid giving publicity to the fact because they anticipated the rise of exaggerated fears in the local white community concerning their Negro employment programs.

The proportion of Negro applicants rejected was substantially greater in Southern plants than in Northern establishments. The principal factors accounting for the higher rejection rates were low educational attainments, deficiencies in industrial background and experience, and failure to meet minimum health and physical standards. Despite the high rejection rate among Negro applicants, sizable numbers of qualified Negroes were obtained whenever sufficiently large numbers of applicants were tested.

In selecting a job, or a group of jobs, in which to place Negroes for the first time, managements gave great emphasis to factors they felt would enhance acceptance of the change by white employees. They usually tried to select jobs (1) that were in the lower or medium skill brackets and hence bore some similarity to tradition-

ally Negro jobs, (2) that were supervised by foremen re
sympathetic to the change, and (3) that would permit rel
wide and hence sparse distribution of Negroes in heretofore
jobs in the plant. Most of these firms conducted special cou
programs for new Negro employees, and sometimes also for
employees, in the initial stages of their new employment pro
In all instances such programs were discontinued once integrated
employment patterns had become customary.

Company experience in upgrading and promoting Negroes was
quite different in the South from in the North because of the more
rigid distinction between white and Negro jobs in the South. In
addition, promotion was complicated by the existence of separate
seniority and promotion arrangements based on race, which restricted Negroes to an extremely limited range of jobs. Promotion
of Negroes to positions in which they would supervise work groups
composed of whites and Negroes had not occurred in any of the
Southern plants studied. There are very few Negro supervisors of
racially integrated work crews even in the North. In the North,
however, no racial employment custom prevails with anywhere
near the force or pervasiveness of the traditional view of Southern
whites that no Negro should supervise a white. Negro supervisors
are not entirely unknown in the South, but almost invariably they
supervise other Negroes only.

In the South, promotion or hiring of Negroes more frequently
led to difficulties on the job between white and Negro employees
than was the case in the North, and the problems were more difficult to resolve. White employees, for example, sometimes objected
openly to working with Negro employees in departments where
Negroes had never been employed. In all of the Southern plants
surveyed, managements refused to yield to such objections. Demurring employees were reminded of the company's fair employment policy and were told that if they did not wish to work with
Negro employees, their only alternative was to quit. Faced with
such alternatives, Southern whites, like their Northern counter-

parts, almost invariably chose to withdraw their objections and keep their jobs. In one plant a fight between a white and a Negro followed an attempt by the white to bully the Negro into doing some work assigned to the white. The matter was settled by the discharge of the white employee. Although it was predicted that this disciplinary action would result in a strike, there were no repercussions among other white employees.

At the time of the survey (1957–58), none of the plants had attempted to eliminate segregated toilet, cafeteria, and related facilities. Managements felt that a merit employment policy could be introduced with fewer adverse reactions among white employees if they did not force interracial use of such facilities. Most management representatives felt, however, that it was desirable to plan for and work toward an ultimate arrangement of single facilities and that such arrangements would be accepted by employees. A number of managements intended to use single facilities in any new plants or in any extensions of existing plants to be built in the future.

Discrimination by Employment Agencies

In order to round out our overview of management racial practices, it is necessary to take brief account of employment agencies, since a primary purpose of these agencies is to recruit and screen prospective employees as a service to management. Both private and public employment agencies are common throughout the country, especially in urban areas; hence, attention must be given to both types.

Private agencies tend to specialize in specific occupational categories—for example, technical, clerical, craft, or domestic service. In some instances the agency's fee is paid by the employer, in others by the employee. Forty-four states have laws regulating the conduct of private employment agencies, and all but two of these states require them to be licensed. None of these laws contains any provision prohibiting or limiting discrimination by employment agencies. Such discrimination *is* prohibited, however, in all states and municipalities having enforceable FEP laws, the stricture being incorporated in the latter statutes rather than in the laws dealing exclusively with employment agencies.

The development of public employment agencies on a widespread basis began in 1933, when Congress passed the Wagner-Peyser Act establishing a "national system of public employment offices." Nominally, it is a joint Federal-state system. While the local public employment offices are administered by separate state agencies ("employment services") in each state, the entire cost of operating the offices is borne by the Federal government. Moreover, the Federal government can theoretically exercise a considerable degree of control over the operation of the local offices, since the law authorizes the USES (a unit of the U.S. Department of Labor) to set uniform policies and operating standards applicable to all state employment agencies. In actual practice, however, the Federal government has exerted only a very minor influence over the state agencies; and for practical purposes the latter have been—and still are—virtually autonomous. While the USES has issued many regulations concerning the operation of the public employment offices, little effort has been made to secure observance of these regulations by the state agencies; and in some states the Federal rules and standards have been ignored or even openly flouted.

It is a safe generalization that most employment agencies, both private and public, discriminate against Negroes and other racial minorities in greater or lesser degree. Most commonly they do so by accepting and complying with employer requests for workers specifying "whites only." Many agencies, however, refer only white applicants even when the employer makes no racial specification.

Although little specific information is available concerning the extent of discrimination by private employment agencies, it is well

known that many of these agencies regularly accept and fill employer job orders on a "whites only" basis. Indeed, in the South
the great majority of private employment agencies openly refuse
to cater to Negro applicants. Such overt discrimination is seldom
found among private agencies in the North, since the FEP laws
established in most Northern states prohibit discrimination by employment agencies as well as by employers and unions. Nevertheless, it is common knowledge that many Northern private agencies,
while outwardly complying with FEP laws, often accede to discriminatory job orders by referring only white applicants.

Racial discrimination is no less common among public employment agencies. It is undoubtedly most prevalent in the South, but
it is by no means uncommon in the North. The state-controlled
local employment offices in the eleven states comprising the "South
proper" were established on a racially segregated basis at the outset. As a result of persuasive efforts by the USES, several local
offices in Florida and North Carolina have been integrated during
the past two years; but the great majority of public employment
offices in the South still conduct separate operations for whites and
Negroes. Owing to the manner in which employer requests for
workers are distributed between the "white" and "Negro" public
employment offices, wholesale discrimination in the allocation of
jobs is practically mandatory in the Southern states. In the typical
situation, the great bulk of job orders involving middle-level jobs
and virtually all upper-level job orders are routed to the white
offices, while the bulk of orders for workers to fill menial and unskilled jobs are routed to the Negro offices. The inevitable effect of
this system of allocating public employment office business is, of
course, to perpetuate the traditional confinement of Negroes to the
lowest level occupations. The following summation of nonfarm
placements by the state-controlled offices in North Carolina in
1959 is typical: out of a total of 73,473 nonwhite placements,
67,572, or 92 percent, were in "service" and unskilled jobs; and out

of 95,576 white placements 74,095, or 77 percent, were in the middle- and upper-level categories, ranging from semiskilled to professional and managerial occupations.[9]

It is worth re-emphasizing that this system of built-in discrimination in referring people to jobs still exists throughout most of the South, despite the present Federal administration's declared support of racial equality in employment and in face of the fact that operation of the public employment offices is financed entirely by Federal funds. In 1961, it is true, the USES incorporated in its "Policy Manual" a policy declaration against acceptance of discriminatory job orders from private employers. (Previously the policy statement had applied only to Federal agencies and private employers engaged in work on Federal contracts.) The policy statements of the USES are, however, by long-accepted custom not mandatory on the state organizations, but merely advisory. Hence, the Southern state organizations are still free to operate the public employment offices on the present segregated and openly discriminatory basis; and it is apparent that in most instances they intend to continue doing so.

Public employment offices in the North are operated on an integrated basis—there are no segregated offices outside of the Southern states. Acceptance of discriminatory job orders by public offices and referrals of applicants in accordance with such orders are, nevertheless, common throughout the Northern states, although not as widely prevalent as in the South. Even in the twenty-two states having enforceable FEP laws, which explicitly prohibit discrimination by employment agencies, public employment offices frequently process job orders in this manner.

The widespread discriminatory referral of workers by public employment agencies in the North, despite the absence of segregated offices, is attributable in large part to the fact that the USES, in allocating Federal funds to the various local offices, does so pri-

[9] "North Carolina: 1961 Report to the Commission on Civil Rights from the State Advisory Committee," in U.S. Commission on Civil Rights, *The 50 States Report*, p. 494.

marily on the basis of the individual office's past record of number of workers placed in jobs. Because of this method of determining agency budgets, local office managers and personnel have a compelling incentive to make as many placements as possible and a concomitant incentive to accede to the wishes of employers who specify "whites only," rather than run the risk of losing the placement business involved. This and the various other factors accounting for the frequent occurrence of discriminatory referrals by public employment agencies in the North are discussed in detail in Chapter 6.

3

UNION RACIAL PRACTICES

Labor union racial practices cover as wide a range of behavior as the employer practices described in Chapter 2. At one extreme are unions that will not admit Negroes to membership unless compelled to do so; at the other are unions that readily admit Negroes to membership and attempt in various ways to protect, or even enhance, their occupational status. Most unions, like most employers, fall somewhere between these extremes and display both discriminatory and nondiscriminatory behavior. Practices rather than policies, particularly those of local unions rather than international unions, determine Negro access to job opportunities just as plant practice rather than company policy determines the racial employment pattern in multiestablishment firms. Union practice is a much less important determinant of Negro employment patterns than is employer practice, if only because union membership totals little more than one-third of nonagricultural employment. Nevertheless, union practice is an important determinant of Negro employment patterns in certain industries, occupations and geographic areas. During the last thirty years overtly discriminatory union racial practices have become somewhat less common, but many unions still limit Negro employment opportunities by informal means. The principal union racial practices which limit Negro employment opportunities are exclusion from membership, maintenance of racially segregated local unions, control of hiring through referral systems, and control of job opportunities through seniority arrangements. This chapter reviews such practices, some union racial practices peculiar to the South, and union fair practice programs.

Formal Discriminatory Union Practices

RACIAL BARS IN UNION CONSTITUTIONS

In 1930, at least twenty-two national unions barred Negroes from membership by explicit racial provisions in their constitutions or rituals. This group of openly discriminatory unions was composed primarily of railroad unions but also included the Boilermakers, the Machinists, and the Airline Pilots. The membership provisions of the constitutions of many of these unions were obviously based on the concept of white superiority. One union of railroad workers, for example, restricted its membership to persons who were "white born, of good moral character, sober and industrious."[1] By 1943, mergers and changing racial practices had reduced to thirteen the number of national unions with formal race bars to membership. By 1960, only three unions retained their formal race restrictions: the Order of Railway Telegraphers, the Brotherhood of Locomotive Engineers, and the Brotherhood of Locomotive Firemen and Enginemen.

"FEDERAL" NEGRO LOCALS

In certain unions, notably the Boilermakers', the Machinists', and the Railway Clerks' Unions, the problem of Negro admission to union membership was avoided for a time by arrangements under which the excluding union would have Negroes in its jurisdiction organized directly by the AFL and given membership in a "Federal local" attached to the national office of the Federation rather than the discriminatory national union. In other cases, these unions arranged to have Negro workers within their jurisdictions organized by other national unions which did not bar Negroes from membership. Such arrangements proved unsatisfactory to the discriminating unions and to Negroes: the Negroes were inade-

[1] Brotherhood of Locomotive Firemen and Enginemen, *Constitution*, as amended January 8, 1960. In 1963, a national convention of this union voted to strike the race bar to membership from its constitution, despite vehement protests from Southern delegates.

quately represented, and the national unions could not collect their dues. In at least one industrial plant, a local union dealt with the problem by admitting Negro employees to membership, despite a race bar in the constitution of the national union, and carrying them on its membership rolls as American Indians.

AUXILIARY NEGRO LOCALS

A number of international unions which did not bar Negroes from membership restricted them to a sort of second-class membership in auxiliary locals composed entirely of Negroes. These locals were subordinate to parent white locals, and their affairs were conducted by officers of the white locals. Negroes were seldom permitted to hold office in such auxiliary, subordinate locals. About the only function performed by the Negro members of these locals was the payment of dues. The arrangement was usually adopted in lieu of outright exclusion by formal means and was sometimes the first change in a union's racial practices following the elimination of formal racial bars to union membership. At least twelve national unions are known to have formed such auxiliaries.[2] All but two of these unions were affiliated with the AFL. Auxiliary locals were weakened by court decisions which prohibited the closed shop where auxiliaries existed, by state FEP laws, by the Taft-Hartley and Railway Labor Act Amendments making the union shop unenforceable if all workers were not admitted on equal terms; and, finally, by the Landrum-Griffin Act of 1959, which made it possible for Negro employees to bring action to abolish auxiliary locals. A few auxiliary locals remained in 1959, but had become relatively unimportant by that date.

[2] These unions were International Brotherhood of Boilermakers, Iron Shipbuilders, Blacksmiths, Forgers and Helpers (AFL); Motion Picture Operators' International Union (AFL); National Rural Letter Carriers' Association (independent); National Federation of Rural Letter Carriers (independent); Brotherhood of Maintenance of Way Employees (AFL); Sheet Metal Workers' Alliance (AFL); Brotherhood of Railway and Steamship Clerks, Freight Handlers, Express and Station Employees (AFL); American Federation of Railroad Workers (AFL); Rural Letter Carriers' Association (AFL); International Association of Machinists (AFL); Seafarers' International Union of North America (AFL); Brotherhood of Railway Carmen (AFL). Sources: Union publications and interviews with union officers and members.

Segregated locals are theoretically different from auxiliary locals in that Negro and white locals elect their own officers, receive separate charters, and nominally enjoy equal status within the national union. The distinction is sometimes more theoretical than real, however, because a white local may, in fact, represent a Negro local. In 1962, for example, Local 189–A (Negro) of the United Brotherhood of Paper Makers and Paper Workers at Bogalusa, Louisiana, brought legal action to secure unemployment compensation for eight months while Local 189 (white) was on strike. The company and the white union contended that Local 189–A was a part of Local 189. The Louisiana Division of Employment Security refused to pay the Negroes unemployment insurance on the ground that they were on strike, although the Negroes stated that their segregated local did not vote to go on strike. Local 189–A was not registered with the Bureau of Labor and Management Reports of the U.S. Department of Labor as a separate labor organization when the action was begun, so that its independence of Local 189 seems questionable. It seems safe to conclude from this and other similar experiences that segregated Negro locals are frequently only theoretically the equals of white locals and that the auxiliary form continues in many cases after it has been formally abolished.

At least twenty-three national unions are known to have had segregated locals within their organizations in very recent years.[3]

---

[3] These unions were Journeyman Barbers', Hairdressers', Cosmetologists', and Proprietors' International Union; International Brotherhood of Boilermakers, Iron Shipbuilders, Blacksmiths, Forgers, and Helpers; Bricklayers', Masons', and Plasterers' International Union of America; United Brotherhood of Carpenters and Joiners of America; Amalgamated Clothing Workers of America; United Glass and Ceramic Workers of North America; National Association of Letter Carriers of the United States of America; National Rural Letter Carriers' Association; International Longshoremen's Association; International Association of Machinists; Brotherhood of Maintenance of Way Employees; International Molders and Foundry Workers of North America; American Federation of Musicians; Oil, Chemical, and Atomic Workers' International Union; Brotherhood of Painters, Decorators, and Paperhangers of America; United Papermakers and Paperworkers; Brotherhood of Pulp, Sulphite, and Paper Mill Workers; Brotherhood of Railway Carmen of America; Brotherhood of Railway and Steamship Clerks,

Most of these national labor organizations belong to the AFL–CIO. Segregated locals are more commonly found in craft unions than in industrial unions and are usually located in the South. The only national unions with a significant number of segregated locals in the North and West are the Carpenters, the Musicians, and the Railway Clerks. A number of national unions have decided to charter no more segregated locals. It seems fairly certain that segregated locals, like auxiliary locals, will decline in importance because the practice of establishing segregated locals has been almost completely discontinued. Even such a labor organization as the Tobacco Workers, with a predominantly Southern membership, decided as long ago as 1946 to form no more segregated locals. Other national labor organizations have taken measures to integrate their segregated locals, and the national AFL–CIO has taken a formal position against segregated locals but has refused to invoke sanctions to compel mergers or to establish a time by which segregated locals must integrate.

While these considerations indicate that segregated locals may disappear in due course, the following factors tend to make the process more time-consuming than in the case of auxiliary locals. Negroes in the South frequently favor a continuation of segregated locals because, when two segregated locals of whites and Negroes merge, Negroes usually form a minority in the integrated local, and Negroes have reason to fear that whites would discriminate against them in such an integrated local. Also, Negro locals sometimes have their own buildings and other property and always have Negro officers with a vested interest in perpetuating segregation. It seems likely that, at least in the South, Negroes will tend to resist integration of segregated locals unless integration takes place under such conditions that Negroes stand little chance of losing whatever advantages they derive, or believe they derive, from a

Freight Handlers, Express and Station Employees; Sheet Metal Workers' International Association; Textile Workers' Union of America; United Textile Workers of America; Tobacco Workers' International Union. Sources: Interviews with union officials and members.

segregated arrangement. This is because under segregation there is usually a formal division of work along racial lines which Negroes believe gives them at least some protection in certain jobs. Negro resistance to integration has been reduced when special arrangements have made it possible for them to have some control over their own affairs. Recently, for example, segregated local unions of the International Association of Machinists at the Marietta, Georgia, plant of Lockheed were integrated even though Negroes were in the minority. Integration became possible when Negroes were guaranteed positions in the local machinists' joint council. Negro leaders of the segregated Negro local resisted integration for years until such guarantees were given.

The preceding discussion can be summarized as follows. Each of the formal discriminatory practices described above—racial bars to union membership and formation of segregated and auxiliary locals—has the effect of limiting the economic opportunities open to Negroes. Outright racial bars to union membership are obviously intended to prevent *any* Negroes from entering certain occupations or industries, most commonly skilled craft occupations. When segregated locals are chartered, a division of work on a racial basis is intended. Although some Negroes oppose the integration of segregated locals because they believe they enjoy a measure of job security under these arrangements, it is likely that such beliefs are groundless. Many segregated locals of Negro building craftsmen in the South, for example, have lost ground to white locals in recent years. In industrial establishments segregated locals and auxiliary locals are frequently used to limit Negroes to a narrow range of unskilled, poorly paid jobs from which promotion is impossible.

Informal Discriminatory Union Practices

EXCLUSION FROM MEMBERSHIP

The decline in the use of overtly exclusionist practices by national unions does not mean that discrimination has disappeared from these organizations. Local union practice is frequently more important than national union policy in determining admission to membership. The locals of some national unions, particularly those composed primarily of skilled workers in the railroad, construction, printing and metalworking industries, often bar Negroes from membership by informal means. Such means include agreements not to sponsor Negroes for membership, refusal to admit Negroes to apprenticeship programs, refusal to accept applications for membership from Negroes, or simply ignoring their applications, general "understandings" to vote against Negroes if they are proposed for membership (for example, three members of a Brotherhood of Railroad Trainmen or Brotherhood of Railway Clerks lodge can bar an applicant from membership by voting against acceptance of his application when the matter comes before the membership at a lodge meeting), use of trade examinations to exclude Negroes from journeyman status by rigging the examinations so that Negroes cannot pass them while at the same time admitting whites who have not been required to take the examination, and use of political pressure on local governmental licensing agencies to see to it that Negroes fail tests they must pass before they can secure licenses to follow such trades as plumber or electrician.

Union practice in the matter of exclusion from membership by informal means is so diverse that generalization is difficult. Nevertheless, we believe the following conclusions can be supported:

Racial exclusion by informal means is not restricted to any particular geographic area, although it is undoubtedly more common in the South than elsewhere because there is a clearer and more rigid separation of work into "Negro jobs" and "white jobs" in the South. Exclusion from membership is most common among craft unions, although some craft unions have egalitarian racial policies and a number of industrial union locals refuse to admit Negroes to membership. When craft unions can control the number of craftsmen in a local labor market, they frequently exclude

Negroes from membership, and hence employment, as a way of reserving employment opportunities for a select coterie, frequently composed primarily of relatives and friends of incumbent members. Local unions of electricians, plumbers, steamfitters, sheet-metal workers, ironworkers, and operating engineers, for example, rarely have any Negro members. In these locals, various admission requirements are used to exclude Negroes from membership. Negroes are also frequently excluded by such means from other craft unions in the building trades, printing trades, and metal trades. In establishments organized by industrial unions, hiring is almost invariably a unilateral function of management. Consequently, since the union cannot prevent Negroes from being hired, it stands to gain more by admitting them to membership than by excluding them.

While exclusion from membership because of race is *per se* a discriminatory practice, the extent to which it will deprive Negroes of employment opportunities that might otherwise be open to them is related to the power of unions to control access to employment. In certain cases, union power over such matters is very great, but in others it is so slight as to exert little if any effect on the operation of the labor market. The ability of unions to discriminate through denial of membership is greatest when employers depend primarily upon unions for their supply of labor. Union employers in certain parts of the construction, hotel, restaurant, maritime, longshore, and trucking industries, for example, look to the unions with which they deal as their primary sources of manpower. Unions whose members are employed in these industries frequently maintain private employment agencies, usually termed "hiring halls," open only to union members. Employers who have signed labor agreements with such unions fill their labor requirements through union hiring halls rather than through public or private employment agencies. In such situations, denial of union membership is equivalent to denial of employment. When a union plays no part in the selection of employees, as is the case in nearly all manufacturing establishments, denial of membership may not in itself adversely affect Negro employment opportunities.

CONTROL OF JOB OPPORTUNITIES

Unions can influence the number of job opportunities open to Negroes through control of job referral systems and admission to apprenticeship and on-the-job training programs, by pressure on employers to hire—or refrain from hiring—members of a particular minority, and by control over transfer, promotion, and layoff within plants. Union referral systems are used by some unions to discriminate against Negroes by referring them to poorer jobs or by not referring them at all. These forms of discrimination sometimes occur when there is no formal referral system or where the formal system is used only for Negroes, whites being referred through an informal system to the better jobs. Until recently, for example, a union referral system in the brewery industry of a Northern city was used to exclude Negroes from desirable jobs by the simple expedient of making certain that Negroes very seldom accumulated enough seniority during the summer busy season to qualify for seniority status that would protect their jobs during the winter slack season. Negroes were required to use the union referral system and report to the union office to secure employment. Union representatives frequently notified whites of job openings by telephone at their homes.[4] Practices such as these are most common in the skilled building trades unions (i.e., those which do not *exclude* Negroes); but they are also found in certain parts of the longshore, maritime, and trucking industries.

Apprenticeship programs exist in only a minority of unions but play a significant role in controlling access to skilled jobs in a number of industries, particularly construction, printing and publishing, and precision metalworking. Very few of the apprentices

[4] Gladys Engel Lang, "Discrimination in the Hiring Hall: A Case Study of Pressures to Promote Integration in New York's Brewery Industry," *Discrimination and Low Incomes* (New York, New York State Commission Against Discrimination, 1959), pp. 195–247.

of the skilled craft unions of these industries are Negro. Apprenticeship "screening," which often turns on such extraneous matters as family relationships or friendships, may bar Negroes but not whites either at entry or somewhere during the course of training. Negroes are sometimes required to serve apprenticeships that are waived for whites if they can pass trade tests. Responsibility for apprenticeship discrimination is difficult to establish because governments, employers, and unions are all involved in the matter. In the building trades, for example, unions frequently have exclusive control over the selection of apprentices. Responsibility for discrimination is difficult to establish, however, because apprenticeship programs are nominally under joint union-employer control, and the practices of local government licensing agencies and vocational schools often lend support to discriminatory practices. Many public school systems, both in the North and in the South, enroll only those persons in apprenticeship training courses who are sponsored by local union-management apprenticeship committees in the several skilled trades. Since these committees seldom select Negroes for apprenticeship, few Negroes are enrolled.[5] When any one of these groups is accused of discrimination, responsibility is shunted back and forth among all of them in such a way that it is difficult to establish which group is responsible. With good reason, Negroes refer to such a situation as a "merry-go-round."

The main way in which industrial unions affect job opportunities is through pressure on employers to influence their hiring, transfer, promotion, and layoff policies and practices. Many employers are convinced that if they move Negroes into previously white occupations, their white workers will strike. Whether or not white workers strike over such matters is frequently determined

[5] See, for example, testimony of Samuel M. Brownell, Superintendent of Schools, Detroit, *Integration in Public Education Programs*. Hearings before the Subcommittee on Integration in Federally Assisted Public Education Programs of the Committee on Education and Labor, House of Representatives, Eighty-Seventh Congress, Second Session, on H.R. 6890, H.R. 9824, H.R. 10056, H.R. 10783, March 15, 1962 (U.S. Government Printing Office, Washington, D.C., 1962), p. 425.

by employer attitudes and firmness and by attitudes of national unions; it is rarely possible for a group of rank-and-file employees to block the employment of Negroes without the aid of either the employer or the national union.

Union Racial Practices in the South

Discriminatory practices are undoubtedly more common among Southern unions than among unions in the remainder of the country. While Negroes in the North are frequently excluded from local unions in the more highly skilled crafts, such as electricians, plumbers, sheet-metal workers, operating engineers, and the "operating" railroad occupations, in the South they are almost invariably excluded from such unions—and to a considerable extent also from most other craft unions. Furthermore, while most Southern industrial unions admit Negroes to membership, some of these unions exclude them, and many others confine them to segregated locals. Each of the following industrial unions, for example, had segregated locals in one or more places in the South in 1962: the Textile Workers; the Oil, Chemical, and Atomic Workers; the Tobacco Workers; the Amalgamated Clothing Workers; the Amalgamated Meat Cutters; the Pulp, Sulphite, and Paper Mill Workers; and the United Papermakers. Moreover, there have been many cases of discrimination against Negroes by locals of industrial unions in such matters as promotion, layoff, and transfer.

The union contracts in many Southern manufacturing plants contain provisions for separate racial lines of progression. These provisions establish separate seniority rosters for white and Negro workers and separate avenues of promotion, confined respectively within the range of "white" and "Negro" jobs. Under most such arrangements, Negroes cannot transfer from a Negro to a white line of progression and hence are permanently confined to menial, laborer, and other unskilled jobs. In a small minority of contracts, transfers are possible for Negroes, but only at the cost of forfeiting all seniority accumulated in the Negro line of progression.

Racially segregated lines of progression have been eliminated in certain Southern establishments in the petroleum-refining, automobile, steel, aircraft, meat-packing, and electrical equipment industries during the last ten years, but still remain in force in most manufacturing plants in the South. In many of these plants the separate promotion lines antedate unionism and are frequently as rigid in nonunion as in union firms. For example, the relatively unorganized Southern textile industry is widely known as "white man's work," and few Negroes have ever been promoted from menial or laborer occupations in Southern textile mills. Even in the unionized industries, the net result of unionization has often been to codify and make somewhat more rigid existing racial employment practices. When a plant is unionized, its racial practices are likely to be reflected in the union contract. Thereafter, change becomes more difficult, not easier, because change can come about only by agreement between the union and management—not by unilateral employer decision. In Northern establishments, formal segregation of seniority rosters on the basis of race is rare, but informal arrangements frequently exclude Negroes from skilled occupations.

Although there are many "integrated" unions in the South, the term may mean very little because many industrial plants in the South have very few Negro employees. An integrated local might thus have a few Negro members who are janitors in the plant but who never come to union meetings.

Certain Southern industries, however, employ Negroes in substantial numbers. Among the Southern manufacturing industries which had a relatively high proportion of Negroes in 1960 are the fertilizer, food-processing, logging, lumber (sawmills), meat-packing, and steel industries. Negroes are employed in production and other semiskilled jobs in these industries and to some extent even in relatively skilled occupations. The three last-named industries are fairly well unionized, and the Negro and white workers usually belong to the same local unions. Separate progression lines are still in effect in some unionized Southern steel plants, but are almost, if not entirely, absent in organized meat-packing plants.

Despite the relatively favorable picture in these industries, however, the predominant pattern of union racial practices in the South is one of widespread discrimination, characterized by pervasive exclusion of Negroes in the craft-oriented industries and of job segregation in the industries organized by industrial unions. Thus, one must conclude that, on balance, unions have impeded rather than enhanced the Southern Negro's occupational progress.

Union Fair Practice Programs and Activities

This chapter is primarily concerned with unions that discriminate—through denial of membership, segregated locals, or seniority rosters, or in other ways—since it is these unions that adversely affect the employment status of racial minorities and hence fall within the jurisdiction of FEP laws. It would, however, convey a distorted and misleading picture of organized labor in this context if it ignored the many unions that actively seek to protect, and in some instances even to improve, job opportunities for Negroes. These organizations include—at least at the national union level—a majority of the larger industrial unions as well as a number of smaller ones. Prominent among them are the United Automobile Workers, the Amalgamated Clothing Workers, the International Ladies' Garment Workers' Union, the International Union of Electrical Workers, the United Packinghouse Workers, the United Steel Workers, and the National Maritime Union.

Universal admission of Negroes as members was a practical necessity in these unions from the outset, since the industries in which they operate already employed many Negroes and since the unions adhered to the principle of including all workers in a given firm or plant in the same organizational unit. The unions listed, however, and a number of others as well, have gone beyond the mere acceptance of Negroes as members, albeit in varying degrees. All have sought to obtain, and in many instances have succeeded in obtaining, clauses in their contracts prohibiting discrimination in layoffs, promotions, and other terms of employment. Several of the unions, notably the UAW and the Packinghouse Workers, have succeeded in broadening these clauses to prohibit discrimination in hiring—usually against strong employer resistance. The significance of these clauses lies in the fact that Negro and other minority-group individuals who believe they have been treated unfairly can invoke the contractual grievance machinery and obtain the union's assistance in arguing their case with management and ultimately before an impartial arbitrator.

The United Packinghouse Workers has undoubtedly been the most aggressive and persistent in pressing for elimination of discrimination against Negroes, particularly in Southern plants, where the problem presents the greatest difficulties. In the early 1950s the national leaders of this union negotiated inclusive nondiscrimination clauses in the master contracts with all of the "Big Four" packers. By insisting on the observance of these clauses, they subsequently succeeded in eliminating segregation of work forces and separate facilities in many of the Southern plants of these companies.[6]

The national leaders of the UAW have also taken action on behalf of the union's Southern Negro members on numerous occasions—sometimes against managements but more often against predominantly white Southern locals—though not to the same extent as the packinghouse union. Thus, for example, the UAW leadership expelled a local in Dallas for refusing to admit nonwhites to membership; and by siding with management on the issue of work force integration, it forced the white membership of a local in Memphis to accept upgrading of Negroes to skilled occupations.

[6] See Hope, *Equality of Opportunity*.

Despite these evidences of active concern for their Negro members, however, the record of the industrial unions in certain other areas is far from impressive. This is particularly the case with respect to their skilled-trades departments. With the exception of the Packinghouse Workers, none of these unions has succeeded in opening up equal opportunities for Negroes in tool and die making, maintenance craft, and other skilled occupations. President Walter Reuther of the UAW, in a recent public statement, admitted that his union has failed in this area, attributing it in part to anti-Negro bias on the part of incumbent skilled workers, in part to management's insistence on retaining sole discretion in selecting skilled-trades apprentices, and in part to lack of qualified Negro candidates. While asserting that the union was endeavoring to overcome the resistance of its skilled-trades members, he conceded that the problem was still far from being resolved.[7]

A number of industrial unions, including most of those listed above, have established civil rights departments to deal with internal union racial practices and have urged their local unions to elect fair practice committees. Although a number of such local committees exist, they are frequently inactive. Staff members of one state FEP commission, for example, attempted to meet with union fair practice committees in their state, but abandoned their efforts when they found that union committee members seldom attended committee meetings. The staff of this commission concluded that the union fair practice committees in the state existed only on paper.

When local union fair practice committees have been more active, their activities have sometimes been frowned upon by officials of international unions, unless they were confined to internal union problems. In 1960, for example, the fair practice committee of UAW Local 1250 filed a complaint with the Ohio Civil Rights Commission concerning the hiring practices of a Cleveland plant

[7] U.S. Commission on Civil Rights, *Hearings Held in Detroit, Michigan, December 14 and 15, 1960* (U.S. Government Printing Office, Washington, D.C., 1961), pp. 49, 55.

of the Ford Motor Company. When the national union learned of this action, the director of the national union's Fair Practices Department rebuked the local committee for filing a complaint with the state Commission and indicated that internal union channels should be used rather than public agencies.

Despite the meager accomplishments of the civil rights departments and local committees, however, and despite the failure of the industrial unions to open up opportunities in the skilled trades, the efforts of these unions to reduce discrimination on the job and in the local organizations have on balance benefited Negro workers in the mass-production industries.

4

EMPLOYMENT AND OCCUPATIONAL STATUS
OF NEGROES

For a well-rounded comprehension of the nature and extent of employment discrimination, it is essential to have before us, in addition to the foregoing review of management and union racial practices, an aggregative picture of the current employment status of the nation's Negro minority. The purpose of this chapter is to convey such a picture, with appropriate attention to the significant differences that exist between the South and the North. The growth, current size, and distribution of the country's nonwhite population are first reviewed to provide the necessary setting for the analysis of the Negro's employment and occupational situation. The chapter also deals briefly with Negro incomes and with the relative level of nonwhite education and its relationships with the Negro's disadvantaged occupational status.[1]

The statistical summarizations in the chapter, derived from the decennial Census reports and other publications of the Bureau of the Census, relate to all nonwhites rather than to the Negro group alone. Most of the racial data on employment and related matters in the Census reports are presented only in terms of the white-nonwhite dichotomy. Since, however, Negroes constitute approximately 95 percent of all nonwhites in the population, the figures under the latter heading can be taken as equivalent to statistics for the Negro group without affecting the validity of the analysis to any significant degree.

---

[1] The changes and trends in Negro population, employment, and occupational status prior to 1940 are examined in detail by Myrdal, *An American Dilemma*, Parts III and IV. The developments between 1940 and 1950 are detailed and analyzed by Ginzberg, *The Negro Potential*, Ch. II.

Size of the Negro Population

At the time of the first Census in 1790, Negroes formed almost 20 percent of the population of the country. Thereafter Negroes declined steadily as a percentage of the nation's population, even though importation of Negro slaves was not prohibited until 1808 and an illicit slave trade continued until 1861. Negroes declined relative to other segments of the population because of their high death rates and the immigration of large numbers of white Europeans. The relative decline of Negroes did not cease until some time during the 1930s, when a reversal of the long-term decline occurred and Negroes began to increase as a percentage of the nation's population.

The Negro population has constituted a nearly constant fraction of the total population in the years since 1900, varying only from 11.6 percent in that year to 9.7 percent in 1930 and back to 10.6 percent in 1960.[2] This basic demographic fact helps to explain the difficulties encountered by Negroes in improving their economic status. Because of their relatively small representation in the total population and because they are denied the franchise in many areas of the South, they have been unable to exert sufficient economic or political power to command national attention to their problems. Moreover, while the Negro population has been increasing at a somewhat more rapid rate than the white population in recent years, it will take many decades for the Negro population ratio to rise significantly above its present level.

Migrations of the Negro Population

In the years since 1900, the most fundamental change in the status of the Negro population has been a major shift in place of

[2] 1900–1950: U.S. Bureau of the Census, *Historical Statistics of the United States, Colonial Times to 1957* (1960), Series A17–21, A34–50, and A59–70. 1960: U.S. Bureau of the Census, *Statistical Abstract of the United States, 1962* (1963), Table 24.

residence from rural to urban areas in the South, and from the South as a region to the larger cities outside the South.[3] The effect of this revolutionary migration on the distribution of the nation's nonwhite population is shown in Table 4.1.

Table 4.1

PERCENTAGE DISTRIBUTION OF NONWHITE POPULATION

	1900	1910	1920	1930	1940	1950	1960
South:	87	86	83	76	74	66	57
Urban	15	18	21	24	27	31	33
Rural	72	68	62	52	47	35	24
Remainder of							
United States:	13	14	17	24	26	34	43
Urban	8	9	13	19	21	30	39
Rural	5	5	4	5	5	4	4

Sources: U.S. Bureau of the Census, *U.S. Census of Population, 1920:* Vol. II, *U.S. Summary,* Table 72 (includes data for 1900 and 1910). *1930:* Vol. II, *U.S. Summary,* Tables 10, 21, and 22. *1940:* Vol. II, Part 1, *U.S. Summary,* Table 21, and special report, "Characteristics of the Nonwhite Population by Race," Table 3. *1950:* Vol. II, Part 1, Tables 58 and 60, and separate state parts for Southern states. *1960:* Final Report PC(1)–1B, Tables 42 and 52. Data revised to exclude Mexicans, who were classified as nonwhite in the 1930 Census reports. Data for Alaska and Hawaii excluded.

MIGRATION FROM RURAL TO URBAN AREAS IN THE SOUTH

In 1900, nearly 90 percent of the nation's 9 million nonwhites lived in the South, where more than four-fifths of the region's non-whites lived in rural areas and were employed primarily in agriculture. By 1960, when the nonwhite population had increased to about 20 million, the proportion of nonwhites living in rural areas of the South had shrunk to 24 percent and the proportion living in Southern urban areas had more than doubled, rising from 15 percent in 1900 to 33 percent in 1960. Within the South much of the increase in the urban percentage was occasioned by an increase in

[3] The South includes the District of Columbia and the states of Delaware, Maryland, West Virginia, Virginia, North Carolina, South Carolina, Georgia, Florida, Alabama, Mississippi, Tennessee, Kentucky, Louisiana, Arkansas, Texas, and Oklahoma. If the border areas of Maryland and the District of Columbia were excluded from the South and treated as part of the North, the migration of Negroes from the South to the North would appear to be larger than that shown in Table 4.1. The Negro populations of Baltimore and Washington have increased sharply in recent years.

the Negro populations of a few large cities, notably Atlanta, Baltimore, Birmingham, New Orleans, and Washington. The percentage of nonwhites living in urban areas outside the South increased even more sharply during these years, rising from 8 percent in 1900 to 39 percent in 1960—a fivefold increase.

During these sixty years, the shift from rural to urban areas was more pronounced among nonwhites than among whites. In 1900, 77 percent of the nonwhite population and 42 percent of the white population lived in rural areas, but in 1960, only 28 percent of the nonwhites remained in these areas, while 30 percent of the white population still lived in rural places. The increase in the percentage of nonwhites living in urban areas was occasioned almost entirely by a shift from rural Southern areas to urban areas in the South and the North. The proportion of nonwhites living in rural areas in the North remained nearly constant at about 5 percent throughout the period.

MIGRATION FROM SOUTH TO NORTH

Dispersion of the nonwhite population to areas outside the South on a major scale began during World War I. Between 1920 and 1930, migration proceeded at a more rapid pace, but was retarded by depression during the 1930s, only to resume with even greater vigor during the 1940s and 1950s. The migration from the South began as a response to the severe labor shortages in Northern industrial centers engendered by the armament program and the coincident sharp decline in immigration from Europe. The legal restrictions on immigration established by Congress in 1921 and made more drastic in 1924 were also a major factor accounting for the continued migration during the 1920s. During the 1940s, the migration resumed in response to the mechanization of Southern agriculture, a shift from traditional products to livestock, and relatively high levels of employment in the remainder of the country, especially during World War II. If, as appears likely, Negroes continue to migrate from the South at the same rate as in the past two decades, more than half of the nonwhite population of the country will be living outside the South before the end of the present decade.

Another way to view the nonwhite migration from the South is to examine its effect on the proportion of nonwhites in the population of the South and on the corresponding proportion for the rest of the country. In 1900, nonwhites constituted nearly one-third of the population of the South, but by 1960 the proportion was barely one-fifth. In the former year, nonwhites comprised only slightly more than 2 percent of the population living outside the South; but by 1960 the figure had increased to nearly 7 percent—more than three times the proportion in 1900.[4]

During the single decade 1950–60, net migration of nonwhites from the South totaled 1,457,000 persons. Every state in the South proper except Florida experienced a net loss of nonwhites during the decade. Net outmigration was greatest from Alabama, Georgia, Mississippi, North Carolina, and South Carolina, each of which had losses of more than 200,000 nonwhites.[5]

CONCENTRATION OF NONWHITES IN NORTHERN AND
WESTERN METROPOLITAN AREAS

The above-cited figures showing the growth of the nonwhite population in areas outside the South fail to disclose certain significant facts concerning the location of Negroes within these areas. In the South, nonwhites are fairly well dispersed throughout the total population. In the North, however, nonwhites are heavily concentrated within the larger metropolitan areas, where they constitute much higher percentages of the populations than in the

[4] U.S. Bureau of the Census, U.S. Census of Population, 1920: Volume II, U.S. Summary, Table 72 (includes data for 1900 and 1910). 1930: Volume II, U.S. Summary, Tables 10, 21, and 22. 1940: Volume II, Part 1, U.S. Summary, Table 21, and special report, "Characteristics of the Nonwhite Population by Race," Table 3. 1950: Volume II, Part 1, Tables 58 and 60, and separate state parts for Southern states. 1960: Final Report PC(1)–1B, Tables 42 and 52. Data revised to exclude Mexicans, who were classified as nonwhite in the 1930 Census reports. Data for Alaska and Hawaii excluded.

[5] U.S. Bureau of the Census, News Release of December 27, 1961 (CB61–167).

North as a whole. Table 4.2 lists the areas with the largest non-white populations.

Table 4.2

NONWHITES AS PERCENTAGE OF POPULATION IN SELECTED NORTHERN
METROPOLITAN AREAS AND THEIR CENTRAL CITIES

	METROPOLITAN AREAS			CENTRAL CITIES		
	1940	*1950*	*1960*	*1940*	*1950*	*1960*
Chicago	7.3	11.0	14.8	9.3	14.1	23.6
Cincinnati	8.8	10.6	12.0	12.2	15.6	21.8
Cleveland	7.2	10.5	14.5	9.6	16.3	28.9
Dayton	8.0	9.4	10.2	9.6	14.1	22.0
Detroit	7.5	12.0	15.1	9.3	16.4	29.2
Gary [a]	...	...	...	18.4	29.4	38.9
Los Angeles	4.4	6.3	8.8	6.5	10.7	16.8
New York	5.8	8.1	11.0	6.4	9.8	14.7
Newark [b]	...	...	...	10.7	17.2	34.3
Oakland [c]	...	...	...	4.7	14.5	26.3
Philadelphia	11.0	13.2	15.7	13.1	18.3	26.7
Pittsburgh	5.8	6.2	6.8	9.3	12.3	16.8
San Francisco	4.3	9.4	12.4	5.1	10.5	18.3
St. Louis	10.9	12.9	14.5	13.4	18.0	28.8

Sources: U.S. Bureau of the Census, *U.S. Census of Population, 1940:* Vol. II, Part 1, Tables 36 and 45. *1950:* Vol. II, Table 53. *1960:* Final report PC(1), Table 72. All the above citations refer to the separate volumes for the several states in which the metropolitan areas are located. Unadjusted for changes in the definitions of standard metropolitan areas.
[a] Included in Chicago Metropolitan Area.
[b] Included in New York Metropolitan Area.
[c] Included in San Francisco Metropolitan Area.

The conventional view that Northern Negroes live in racial ghettos, such as Harlem and Chicago's South Side, has a solid basis in fact. In 1960, about 5,750,000 nonwhites lived in these metropolitan areas, a little more than two-thirds of all nonwhites living outside the South. Only about one-third of the white population outside the South lived in these same areas. Within the metropolitan areas, nonwhites were concentrated in the central cities and their principal satellite cities, such as Newark and Oakland. In 1960, almost 54 percent of the nonwhites living outside of the South were to be found in the fourteen principal cities of these metropol-

itan areas, but only about 15 percent of the white population living
outside of the South dwelt in these same cities. Between 1940 and
1960, nonwhites increased as a percentage of the population in each
of these metropolitan areas and cities; but the most rapid rates of
increase were in the central cities rather than the metropolitan areas.
In eleven of these fourteen cities, nonwhites formed a larger fraction of the population in 1960 than they did of the South as a whole.

The migration of Negroes to urban places in the South and the
remainder of the country transformed them in the space of a few
decades from a predominantly rural agricultural group to a largely
urbanized population. Negro employment problems became national in scope rather than regional. The change in place of residence caused increased competition between Negroes and whites
for the employment opportunities of the industrial and commercial
world of large metropolitan centers. The Negro population has
been urbanized at a particularly rapid rate since 1940, but employment practices have changed more slowly. Many unresolved
social and economic problems stem from the Negro migration to
urban areas. Employment patterns and practices that were accepted
with relatively little protest by the predominantly rural Negroes
of earlier generations are increasingly unacceptable to the Negroes
of the present generation.

The Occupational Status of Negroes

The great migration of Negroes from the rural South to the
urban areas of the South and North was accompanied by major
changes in their occupational status. On balance, migration improved the economic status of Negroes in the nation by reducing
their concentration in Southern rural areas, where occupational
choices are severely limited and family income is exceptionally low.

THE NATION

One way to measure the occupational progress of Negroes is
to examine changes in the percentage of nonwhites in each of the

major occupation groups used by the Bureau of the Census in classifying all occupations. Such percentages are given in Table 4.3, by ten-year intervals, beginning in 1920.[6]

The occupation groups are arranged roughly in the order of their desirability from the standpoint of social status and economic rewards. The first three groups—professional and technical workers; managers, officials, and proprietors; clerical and sales workers— comprise the bulk of the nation's white-collar workers, with clerical and sales workers ordinarily falling into the lower part of these groups of occupations. Craftsmen and operatives are composed respectively of skilled and semiskilled manual workers in the manufacturing, construction, mining, transportation, and utility industries. A number of service industry occupations are also included in these occupation groups. Median annual earnings of male craftsmen are slightly higher than those of male clerical and sales workers, so that the craftsmen occupation group includes many desirable jobs. The service-worker group is composed primarily of occupations of relatively low status and pay—attendants, cooks, waiters, janitors, porters, and the like—but includes a few relatively desirable occupations such as firemen and policemen. From the standpoint of social status and pay, the farm-worker group is the least homogeneous group of occupations; it includes both affluent farm owners and poverty-stricken migratory farm laborers. Negroes are concentrated in the least desirable sectors of the farm-worker group—sharecroppers and migratory laborers. The remaining occupation groups require no explanation.

Table 4.3 shows that the percentage of Negroes is small in the most desirable occupation groups and relatively large in the least desirable groups. The only occupation group where there was a large decline in the percentage of Negroes was the farmer and farm-laborer group, a consequence of the migration of Negroes to urban areas of the North and South from rural areas of the South.

[6] The data shown in Table 4.3 include both the employed and the unemployed because employed and unemployed persons were not enumerated separately prior to the census of 1940. Tables 4.4 and 4.5 give data for employed persons only.

Table 4.3

NONWHITE AS PERCENTAGE OF TOTAL CIVILIAN LABOR FORCE, UNITED STATES

Occupation group	PERCENTAGE NONWHITE					INDEX OF NONWHITE PARTICIPATION				
	1920	*1930*	*1940*	*1950*	*1960*	*1920*	*1930*	*1940*	*1950*	*1960*
Professional, technical, and kindred workers	3.6	3.8	3.7	3.9	4.7	29	32	34	38	45
Managers, officials, and proprietors, except farm	1.8	1.9	1.7	2.3	2.1	15	16	16	22	20
Clerical and sales workers	1.3	1.3	1.4	2.6	3.7	10	11	13	25	36
Craftsmen, foremen, and kindred workers	2.8	3.0	3.0	4.0	4.7	23	25	28	39	45
Operatives and kindred workers	6.0	6.9	6.2	9.7	10.8	48	58	57	94	104
Service workers, except private household	22.2	21.1	17.2	20.3	20.2	179	179	159	197	194
Private household workers	44.6	47.1	48.4	58.1	54.3	360	399	448	564	522
Laborers, except farm and mine	20.2	21.6	20.6	25.8	25.7	163	183	191	250	247
Farmers and farm laborers	21.3	19.9	18.2	16.2	14.4	172	169	169	157	138
Total, all employed persons	12.4	11.8	10.8	10.3	10.4					

Sources: 1920–40: The data from which the percent of nonwhites in each occupation group was derived were prepared by David L. Kaplan, Assistant Chief, Population Division, U.S. Bureau of the Census. For 1920 and 1930 the figures for total persons were taken from U.S. Bureau of the Census, *Working Paper No. 5*, and the figures for nonwhites were estimated from other published and unpublished Census Bureau data.

1940: *Census of Population*, Vol. III, Part 1, Table 62, and *The Labor Force* (*Sample Statistics*), *Usual Occupation*, Table 4. The data for 1940 were compiled from figures on current occupation of employed persons, usual occupation of persons on public emergency work, and last occupation of experienced workers seeking work. These data were not fully adjusted for comparability with the 1950 and 1960 occupational classification systems, but are considered satisfactory for the purpose of showing nonwhite proportions. Thus, the data from which the 1940 nonwhite proportions were computed differ from the historical series in Census Bureau *Working Paper No. 5* because of differences in occupational classification, because certain complete count data were used in their preparation, and because persons who did not report their occupations were excluded.

1950: U.S. Bureau of the Census, *Census of Population*, Special Report P–E No. 1B, Table 3 (based on 3½% sample).

1960: U.S. Bureau of the Census, *U.S. Census of Population, United States Summary*, Final Report PC(1)–1C, Tables 88 and 90. Alaska and Hawaii excluded.

Changes in the occupational status of nonwhites in the nation relative to whites can be shown most accurately by indexes of nonwhite participation in each occupation group. Such indexes can be computed by dividing the percentage of nonwhites in any occupation group by the percentage of nonwhites in the total labor force. If the distribution of nonwhites by occupation group were the same as that of the total population, each index number would be 100; an index number less than 100 indicates that nonwhites are underrepresented in the occupation group, while an index number greater than 100 indicates that nonwhites are overrepresented. The indexes corresponding to the percentages for the United States as a whole are given in the second half of Table 4.3.

The indexes show that Negroes gained some ground in the desirable professional, managerial, clerical, and craftsmen groups between 1920 and 1960, but were still seriously underrepresented in each of these groups in 1960. Negroes were still largely concentrated in the least desirable occupations in 1960. In a sense, Negroes experienced both gains and losses in occupational status during these forty years. Participation in the more desirable occupation groups increased somewhat; but participation in certain of the least desirable occupation groups—service workers, private household workers, and nonfarm laborers—increased also. The fact that Negroes who moved out of agricultural occupations in rural areas of the South usually found their first jobs in urban areas among service and laborer occupations accounts in large part for the sharp rise in the indexes of nonwhite participation in the least desirable nonagricultural occupations.

The indexes also show that gains in the occupational status of Negroes are most likely to occur when there are labor shortages. Between 1920 and 1960, improvements in the occupational status of Negroes were most pronounced in two decades, 1920–30 and 1940–50. In the earlier decade, curtailment of the immigration of white Europeans happened to coincide with a period of industrial expansion in the Northern states. During the 1940–50 decade,

Negro gains resulted from war and postwar manpower shortages. The decade-to-decade changes in the index of nonwhite participation in the operatives group illustrate the point. Between 1920 and 1930, the index rose 10 points; during the depressed decade of the 1930s, Negroes failed to gain ground; between 1940 and 1950, the index rose 37 points to near parity with whites. During the 1950s, Negro gains were more modest. The operatives group contains many semiskilled occupations for which relatively poorly educated Negroes can qualify. For many Negroes, employment as an operative is the next step up the occupational ladder from the largely unskilled occupation groups of service workers, household workers, and laborers, in which many of them were first employed when they abandoned farming.

It is significant that the operatives group is the only one above the laborer and service categories in which Negroes succeeded in attaining parity with whites between 1920 and 1960, given serious underrepresentation at the beginning of the period. Negroes made progress in this occupation group for several reasons: many occupations in the group could be filled quite easily by inexperienced persons after only brief on-the-job training; in two of the four decades, labor market conditions forced employers to change their racial hiring practices in order to meet their needs for manpower; at least in the North, discriminatory practices and attitudes are much less prevalent and intense in the case of occupations of relatively low status and pay than they are in the case of occupations higher on the scale of desirability. Negro progress in skilled manual occupations, white-collar work, and professional jobs was much less pronounced than it was in occupations of lower status.

In some respects, the broad occupation groups shown in Table 4.3 give a false impression of the occupational status of Negroes because each group is an aggregate of many specific occupations and because Negroes are frequently concentrated in the lower-paid or otherwise less desirable occupations within each group. In the professional-technical category, for example, the Negro aggregate is composed largely of clergymen, teachers, and nurses. In the higher-paid professions, such as medicine, accountancy, engineering, and the natural sciences, Negroes are grossly underrepresented. Negroes are also greatly underrepresented in the manager-proprietor category, and Negroes employed in this occupation group are most frequently self-employed persons in retail trade, eating and drinking establishments, and similar small businesses. In 1960, less than ½ of 1 percent of the salaried managers and officials of manufacturing establishments were Negro.[7] Concentration of Negroes in relatively undesirable occupations could also be observed in the craftsmen and operatives occupation groups in 1960.[8]

Another matter not taken into account in Table 4.3 is the effect of segregation on racial patterns of employment by occupation. In the South, many of the Negroes employed in the more desirable occupation groups are engaged in performing services almost exclusively for other Negroes rather than for the community at large. In that region, Negro teachers, clergymen, lawyers, physicians, and dentists serve all-Negro clienteles. The same statement is true of Negro proprietors of retail businesses, the sales and clerical workers employed in such places, and employees of Negro banks, insurance companies, and other establishments that cater to Negroes. In the North, Negro establishments are a less important source of Negro employment.

THE NORTH

Table 4.4 gives indexes of nonwhite participation in 1940, 1950, and 1960 for the North and West (which for brevity we will call simply the North) in each of the major census occupation groups. Considering first the decade 1940–50, we note that the index of nonwhite participation in the operatives group rose from 79 in 1940 to 120 in 1950, or an increase of approximately 50 percent. Moreover, the fact that the 1950 index was over 100 shows that

[7] U.S. Bureau of the Census, U.S. Census of Population, 1960: Detailed Characteristics, U.S. Summary, Final Report PC(1)–1D, Table 205.
[8] Ibid.

Negroes were by that time somewhat better than equitably represented in operative jobs in the North. In the clerical and sales group,
the index also rose by about 50 percent; and in the craftsmen and
foremen group, it rose by approximately 30 percent.   In both

Table 4.4

NONWHITE AS PERCENTAGE OF ALL EMPLOYED PERSONS IN THE NORTH

Occupation group	PERCENTAGE NONWHITE			INDEX OF NONWHITE PARTICIPATION		
	1940	*1950*	*1960*	*1940*	*1950*	*1960*
Professional, technical, and kindred workers	1.3	1.8	3.2	38	36	50
Managers, officials, and proprietors, except farm	1.1	1.5	1.6	32	30	25
Clerical, sales, and kindred workers	0.9	2.0	3.3	26	40	52
Craftsmen, foremen, and kindred workers	1.2	2.3	3.2	35	46	50
Operatives and kindred workers	2.7	6.0	8.2	79	120	130
Service workers, except private household	9.3	12.4	12.9	273	248	204
Laborers, except farm and mine	7.3	13.5	13.9	214	270	220
Private household workers	21.5	34.5	30.1	632	690	477
Farmers and farm laborers	2.2	2.3	2.4	64	46	38
Total, all employed persons	3.4	5.0	6.3			

Sources: U.S. Bureau of the Census, *U.S. Census of Population, 1940:* Vol. III,
Part 1, Table 63. *1950:* Vol. II, Part 1, Table 159. *1960: General Social and Economic Characteristics, U.S. Summary,* Final Report PC(1)–1C, Table 88 and separate state volumes, Table 58. Alaska and Hawaii excluded to make 1960 data
comparable to those for 1940 and 1950.

these groups, however, Negro representation was still less than
one-half of parity with the white population in 1950. The managerial and technical-professional groups, unlike the operatives, clerical-sales, and craftsmen groups, showed no increase in the Negro
participation index between 1940 and 1950; indeed, in both groups
the index fell slightly over the decade.

Without doubt the principal factor accounting for the gains

made by Negroes in the operatives category between 1940 and 1950 was the advent of World War II and the resultant severe shortage of labor. The immense expansion of production and the withdrawal of millions of young workers into the armed forces created a manpower gap that could only be filled by recruitment from the nonindustrial labor force and from among the unemployed; and Negroes comprised an important proportion of both these groups. Hundreds of firms engaged in war production that had never previously utilized Negroes now employed them in substantial numbers, largely for semiskilled production jobs. The President's Committee on Fair Employment Practice and other government agencies concerned with wartime manpower problems also played some part in the process by persuading reluctant employers to speed up their hiring of Negro workers. The basic causative factor, however, behind the substantial occupational progress of Negroes in the North during the war period was the critical scarcity of available manpower. The gains made during the war were in large part held in the postwar period, as evidenced by the fact that the index of nonwhite participation in the operatives category in 1950 exceeded the 1940 index by more than 50 percent.

The 30 percent increase in the index for the craftsmen and foremen group during the 1940s was also due in large part to the wartime labor shortage. The rise in the index tends, however, to overstate the actual gain made by Negroes in this category, since gains were concentrated for the most part in such lower-level crafts as cement-finishing and painting. Very few Negroes gained access to such high-level crafts as electrician and plumber or to positions as foremen. The 50 percent rise in the clerical and sales index between 1940 and 1950 is traceable in part to a substantial increase of Negroes in postal and other Federal government jobs in the North during the decade. While labor shortages probably had much to do with this gain, the official policy of nondiscrimination in Federal employment, which was reasonably well enforced in the postal and some of the other Federal services in the

North, was undoubtedly also an important contributing factor.[9]

The changes in the middle- and upper-level indexes between 1950 and 1960 indicate that Negroes made some further occupational gains in the North during this decade. The rate of progress appears, however, to have been considerably slower in the 1950s than in the 1940s. The indexes for the operatives and craftsmen groups rose by less than 10 percent and that for the clerical and sales group by about 30 percent (as compared with 50 percent in the preceding decade). The professional and technical group index, it is true, rose by about one-third—mainly because of an unusually large increase in Negro nurses. On the other hand, the managerial group index *fell* by one-sixth, reflecting mainly a decrease in the number of self-employed Negroes in retail trade, accompanied by a substantial increase in the Negro labor force in the North. At the end of the decade, in 1960, the operatives group index was well above the 100 mark—as indeed it had been in 1950. Allowing for the fact that Negroes were still somewhat concentrated in the lower-paid occupations in this group, this fact can be interpreted as meaning that Negroes in the North had by 1960 achieved approximate parity with whites in semiskilled blue-collar work.

In the two next higher groups, however—craftsmen and foremen, and clerical and sales—the indexes indicated that Negroes still had only about one-half the representation that their numerical strength in the total work force would imply. Negro representation of approximately one-half of parity with whites was also indicated in the professional and technical category; but within this group of occupations Negroes were heavily concentrated in nursing and other lower-level professional occupations, so that this fraction exaggerates Negro gains in professional occupations. In the managerial category, the indicated status of Negroes was only one-quarter of parity with whites; and even this low figure over-

[9] This analysis of the factors accounting for the Negro's occupational gains between 1940 and 1950 is based in part on Ginzberg, *The Negro Potential*, Ch. II.

stated their actual status, owing again to concentration of Negroes in lower-level occupations within the group. In sum, Negroes in the North were still greatly under-represented in all four upper-level categories in 1960 and—as Table 4.4 shows—greatly overrepresented in all the lower-level categories except farm workers. Only in the middle-level operatives group were they approximately on a par with the white majority.

It is not easy to assess the factors accounting for the modest gains in Negro occupational status in the North between 1950 and 1960. Unlike the 1940s, the 1950s were not characterized by general shortages of unskilled and semiskilled labor. Indeed, except for the Korean War period in 1951–52, a small but growing surplus of unskilled labor was in evidence throughout the decade. Moreover, it is doubtful whether a continuing labor shortage would have resulted in employment of Negroes in such predominantly white-collar activities as banking, insurance, and retail selling, since this did not occur even during the extreme shortages of the later years of World War II. It appears likely, however, that gains in blue-collar employment were due in part to local labor shortages in particular metropolitan areas in the North where the Negro population was growing rapidly. The advent of FEP laws in a number of the industrial states of the North and West accounted for part of the indicated gains—both in blue-collar and white-collar employment. Since, however, only two states with substantial Negro populations—New York and New Jersey—had FEP laws throughout the decade and since most of the other states in this category enacted their laws late in 1959 and 1960, this factor could not have had a major influence on the North and West as a whole. The effects of the long-established FEP laws on the occupational status of Negroes within the respective states are discussed in Chapter 6. Still another factor that contributed to the indicated gains in the clerical and sales category was a substantial further increase in the employment of Negroes in post offices and other Federal government establishments in the major urban areas of the North. As in the preceding decade, the increase was attributable in considerable part to the official policy of nondiscrimination in Federal employment. This development is dealt with in more detail in Chapter 8.

THE SOUTH

Examination of census data for 1940, 1950, and 1960 reveals that the occupational progress of Negroes over the twenty-year period was considerably slower in the South than in the rest of the country. This difference is brought out in Table 4.5, which shows indexes of Negro occupational participation for the South corresponding to the indexes for the North shown in Table 4.4. Again the analysis will be facilitated if we consider the two decades separately.

Table 4.5

NONWHITE AS PERCENTAGE OF ALL EMPLOYED PERSONS IN THE SOUTH

Occupation group	PERCENTAGE NONWHITE			INDEX OF NONWHITE PARTICIPATION		
	1940	1950	1960	1940	1950	1960
Professional, technical, and kindred workers	10.6	9.9	9.2	40	45	47
Managers, officials, and proprietors, except farm	3.2	3.9	2.9	12	17	15
Clerical, sales, and kindred workers	2.4	3.9	4.2	9	17	22
Craftsmen, foremen, and kindred workers	7.8	7.9	8.1	30	36	42
Operatives and kindred workers	15.6	18.6	17.8	60	85	92
Service workers, except private household	35.0	40.1	37.4	135	183	194
Laborers, except farm and mine	49.4	49.8	47.6	190	228	247
Private household workers	81.6	84.4	79.8	315	387	415
Farmers and farm laborers	33.4	30.8	30.1	128	141	156
Total, all employed persons	25.9	21.8	19.2			

Sources: U.S. Bureau of the Census, *U.S. Census of Population, 1940:* Vol. III, Part 1, Table 63. *1950:* Vol. II, Part 1, Table 159. *1960: General Social and Economic Characteristics, U.S. Summary,* Final Report PC(1)–1C, Table 88, and separate state volumes, Table 58. Alaska and Hawaii excluded to make 1960 data comparable to those for 1940 and 1950.

Between 1940 and 1950, the index for the operatives group rose from 60 to 85—a 40 percent increase. The index also rose in each of the higher-level groups—craftsmen and foremen, clerical and sales, managerial, and professional and technical. Only in the operatives group, however, did the 1950 index indicate a Negro status anywhere near parity with whites. In the clerical and sales and managerial groups it was less than two-tenths of parity, and in the craftsmen and foremen group about one-third. The professional and technical index was 45, indicating a Negro representation of nearly one-half of parity; but this figure greatly overstated the true situation, since about two-thirds of the Negroes in the group were clergymen and teachers—both low-paid occupations—as compared with only one-fifth of the whites. If the nonwhite index were recomputed with these occupations omitted, it would drop from 45 to 15, or less than two-tenths of parity with whites.

In the South, as in the North, the substantial gain made by Negroes in the operatives category was attributable in large part to the labor shortage occasioned by the war effort. Negroes in the South, however, were not hired for production jobs in defense plants as they were in the North, nor did they gain access to such jobs in civilian manufacturing—except in such establishments as laundries, sawmills and fertilizer plants, where Negroes were already employed in substantial numbers. Instead, they found increasing employment as truck drivers, gasoline station attendants, laundry operatives, and the like when white workers left these occupations for defense plant employment. Thus, while Southern Negroes made a notable gain in the semiskilled category as a whole, the traditional racial pattern of segregated employment in Southern industry remained substantially unchanged.

A similar development probably accounted for most of the small gain indicated in the craftsmen and foremen group. In the South, Negroes in the construction crafts have long been heavily concentrated in bricklaying, plastering, and cement-finishing; and their representation in these trades may have improved during the

1940s. Negroes also gained increasing access to jobs as automobile repair mechanics during these years—largely, one may assume, as a further consequence of the general shortage of labor during the war years.

There is little evidence that wartime labor shortages or other market factors had any significant effect on the status of Southern Negroes in the professional, managerial, and clerical occupation groups during the 1940s. Except in a few border-area cities included in the Census definition of the South, notably Washington, D.C., the traditional pattern of nearly complete exclusion of Negroes from "white" office work and retail trade establishments still remained virtually intact in 1950; and the same was true with respect to managerial and professional employment. It is, therefore, safe to conclude that the small gains indicated in these three categories were largely a manifestation of additional employment opportunities within the segregated Negro community, resulting from the increasing Negro migration from rural to urban areas in the South.

A comparison of the 1950 indexes for the South with those for 1960 gives evidence of some further improvement of the Negro's status in the middle and higher occupational categories. The indicated gains were much smaller in the 1950s, however, than in the preceding decade, with the result that Negroes in the South were still grossly underrepresented in all four higher-level categories in 1960—substantially more so, in fact, than in the North—except for the professional and technical category, where the continued presence of a large number of Negro clergymen and teachers inflated the index of nonwhite participation. Only in the middle-level operatives group did the index indicate any close approach to Negro parity with the white majority, and even this figure, as we have seen, considerably overstated the southern Negro's true status in semiskilled occupations.

The persistence of low index values in the higher-level categories in 1960—and concomitantly of high index values in the lower-level categories—is corroborated by the results of recent field surveys in several Southern cities, as indicated in Chapter 2. Thus, for example, it is apparent that Southern Negro representation in the construction crafts is still heavily concentrated in the "trowel trades," with little evidence of appreciable progress in any other skilled building occupations. Further, apart from work in the segregated Negro community, Southern Negroes are still almost entirely debarred from clerical and retail sales positions, as well as from managerial and professional employment except in "Negro" businesses.

While it is not possible to trace all of the reasons accounting for the slower occupational progress of Negroes in the South than in the North in the 1950s, some of the more obvious contributing factors may be noted. The labor surplus that developed in the middle and later 1950s was substantially larger in the South than in the North. At the beginning of the decade, the South had a larger reserve of agricultural labor than any other region of the country— 16.2 percent as opposed to 9.2 percent in the nation as a whole.[10] The migration of whites from rural to urban areas of the South provided a sufficient supply of labor to meet the manpower requirements of Southern urban areas without significant deviation from customary racial employment patterns.

Another contributing factor, without doubt, was the widespread and deep-rooted practice of segregated employment and separate facilities in Southern industry. This practice constitutes a built-in deterrent to the employment of Negroes in white-collar and upper-level blue-collar jobs. A corollary factor was that, while most of the industrial states in the North adopted FEP laws during the period, no such development occurred in the South. Indeed, several Southern states and cities enacted laws designed to *prevent* racial integration in employment. It is hardly surprising, therefore,

10 U.S. Bureau of the Census, *U.S. Census of Population, 1950:* Vol. II, *Characteristics of the Population*, Part 1, *U.S. Summary*, Table 79.

that Negroes made little occupational progress in the South following the disappearance of the war-created labor shortages.

Unemployment among Negroes

Unemployment rates have been higher for Negroes than for whites over the entire period of time for which data are available. Table 4.6 shows unemployment rates, by sex and color, in 1940, 1950, and 1960.

Table 4.6

PERCENTAGE OF CIVILIAN LABOR FORCE UNEMPLOYED, UNITED STATES

	1940	1950	1960
Both sexes:			
White	14.2	4.5	4.7
Nonwhite	16.8	7.8	8.7
Total	14.5	4.8	5.1
Male:			
White	14.6	4.6	4.6
Nonwhite	17.8	7.8	8.8
Total	14.9	4.9	5.0
Female:			
White	13.0	4.1	4.9
Nonwhite	14.5	7.9	8.5
Total	13.3	4.6	5.4

Source: U.S. Bureau of the Census, *U.S. Census of Population, 1960: General Social and Economic Characteristics, U.S. Summary*, Final Report PC(1)–1C, Table 83.

Total unemployment was so great in 1940 that white-nonwhite differences in unemployment rates were relatively slight. During the postwar period, the unemployment rate among nonwhites has been very much higher than among whites; and the difference between white and nonwhite rates has tended to grow larger with the passage of time. One author who computed unemployment rates for whites and nonwhites in 1949–50 and 1959–60, periods of roughly similar total unemployment and labor force participation rates, found that the rate of unemployment among whites had declined about 6 percent while increasing 19 percent among nonwhites.[11] Unemployment rates are higher among nonwhites than whites in each region of the country, in each age and sex group, and at every level of educational attainment.

The rate of unemployment is particularly high among young Negro males and may have reduced their rate of participation in the labor force. Between 1940 and 1960, the percentage of nonwhite males fourteen years of age and over not in the labor force increased from 20.0 to 27.8. Among white males the percentage not in the labor force was about 21 percent in both years. Persons not in the labor force are not at work and are not looking for work. The much higher rate of nonparticipation in the labor force among nonwhite males probably indicates that many of them are so convinced of the futility of seeking employment that they do not even look for work.

If data from *Current Population Reports* of the Census Bureau are used to measure racial differences in unemployment, instead of data from the decennial Censuses, white-nonwhite differences in unemployment rates appear to be even greater than those shown in Table 4.6. In each of the years 1957–61, according to these reports, the annual average rate of unemployment among nonwhite males was more than twice what it was among whites. Among females, racial differences were not quite so great, the unemployment rate for nonwhite females being about 175 percent of the rate for whites. Data from the *Current Population Reports* may reflect reality more accurately than those of the decennial Censuses because the former are collected by more carefully trained personnel and give particular attention to the measurement of unemployment.

Table 4.7 shows that during recent years, unemployment rates

[11] Clarence D. Long, "An Overview of Postwar Labor Market Developments," *The Labor Market and Social Security, Proceedings of the Fourth Annual Social Security Conference,* University of Michigan and Wayne State University (Kalamazoo, Mich., The W. E. Upjohn Institute for Employment Research, 1962), p. 19.

have been higher for nonwhites than whites in each major occupation group. In the most desirable occupation groups, where Negroes are underrepresented, the difference between white and nonwhite unemployment rates is particularly large and has shown relatively little tendency to decrease. In both 1950 and 1960, for

Table 4.7

EXPERIENCED UNEMPLOYED AS PERCENTAGE OF EMPLOYED, UNITED STATES

Occupation group	1950		1960	
	White	*Nonwhite*	*White*	*Nonwhite*
Professional, technical, and kindred workers	1.6	2.7	1.3	2.3
Managers, officials, and proprietors, except farm	1.2	2.4	1.4	3.1
Clerical and kindred workers	2.5	6.9	3.2	6.3
Sales workers	3.0	6.1	3.4	7.5
Craftsmen, foremen, and kindred workers	4.9	10.1	5.5	9.5
Operatives and kindred workers	5.1	8.1	7.7	10.4
Service workers, except private household	5.1	7.0	5.3	8.1
Private household workers	5.1	6.5	4.9	6.4
Laborers, except farm and mine	9.8	11.2	13.3	14.5
Farmers and farm laborers	1.9	2.8	2.7	7.8
Total, all occupations	3.7	6.8	4.6	8.7

Computed from the following sources: U.S. Bureau of the Census, *U.S. Census of Population, 1950:* Special Report P–E No. 1B, Table 3 (based on 3½ percent sample). *U.S. Census of Population, 1960: General Social and Economic Characteristics, U.S. Summary, Final Report* PC(1)–1C, Tables 88 and 90. Excludes persons who did not report their occupations, and those who lived in Alaska and Hawaii. Unadjusted for Bureau of the Census changes in the definition of unemployed persons.

example, the rate of unemployment among nonwhite managerial and sales personnel was twice the white rate or more. In the less desirable occupation groups, differences tend to be somewhat smaller. In the operatives group, where Negroes have made substantial progress in recent decades and sometimes benefit from the seniority provisions of labor agreements, the difference between nonwhite and white unemployment rates decreased between 1950 and 1960.

The high rates of unemployment among nonwhites probably result from the following factors: nonwhite concentration in unskilled and semiskilled occupations where intermittent employment occasioned by layoffs and casual work produces high unemployment rates; a tendency for nonwhites to be clustered within each major occupation group in suboccupations particularly subject to unemployment; lower levels of educational attainment and achievement among nonwhites than whites; and, at least in some instances, employer preference for white rather than Negro employees. The fact that Negro workers are frequently the most recently hired, and hence the first to be released when layoffs occur, also contributes to high Negro unemployment rates.

Incomes of Negroes and Whites

Dependable racial statistics on incomes, like those on unemployment, are available only for recent decades. Table 4.8 shows how the median annual income of the nation's nonwhite families compared with that of white families over the period 1939–60.

Table 4.8

MEDIAN WAGE OR SALARY INCOME OF PRIMARY FAMILIES
AND UNRELATED INDIVIDUALS, UNITED STATES

	1939	1950	1953	1956	1960
White	$1,325	$3,390	$4,201	$4,685	$5,424
Nonwhite	489	1,671	2,357	2,429	3,058
Nonwhite income as percentage of white income	37	49	56	52	

Sources: U.S. Bureau of the Census, *Statistical Abstract of the United States, 1950* and *1960*, and *Current Population Reports*, Series P-60, No. 37 (January, 1962).

From 1939 to 1953, the median dollar income of nonwhite families increased at a considerably faster rate than that of white families,

As of 1939 Negros got 37% of white man medium wage + 1970 only 76%

with the result that the relative magnitude of nonwhite income rose from 37 percent of white income in 1940 to 56 percent in 1953. From 1953 to 1960, however, nonwhite and white dollar incomes increased at approximately the same rate. Hence, nonwhite incomes still averaged only 56 percent of white incomes in 1960.

While the comparison for the nation as a whole indicates the existence of a wide over-all income differential between the Negro group and the white majority, a more accurate and meaningful picture of the disparity is obtained by making separate comparisons for the South and for the rest of the country. Table 4.9, based on sample surveys conducted in 1935–36, 1953, and 1960, shows the median income of *urban* nonwhite families, expressed as a percentage of the corresponding white income, for the respective periods in each of the two major regions.

Table 4.9

MEDIAN INCOME OF URBAN NONWHITE FAMILIES, AS PERCENTAGE
OF MEDIAN INCOME OF URBAN WHITE FAMILIES

Region	1935–36	1953	1960
South	33	52	52
North and West	63	72	73

Sources: For 1935–36, Sterner, *The Negro's Share*, p. 60 (derived from data in *Consumer Incomes in the United States: Their Distribution in 1935–36*, National Resources Committee, 1938, p. 28). For 1953 and 1960, data for the South from U.S. Bureau of the Census, *Current Population Reports*, Series P-60, No. 20 (December, 1955) and No. 37 (January, 1962). Data for the North and West provided by the Census Bureau from unpublished materials.

It is apparent from Table 4.9 that the disparity between the incomes of Negroes and whites has long been, and still is, considerably greater in the South than in the remainder of the country. Thus, in 1935–36, urban Negro family income was, on the average, only one-third that of white income in the South, as compared with about three-fifths of white income in the North and West. In the ensuing years the relative income status of Southern Negroes improved somewhat, so that by 1953 their median income was about one-half that of Southern whites. A similar improvement occurred in the North and West, bringing the level of Northern Negro income up to nearly three-fourths that of Northern white income. Between 1953 and 1960 the ratios in both regions remained virtually unchanged. In sum, despite a modest narrowing of the North-South income gap since the 1930s, the relative (as well as the absolute) income status of the Southern Negro is still substantially below that of his Northern counterpart. Clearly, this disparity is causally related to the continuing North-South differential in the occupational status of Negroes revealed by our earlier analysis.

The Educational Status of Negroes

Racial discrimination in education has been both widespread and severe in this country since the days of slavery. As a result, Negroes have always been less well educated, on the average, than whites. While the differential has narrowed considerably in recent decades, there is still a substantial gap between the average level of education attained by the Negro group and that of the white majority. There is a close relationship between this fact and the Negro's disadvantaged employment and occupational status. The relationship is by no means a simple one, however, since the relatively low level of education among Negroes is both a cause and an effect of the handicapped position they occupy in the labor market. In order to complete the overview of the Negro group's employment and occupational situation, therefore, it is necessary to examine briefly the changes that have occurred in the group's educational attainment level in recent decades and its educational status at the present time relative to that of the white majority.

The 1960 Census figures on years of school completed by persons age twenty-five and over, classified by color, convey a reasonably accurate statistical picture of the current educational status of the Negro and white adult populations. These figures are summarized, as percentage distributions, by categories of school-completion periods, in Table 4.10. The table also includes the corresponding percentages for 1940 to show how the relative educational status of the two groups has changed in recent decades.

Considering first the indicated changes over time, we see that the average level of educational attainment of both whites and Negroes improved substantially over the twenty-year period. The

Table 4.10

PERCENTAGE DISTRIBUTION OF YEARS OF SCHOOL COMPLETED BY PERSONS
TWENTY-FIVE YEARS OF AGE AND OVER, UNITED STATES

	1940		1960	
	White	*Nonwhite*	*White*	*Nonwhite*
College:				
4 years or more	4.9	1.3	8.1	3.5
1 to 3 years	5.9	1.9	9.3	4.4
High school:				
4 years	15.3	4.5	25.7	13.4
1 to 3 years	15.8	8.7	19.3	18.8
Elementary school:				
8 years	29.9	11.9	18.1	12.8
5 to 7 years	17.3	29.9	12.8	23.6
1 to 4 years	7.8	31.3	4.8	18.0
None	3.1	10.5	1.9	5.5
Total	100.0	100.0	100.0	100.0

Computed from the following source: U.S. Bureau of the Census, *U.S. Census of Population, 1960: General Social and Economic Characteristics, U.S. Summary,* Final Report PC(1)–1C, Table 76. Alaska and Hawaii excluded.

proportion of whites in the four upper categories combined—representing the range of levels from some high school education to completion of college or more—rose from 41.9 percent in 1940 to 62.4 percent in 1960, while the corresponding proportion of nonwhites rose from 16.4 to 40.1 percent. Second, the table shows that, despite the greater gain indicated for nonwhites, the educational status of the Negro group is still well below that of the white majority. Thus, in 1960 about two-fifths of all nonwhite adults had educational experience in the categories beyond elementary school, whereas about three-fifths of white adults fell in these upper categories.

It is worth noting, in this connection, that the level of Negro education is substantially lower in the South than in other sections of the country. The magnitude of the North-South differential may be judged from Table 4.11, showing the median number of school years completed by whites and nonwhites age twenty-five and over in 1960 for each of the country's major regions. In briefer summary, it may be said that Negroes in the South have, on the average, attended school 3.3 fewer years than Southern whites, as compared with an average Negro-white differential for the North as a whole of about 1.8 years.

Table 4.11

MEDIAN SCHOOL YEARS COMPLETED BY PERSONS TWENTY-FIVE YEARS OLD
AND OVER, 1960

Region	White	Nonwhite	Difference (white minus nonwhite)
Northeast	10.8	9.2	1.6
North Central	10.8	9.0	1.8
West	12.1	10.0	2.1
South	10.4	7.1	3.3

Source: U.S. Bureau of the Census, *U.S. Census of Population, 1960: General Social and Economic Characteristics, U.S. Summary,* Final Report PC(1)–1C, Table 115.

While the educational level of the Negro group is thus substantially below that of the white majority, the differential is by no means so great as the gap between the occupational status of Negroes and whites, discussed earlier in the chapter. That the occupational gap is wider than the educational gap is apparent if one compares the 1960 indexes of nonwhite participation by occupation groups in Table 4.3 with the statistical picture of relative educational status for that year shown in Table 4.10. In the former table it was shown that the all-U.S. occupational status of Negroes in the four upper-level occupational categories—professional-technical, managers-proprietors, clerical-sales, and craftsmen-foremen —is substantially less than one-half of parity with whites. Table 4.10, on the other hand, indicates that the current attainment level of Negroes in the four upper-level educational categories combined (which gauges, in approximate terms, the degree of qualification for the upper-level occupations) is somewhat more than one-half that of the white majority.

The main causal factor accounting for the greater magnitude of the occupational gap is also fairly apparent. Owing to widespread racial discrimination in employment, a large proportion of Negroes with college education and an even larger proportion of Negro high school graduates are unable to find jobs commensurate with their educational qualifications. This situation has been alleviated to some extent in a few Northern states with established and reasonably well-administered FEP laws. In the remainder of the North, however, there is still a wide disparity between the level of educational attainment among Negroes and their representation in the upper half of the occupational spectrum. The disparity is even wider throughout the South, where Negroes are still debarred from most clerical, sales, and professional jobs and from virtually all managerial employment.

The following conclusions emerge from the foregoing review of the Negro's recent and current educational status. While a low average level of educational qualifications is a major factor holding back the Negro group's occupational progress, racial discrimination is at least an equally important retarding factor. Moreover, discrimination is also a causal factor holding back educational progress among Negroes: owing to the lack of desirable employment opportunities, young Negroes have little incentive to strive for more and better education. Further, the Negro group's low occupational status is itself a cause as well as an effect of its low educational level. Because of the low incomes which accompany low-level occupations, most Negro parents are unable to afford higher education for their offspring. In sum, Negroes cannot make any real gains in the upper-level occupational categories without a major improvement in their educational qualifications; but they cannot become better educated until racial discrimination in employment is eliminated, making available sufficiently better jobs to provide the means and the incentive for young Negroes to seek and strive for more knowledge.

Conclusions

THE LABOR MARKET AND RACIAL EMPLOYMENT PATTERNS

The concentration of Negroes in unskilled and semiskilled occupations of low status is not likely to be relieved in the foreseeable future by normal market mechanisms. In the past, improvements in the occupational status of Negroes tended to occur during periods of severe labor shortages. During these periods, Negroes could move into relatively unskilled occupations in substantial numbers and perform effectively on the job with only brief training by their employers or none at all. In the future such conditions are not likely to recur on the same scale.

When acute shortages arise in more skilled occupations, Negroes who have been trained or are trainable for such work can sometimes enter new fields. There was, for example, a shortage of nurses during the post-World War II years. Negro women entered the occupation in substantial numbers, particularly in the North, although cases we have reviewed in the files of state FEP commissions indicate that resistance to employment of Negro women as nurses was common during the early postwar years. Similarly, many employers, when questioned by state or Federal FEP officials concerning the absence of Negroes from executive, administrative, and professional positions during the postwar years, responded by suggesting that they would be happy to employ qualified Negro engineers or technicians. Since 1950 there has been a fairly persistent shortage of engineers. On the other hand, no single case was encountered in this study in which an employer suggested he would be willing to hire Negroes for employment in executive or administrative positions in management. In recent years, there has been no lack of candidates for such positions. It is worth noting, however, that although there was an acute shortage of clerical and sales personnel during World War II, very few Negroes were hired in either of these categories in the North and virtually none in the South.

Such examples indicate that market forces sometimes operate to facilitate Negro entry into nontraditional occupations, but they also show that there must be a persistent and fairly acute shortage of personnel in an occupation before employers will make use of minorities in occupations from which they have been excluded. In the case of occupations that require a long period of specialized training or education, it usually happens that only a small number of Negroes are ready to take advantage of such developments when they occur. Few Negroes can afford the luxury of expensive, time-consuming preparation for work in a nontraditional occupation on the chance that employer sentiment may have changed by the time their training has been completed. FEP laws, if effectively administered, would assure Negroes of genuine equality of opportunity and reduce the reluctance of many Negroes to qualify themselves for employment in nontraditional occupations.

On a national basis Negroes constitute only a small fraction of the labor force—about 10 percent. Except under conditions of full employment, employers seldom find it necessary to employ Negroes in nontraditional occupations, because the supply of whites is adequate for their needs. Negroes form a sizable fraction of the labor force in a number of large metropolitan areas—currently about 20 percent in Southern and some 10 to 15 percent in Northern metropolitan centers. Even in these areas of greater Negro concentration, however, employers seldom find it necessary to employ Negroes in nontraditional capacities. When, for example, automobile assembly plants were established in Atlanta, Georgia, following World War II, it was possible to staff the plants entirely with whites, except for Negroes employed in janitorial, culinary, laboring, and other traditional Negro occupations. Many other manufacturing plants established during these years in the South followed similar staffing practices without appreciable difficulty. Such practices were feasible because both Negroes and whites abandoned agricultural pursuits in the South at a rapid rate during the postwar years. Movement out of agriculture was somewhat more pronounced among whites than among Negroes, with the result that there was a plentiful supply of whites to fill unskilled and semiskilled production worker occupations in Southern manufacturing plants.

Because Negroes are usually a marginal part of the labor supply in any given labor market, from the standpoint of both numbers and quality, there is little incentive for employers to innovate in the matter of racial personnel policy. When a firm does decide to abandon traditional practices, it frequently feels that it must take special pains to explain its actions to its employees, and sometimes to customers as well. Many firms believe that such matters are so troublesome that they are unwilling to change their practices for the sake of a marginal addition to their labor supply.

Employers must broaden their recruitment activities by extending them to Negro schools and colleges when they change their racial practices. Unless a company makes a real effort to recruit Negro employees for nontraditional jobs, it will usually receive few applications from Negroes for employment in such jobs. Because of poor communication between the white and Negro communities, members of the Negro community are frequently unaware of changes in company employment policy. A perfunctory telephone call from a company personnel office to a local office of a Negro organization such as the NAACP or the Urban League is not likely to produce many job applicants. These organizations are not particularly well equipped to act as employment agencies. In 1961, for example, the national office of the Urban League received requests for referrals of Negro professionals from employers who had signed Plans for Progress sponsored by the President's Committee on Equal Employment Opportunity. The Urban League referred the requests to a single private employment agency for

Negro professionals in Harlem.[12] As long as the supply of whites is adequate, few employers will make special efforts to recruit and train Negroes for employment in nontraditional jobs, because such efforts require investment of time and money to overcome racial barriers.

As long as there are generally recognized patterns of employment by race and occupation in any given market, few employers will deviate from the usual patterns unless forced to do so by labor shortage or pressure from FEP commissions. Each employer is reluctant to change his practices in a way thought to be unacceptable in the community, because he fears loss of business or employee discontent. If, however, it can be made clear to all employers in the market that they must abandon their discriminatory practices, each individual employer will be less reluctant to do so, because all will be similarly situated. The cost to any given employer of changing his racial employment practices is reduced if all employers abandon discriminatory practices at the same time.

NEGRO EMPLOYMENT PROSPECTS

The inferior economic position of Negroes relative to whites tends to be self-perpetuating. Furthermore, recent and prospective changes in the occupational structure of the labor force imply greater difficulties in the future for many Negroes in matters of employment. Many of the occupations in which Negroes traditionally have been employed have formed a declining fraction of total employment in the years since World War II. In certain of these occupations there has been an absolute as well as a relative decline. Production workers in manufacturing industries, for example, decreased in number by about 525,000 between 1947 and 1960.[13] During the same years employment in clerical, professional, administrative, and executive positions rose sharply. In other words, the

[12] Interview with Julius Thomas, formerly Director, Department of Industrial Relations, National Urban League, New York.

[13] An independent study group, *The Public Interest in National Labor Policy* (New York, Committee for Economic Development, 1961), p. 41.

distribution of jobs by occupation changed in such a way that the unskilled occupations, where Negroes have long been concentrated, decreased as a fraction of total employment, while skilled occupations, where they have always been greatly underrepresented, increased.

The post-World War II trends seem certain to continue for some years. The rate of change in the occupational structure of employment may even increase as recent investments in research and development result in the introduction of radical changes in production processes and the adoption of new management techniques that minimize the use of relatively unskilled personnel. Many Negroes will find it increasingly difficult to secure employment unless extraordinary measures are taken to facilitate their entry into occupations in which they have long been underrepresented as the result of discriminatory employment practices and other factors. The U.S. Department of Labor recently estimated that the number of jobs in the desirable professional, managerial, clerical, and sales occupations will increase by 30 to 65 percent between 1960 and 1975. In less desirable occupations, increases will be much smaller, except in service occupations. The Department predicts that the number of jobs in agriculture will decline by more than 25 percent and that the number of nonfarm laborer jobs will remain constant.[14] Thus, during the foreseeable future, employment opportunities will increase sharply in occupations where Negroes are poorly represented and remain relatively constant or decline in most of the occupations where Negroes are now employed in large numbers.

Because of deficiencies in educational attainment or achievement, relatively few Negroes are prepared to enter certain rapidly expanding occupations. There are virtually no Negro students in Northern engineering schools, and Negro colleges in the Southern states have hesitated to develop engineering programs for their students. On the other hand, a small but growing number of young

[14] *Manpower Report of the President*, and U.S. Department of Labor, *A Report of Manpower Requirements, Resources, Utilization and Training* (U.S. Government Printing Office, Washington, D.C., 1963), p. 100.

Negroes attend liberal arts colleges and could enter junior administrative and executive occupations in industry and government on a
wider scale if it were not for discriminatory practices. A few
Negroes have obtained responsible positions in the Federal civil
service, but Negroes still totaled less than 1 percent of all persons
employed in the upper job ranges in 1962.[15] The proportion of Negroes in positions of comparable responsibility in private industry
is even smaller. Under current racial employment practices, many
Negro college graduates are employed at less than their full potential. Many other Negroes could perform effectively in skilled, clerical, and other occupations if given an opportunity to do so.

Between 1958 and 1962, the average annual rate of unemployment, seasonally adjusted, varied from about 5.5 to 6.5 percent,
while total employment rose markedly.[16] Given such levels of employment and unemployment, elimination of discriminatory employment practices would lead to improvement in the economic
status of Negroes through the normal processes of attrition and
turnover. A decline in the rate of unemployment would lead to still
greater improvement. In most industrial communities in the South,
for example, there are large Negro populations and hence an abun-
dant supply of Negro workers. Elementary school education is
sufficient educational qualification for most of the semiskilled jobs
from which Negroes are widely excluded in the South. Hence, the
locally available Negroes are in many instances just as well qualified
for such work as the whites for whom it is traditionally reserved.
In other words, the fact that the educational level of Southern
whites is somewhat higher than that of Negroes does not necessarily
mean that Negroes would not be able to perform effectively in
such jobs if given an opportunity to do so.

[15] The President's Committee on Equal Employment Opportunity, *Negro and Total Employment* [in Federal agencies] *by Grade and Salary Groups, June, 1961, and June, 1962* (Washington, D.C., January, 1963, mimeographed), p. 1.
[16] *Manpower Report of the President*, Tables A-7 and A-8, pp. 143 and 144.

PART TWO

Fair Employment Practice Laws and Executive Orders

5

ORGANIZATION AND FUNCTIONING OF
LOCAL FAIR EMPLOYMENT COMMISSIONS

State and municipal legislation prohibiting discrimination in employment has become increasingly widespread in recent years. Over the past two decades, twenty-five states have enacted laws designed to insure equal job opportunities for members of racial, religious, and ethnic minorities in all types of employment.[1] Twenty-two of these statutes provide for administering agencies with powers to issue enforceable orders. In the other three all-embracing state laws, employment discrimination is declared a court-actionable misdemeanor but no administrative agency is provided for.[2] Three additional states have fair employment laws applying only to establishments that supply the particular state government. During the same

[1] Originally, the prohibitions in all the state FEP laws applied only to discrimination based on race, color, creed, and national origin; seven states have subsequently amended their laws to prohibit employment discrimination based on age. In addition to the strictures against employment discrimination, ten of the state laws have been amended to prohibit discrimination in one or more categories of housing accommodations, and seven of these also prohibit discrimination by educational institutions. Twenty-six states, including nineteen FEP-law states and seven states without such laws, prohibit racial discrimination in public accommodations, such as hotels, restaurants, theaters, and recreation areas. The provisions relating to housing, education, and public accommodations and those barring employment discrimination based on age are outside the scope of the present study.

[2] The twenty-two states having "fully enforceable" FEP laws, in the chronological order of their enactment, are New York and New Jersey (1945), Massachusetts (1946), Connecticut (1947), New Mexico, Oregon, Rhode Island, and Washington (1949), Alaska (1953), Michigan, Minnesota, and Pennsylvania (1955), Colorado and Wisconsin (1957), California and Ohio (1959), Delaware (1960), Illinois, Kansas, and Missouri (1961), Hawaii and Indiana (1963). (Colorado, Wisconsin, Kansas, and Indiana had non-enforceable laws for varying periods of years prior to enacting fully enforceable laws.) The three states which declare employment discrimination a misdemeanor are Idaho (1961), Iowa (1963), and Vermont (1963). The states that prohibit discrimination in firms supplying the state government are Arizona (1961), Nebraska (1961), and Nevada (1961).

interval, numerous local governments, including seven major cities, have also adopted ordinances aimed at combating employment discrimination.[3] With the exception of Delaware and Baltimore, all of these states and cities are in the North and West.

This chapter summarizes the salient provisions of the principal state and municipal laws and the powers, duties and procedures of the commissions charged with administering them. In the next chapter, we trace the experience of the longer-established FEP commissions and attempt to assess the extent of their effectiveness in combating discrimination and promoting equal opportunity in employment.

Prohibition of Discriminatory Practices

The "prohibitory" provisions in the FEP laws are either identical or closely similar in content (though not always in language) in nearly all of the states and municipalities having enforceable laws. The "prohibitory" provisions of the New York law, on which most of the other state laws are modeled, define unlawful practices. These provisions of the New York law are summarized below:

It shall be an unlawful discriminatory practice

(a) For an *employer* because of the . . . race, creed, color or national origin of any individual, to refuse to hire or employ or to bar or discharge from employment such individual or to discriminate against such individual in compensation or in terms, conditions or privileges of employment.

(b) For a *labor organization*, because of the . . . race, creed, color or national origin of any individual, to exclude or to expel from its membership such individual or to discriminate in any way against any of its members or against any employer or any individual employed by an employer.

(c) For any *employer* or *employment* agency to print or circulate or cause to be printed or circulated any statement, advertisement

---

[3] The major cities having actively functioning FEP commissions are Baltimore, Cleveland, Minneapolis, Philadelphia, Pittsburgh, St. Paul, and Toledo. Through special understandings between the respective state and local governments, most of the discrimination cases originating within these cities are handled by the municipal agencies.

or publication, or to use any form of application for employment, which expresses, directly or indirectly, any limitation, specification or discrimination as to . . . race, creed, color or national origin, or any intent to make any such limitation, specification or discrimination, unless based upon a bona fide occupational qualification.

(d) For any *employer, labor organization* or *employment agency* to discharge, expel, or otherwise discriminate against any person because he has opposed any practices forbidden under this article or because he has filed a complaint, testified or assisted in any proceeding under this article.[4]

These provisions, which are self-explanatory, constitute the principal prohibitions in all of the state and municipal laws. Some of the more recently enacted laws, however, contain additional provisions explicitly prohibiting certain discriminatory practices only inferentially covered by the provisions of the New York law. Thus, under the Michigan, Ohio, and Illinois laws, it is an unlawful practice for an *employment agency* to "refuse or fail to accept, register, classify properly, or refer for employment, or otherwise to discriminate against any person" [5] on grounds of race, etc.; under the Michigan and Ohio laws, for an *employer, employment agency,* or *labor organization* "to utilize in the recruitment or hiring of persons any employment agency . . . or any other employee-referring source known to discriminate" [6] on these grounds; and finally, under the Ohio law, for an *employer, labor organization,* or *joint labor-management committee controlling apprentice training programs* to discriminate against any person (on grounds of race, etc.) in admission to or employment in any program established to provide apprentice training.[7] The last of these provisions is particularly noteworthy, since no other state FEP law except Ohio's makes any mention of joint labor-management apprenticeship committees; and consequently it is doubtful whether any other law actually covers

[4] New York State Law Against Discrimination, Para. 296(1). Italics added for emphasis.

[5] State of Ohio, Revised Code, Section 4112.02(B)(1), 1959.

[6] State of Ohio, Revised Code, Section 4112.02(E)(6), 1959.

[7] State of Ohio, Revised Code, Section 4112.02(D), 1959.

discriminatory exclusion from apprentice programs controlled by such committees.[8]

Administrative Agencies—Commissions and Others

In seventeen of the state FEP laws, the task of administering the statute is assigned to a commission, composed of from three to ten commissioners appointed by the governor—usually for five-year staggered terms. The seven municipal FEP ordinances studied provide for similar administrative commissions, appointed by the mayor. In Alaska, Delaware, Hawaii, New Jersey, and Oregon, the laws are administered by specially-created divisions of established state government departments.

Of the seventeen state commissions, only the New York commission is a full-time body in the sense that the commission members themselves devote full time to their duties. The salary prescribed for each of the six commissioners is $19,500 per year and for the Chairman $21,462. In Ohio the commissioners receive annual salaries of $5,000, in Massachusetts $4,000, and in Rhode Island $2,500; but these officials function on only a part-time basis. In the other "commission" states, the commissioners also serve part time and are paid either a small per diem allowance and "expenses" or only "expenses."

Seven state laws lay down rules concerning appointments to commissions: in Colorado and Minnesota, geographical area representation is prescribed; in Michigan, Ohio, and Illinois, no more than three of the five commissioners may be of the same political party; and in Kansas and Wisconsin, the commissions must include representatives of management, organized labor, and the public at large. In the remaining "commission" states, the Governor is given a free hand in making appointments. There is, however, a marked similarity of composition among most of the commissions. Thus, nearly all the commissions include Negro members, and almost as

[8] The New York law was amended in 1962 to include similar provisions.

many have Jewish members. The clergy—in each of the major sects
—and the legal profession are also well represented. There are
labor union officials on approximately two-thirds of the commissions, and business or industrial executives on nearly the same proportion. Finally, a sizable majority of commissions include one or
more housewives in their membership. Thus, while there is a
marked similarity of composition among the commissions, there is
a considerable diversity of membership within each of the several
commissions. Despite this diversity, however, all commission members have one characteristic in common—they are committed to
the objective of reducing discrimination in employment and to the
belief that action under government auspices is necessary to
achieve this objective.

One important distinction among the FEP commissions should
be noted. In some states, the commissions function only as collective entities, to approve proposed actions, hold hearings, etc., while
the day-to-day problem-solving activities are conducted by full-
time staff personnel, whereas, in others the individual members are
"working commissioners"—i.e., in addition to their collective duties
they personally direct and conduct conciliation efforts with employers, unions, and employment agencies aimed at finding solu-
tions to specific employment discrimination problems. The significance of this dichotomy as regards commission effectiveness is
discussed in a subsequent section.

STATUTORY POWERS AND DUTIES OF COMMISSIONS

Each of the state FEP laws contains a set of provisions defining
the powers and duties delegated to the commissions. Most important among these are the provisions which establish the basis for
the commissions' compliance activities as conducted in actual practice. The "standard" powers and duties relating to the handling
and adjustment of complaints, found in practically all of the laws,
may be summarized as follows:

1. The power to receive, investigate, and pass upon complaints

alleging unlawful employment practices. (In ten states the commission is empowered to *initiate* such complaints, and in five of these and six others the attorney general of the state is empowered to do so.)

2. The duty (if investigation reveals probable cause for crediting such allegations) to endeavor to eliminate the unlawful practices by conference, conciliation, and persuasion.

3. The power to hold hearings, subpoena witnesses, compel their attendance, administer oaths, take testimony of any person under oath, and, in connection therewith, to require the production for examination of any books or papers relating to any matter in question before the commission. The commissions can secure enforcement of the subpoena and production-of-record powers through the state courts.

4. The power (where, following a hearing, the commission determines that a respondent is persisting in an unlawful employment practice) to issue an order requiring the respondent to cease and desist from such practice and to take such further affirmative action as in the judgment of the commission will effectuate the purposes of the act, including a requirement of reports of the manner of compliance. Commissions can obtain enforcement of such orders by the state courts.

Most of the state FEP laws also contain two further power-granting provisions, relating to commission compliance efforts of broader scope than the adjustment of individual complaints. While the language of these provisions varies from state to state, the gist of their content is as follows:

1. The power to study the problems of discrimination in all or specific fields of human relationships when based on race, color, religion, or national origin. (The commissions are also empowered to create advisory agencies, local or state-wide, and to authorize these agencies to study such problems and to "foster good will among the groups and elements of the population of the State.")

2. The power to issue such publications and such results of investigation and research as, in its judgment, will tend to promote good will and minimize or eliminate discrimination based on race, color, religion, or national origin.

These provisions, while couched in rather vague general language, have been interpreted as empowering the commissions to investigate employment *patterns*, by race and occupation, over entire plants, companies, or even local or state-wide industries— and, where evidence of a pattern of discrimination is found, to seek to eliminate it through the prescribed procedure of conference, conciliation, and persuasion. These provisions, however, unlike those dealing with the processing of individual complaints, seldom include the power to hold hearings, subpoena witnesses, issue cease-and-desist orders, and secure enforcement by the courts. Only two existing FEP laws—those of Ohio and Philadelphia—contain provisions clearly vesting the respective commissions with these powers when dealing with discriminatory employment patterns. The significance of these provisions in terms of over-all commission achievement in reducing employment discrimination is discussed in a later section.

COMMISSION BUDGETS AND STAFFING

It is necessary to review briefly the procedures followed by the FEP agencies in conducting compliance activities. Commission compliance procedures have a definite bearing on the agencies' effectiveness. Here again, we find that the procedural provisions relating to the processing of individual complaints are identical, or closely similar, in a majority of the states. Hence, the basic stages in formal complaint-handling procedures are also the same or closely similar throughout. With respect to employment-pattern–focused activities, however, this pervasive similarity does not hold. There are wide differences among the state agencies both with regard to the procedures followed and the extent to which the different commissions engage in such employment-pattern–centered activities. These differences are due in large measure to differences in the size and caliber of agency staffs, which in turn are largely due to differences in their financial resources. Before we proceed to discuss the commissions' procedures, therefore, it is necessary to review briefly the budget and staff situation in the several state and municipal agencies.

The New York State Commission for Human Rights (formerly named the State Commission Against Discrimination) has by long odds the largest annual budget and operating staff of any state or municipal FEP agency. In 1960 (the latest year for which comparable figures are available for all state agencies), the New York commission had a budget of approximately $950,000 and a total professional staff of eighty persons (including the five full-time commissioners) and nearly the same number of clerical and related employees. All but nine of the professional personnel were exclusively or primarily engaged in compliance and enforcement work, the exceptions being concerned with educational and community relations activities. The headquarters staff comprised approximately two-thirds of the total and the four regional offices the remaining third.

Even when account is taken of the fact that New York has the largest compliance work load of any state with an FEP law, the budgets and staffs of most of the other state agencies fall far short of New York's. A rough comparison between New York and five other states having comparable (although moderately smaller) aggregate compliance work loads will serve to illustrate this disparity in financial resources and personnel. The Negro population of New York State was 1,417,000 in 1960; and the Negro populations of the other states with FEP laws, expressed as a proportion of the New York figure, can be used as approximate indexes of compliance work loads in those states relative to the work load in New York.

In comparison with the New York Commission's $950,000 budget and professional staff of eighty persons, California, with nearly two-thirds as large a Negro population, had a budget of only $203,000 and a professional staff of fifteen; Ohio, with nearly six-tenths as many Negroes as New York, had a budget of $100,000 and a professional staff of three (raised to $170,000 and eight, respectively, in 1961); and Michigan, with about half as many Negroes as New York had a budget of $148,000 and a professional staff of ten. The New Jersey Division Against Discrimination was somewhat better staffed than the California, Ohio, and Michigan commissions, for, while its budget was approximately the same as Michigan's and its staff slightly larger, New Jersey's Negro population is only four-tenths as large as New York's. The Pennsylvania Commission was also in this category. It had a budget and staff approximately the same as Michigan's. While Pennsylvania's Negro population is about six-tenths as large as New York's, however, this figure exaggerates the Pennsylvania Commission's work load. Since Philadelphia, where more than half the state's Negroes reside, has its own enforceable FEP law and a relatively well-staffed enforcement agency, the Pennsylvania Commission is not required to deal with discrimination problems arising within Philadelphia's boundaries.

Despite the somewhat better situation in New Jersey and Pennsylvania, however, it is apparent that none of the five state agencies referred to above approaches the New York commission in financial and staff resources. Moreover, since our study strongly indicates that even the New York agency's staff is not fully adequate to cope with all of the state's discrimination problems, it follows that the other five state agencies are decidedly understaffed. This generalization also holds for most of the other fifteen state FEP agencies, the only exceptions being those, like Alaska and Idaho, that have rather small minority group populations and hence a correspondingly small aggregative employment discrimination problem.

The only FEP agency that does approach parity with the New York Commission in this respect is the Philadelphia Commission on Human Relations. While Philadelphia's Negro population is approximately one-third as large as New York State's, the Philadelphia agency in 1960 had a professional staff of nineteen, or approximately one-fourth as many as the New York Commission. Thus, the Philadelphia Commission is obviously much closer to parity of staffing with New York State than any state commission. As will be shown in a later section, the Philadelphia agency's record of accomplishment in abating employment discrimination is also fairly comparable to that of the New York Commission.

Procedures

With this comparative picture of agency budgets and staffs in mind, let us turn now to the procedures followed by the FEP commissions in administering and enforcing the ban on employment discrimination. While the basic stages of the complaint-processing procedures are virtually identical in nearly all the states with FEP laws, there are significant differences in detail of practice among the commissions, particularly regarding the extent to which the commissioners themselves participate in the process. The following account summarizes the complaint procedure of the New York State Commission, under which the commissioners, either individually or collectively, personally conduct or directly supervise all stages of the process. The variations from this procedure in other states with "working" commissioners and in states in which the commissions function only as collective entities will be noted in due course.[9]

The key procedural provision in the New York law, which both defines and limits the Commission's power to deal with complaints, reads as follows:

Any person *claiming to be aggrieved by an unlawful discriminatory act* may, by himself or his attorney-at-law, make, sign, and file with the commission a verified complaint in writing which shall state the

[9] For a more detailed account of the procedures followed by the state FEP commissions, see Michael A. Bamberger and Nathan Lewin, "The Right to Equal Treatment: Administrative Enforcement of Antidiscrimination Legislation," *Harvard Law Review*, LXXIV (1961), 526–89.

name and address of the person, employer, labor organization or employment agency alleged to have committed the unlawful discriminatory practice complained of and which shall set forth the particulars thereof and contain such other information as may be required by the commission. The industrial commissioner or attorney-general may, in like manner, make, sign and file such complaint.[10]

It should be noted that this provision limits the Commission to dealing with complaints in which the complainant (or his attorney, the State Industrial Commissioner, or the Attorney General acting on his behalf) alleges that a discriminatory *act* has been committed *against himself*. Nearly all the state and municipal FEP laws contain this same limitation. Only two state laws (Ohio and Rhode Island) and one city ordinance (Philadelphia) explicitly authorize commissions to deal with complaints by persons alleging discriminatory *practices* and complaints filed by complainants *other* than those claiming to be personally victimized. The significance of this distinction will be discussed at a later point in the present chapter.

Under the New York Commission's procedures, complainants usually register their grievances "in person." The complainant appears at one of the Commission's regional offices and commits his complaint to writing with the assistance and guidance of a member of the Commission staff, who endeavors to make certain that all essential facts are included in the complaint. Upon completion, the written complaint is sent to the chairman of the Commission, who assigns one of the commissioners to handle the case to a conclusion.

The first step in the procedure—investigating the complaint—is conducted by a field representative, assigned from the Commission's Regulatory Division to assist the commissioner assigned to the case.[11] (For the sake of simplicity we shall assume that the com-

[10] New York State Law Against Discrimination, Para. 297. Italics added for emphasis.

[11] When commissioners are engaged in handling complaint cases or other specific compliance efforts, they are called "investigating commissioners." This term is something of a misnomer, since the investigative phase of a case is conducted by a field representative and since the most important function of the commissioner himself is conciliation. It seems best, however, to continue using the accepted term despite its ambiguity.

plaint alleges discrimination by an employer—by far the most common kind of complaint filed in practice. Only certain details of the procedure are different when the respondent is an employment agency or a labor union.) The field representative visits the employer's establishment and proceeds to carry out a threefold assignment: first, he endeavors to obtain all pertinent facts bearing on the complainant's grievance; second, he attempts to get a comprehensive factual picture of the employer's general employment policies; and third, he surveys the existing employment pattern in the workplace, in terms of the numbers of minority group members in each occupational category. He does not, however, discuss the merits of the complaint nor does he attempt to obtain any retraction or concession by the employer in favor of the complainant. His findings, embodied in a written report, are submitted to the investigating commissioner.

The commissioner, on the basis of the complaint statement and the investigation report, determines whether or not there is sufficient evidence to support the allegation of discrimination. If sufficient evidence of unlawful discrimination is found, he issues a finding of "probable cause," which is then transmitted to both the respondent employer and the complainant.

The second stage of the procedure is based on the provision in the law requiring that "if [the] commissioner shall determine . . . that probable cause exists . . . he shall immediately endeavor to eliminate the unlawful discriminatory practice complained of by conference, conciliation and persuasion." [12] (Nearly all of the other state and municipal laws contain similar provisions.) The key word here is "conciliation"; the commissioner meets with the appropriate executive of the respondent employer and seeks a commitment from him that the practice complained of will be discontinued and the injury to the complainant redressed. In FEP-law parlance, the term "conciliation" denotes conference approaches and techniques that utilize a combination of persuasion and coercion. The commissioner meets with the noncomplying employer

[12] New York State Law Against Discrimination, Para. 297.

and endeavors to persuade him to correct his practices voluntarily, while, as an aid to the persuasion process, keeping him reminded that his noncompliance is illegal and may, if persisted in, result in unfavorable publicity or even legal sanctions. The law specifies that any discussion that takes place during conciliation conferences must be kept confidential—presumably as an added inducement to the respondent to revise his practices voluntarily.[13]

Under a literal interpretation of the statutory provision, the commissioner would confine his conciliation effort to obtaining an agreement by the employer to eliminate the specific practice referred to in the complaint and provide redress for the individual filing the complaint. And in fact some FEP commissions do confine the conciliation process within this narrow purview. In New York complaint cases, however, the commissioner often carries his conciliation effort beyond the adjustment of the individual complainant's grievance. When, as frequently happens, the investigation reveals evidence of more pervasive discrimination, the commissioner-conciliator endeavors to work out a comprehensive "conciliation agreement" with the respondent employer. While such agreements vary in form and content from case to case, they customarily include three main types of provisions. First, the employer commits himself to correct the particular practice cited in the complaint; second, he agrees to revise his over-all employment policies and practices to conform with the letter and the spirit of the law; and, third, he agrees that the Commission may make periodic follow-up reviews of his employment pattern and practices and that his records will be made available to the Commission on such occasions. Other customary provisions include a requirement that the employer display in his establishment the Commission's poster describing the employment provisions of the law and a commitment that he will inform and educate his employees concerning the problems of discrimination and the requirements of the law.

When the terms of a conciliation agreement have been agreed

[13] *Ibid.*

on, the agreement is committed to writing, either in the form of an interchange of correspondence or of a written statement approved by the commissioner and the employer. The investigating commissioner's approval constitutes official Commission acceptance of the agreement—it is not necessary to have it approved by the full Commission. With regard to this phase of the conciliation process, the New York Commission's practice is unusual. Only two other FEP commissions—those in Massachusetts and Rhode Island—follow New York in authorizing individual "investigating commissioners" to consummate final conciliation agreements. In the remaining agencies formal approval of all negotiated agreements by the full commission is required. In these states the agreements usually take the form of an official consent order drawn up by the commission's staff, which the respondent formally accepts by signature following the commission's approval. In New York State, with the consummation of the conciliation agreement, the commissioner declares the complaint phase of the case "closed." When the agreement covers the employer's over-all practices, however, its acceptance constitutes a nominal rather than an actual conclusion of the case. In conformance with the provision for periodic reviews, the commissioner may—and often does—instruct the field representative to conduct follow-up investigations of the employer's practices and employment pattern, usually at six-month or one-year intervals. If these investigations indicate that the discriminatory practices have been corrected, he will declare the case finally concluded. On the other hand, if the investigations indicate that pattern discrimination is still present or that insufficient progress has been made toward eliminating it, the commissioner will begin follow-up negotiations with the employer to ascertain the reasons for the lack of progress and see that a more affirmative effort is made toward full compliance.

The great majority of complaint cases handled by the New York Commission have been satisfactorily concluded through conciliation, both with respect to adjustment of individual grievances and revision of general policies and practices. If, however—as occasionally happens—the respondent employer refuses to take any corrective action despite the commissioner's conciliation efforts, the agency may order a public hearing. At the hearing, the entire case is reviewed before a panel of three commissioners (not including the commissioner originally assigned to the case). The record of factual evidence from the investigation report is made part of the proceeding, and the employer is required to submit to questioning by the commissioners. The complainant may also appear and testify. The entire hearing is held in public, and all of the evidence and testimony is available for public inspection and publication. If the Commission, on reviewing the case, sustains the original finding of "probable cause," it issues a "cease-and-desist" order to the employer, requiring him to take corrective action. Such orders are enforceable by the state courts, and refusal by a respondent to comply would make him liable to contempt action.

Over the period 1945–60, the New York Commission ordered twenty-nine complaint cases for public hearing, including eighteen involving employment discrimination. The proceedings were carried through to completion and cease-and-desist orders issued in only six of these cases (including three employment cases). Of the other twenty-three cases, fourteen were settled through conciliation agreements or "consent orders" reached either during or just prior to the hearing. (The remainder were still pending as of the end of 1960.) Over the same period, the agency processed more than 3,000 "probable cause" complaints—i.e., cases in which the specific complaint was sustained or other discriminatory practices were found. This appears to indicate that the New York Commission has used the public hearing—its only direct enforcement weapon—very sparingly. The number of hearings actually held, however, is only a part of the total picture. In an unknown but certainly substantial number of cases, commissioners have used the *threat* of a public hearing as an aid in persuading recalcitrant respondents to revise their existing practices. Most employing managements—and unions and employment agencies as well—are very reluctant to have a FEP complaint case involving them go to public hearing, owing to the unfavorable publicity involved. The small number of hearings held, therefore, is just as much a testimonial to the efficacy of the weapon as an indication of restraint by the commission in utilizing it.

Although conciliation efforts focused on employment patterns, as described above, are most frequently conducted as a concomitant of commissioner efforts to adjust individual complaints, this is not always the case. Even in instances where no "probable cause" is found with respect to the complainant's allegation, commissioners often meet with the employers concerned and negotiate conciliation agreements covering their over-all employment policies and practices. Moreover, it is readily apparent that the pattern-centered efforts that stem from complaint cases have a far greater job opportunity potential for racial minorities than efforts directed toward redressing individual grievances. Consequently, for purposes of appraising an agency's effectiveness, it is necessary to consider the two phases of the complaint-handling process as separate activities. From this viewpoint, the pattern-centered aspects of complaint cases constitute one of three types of pattern-centered compliance activities in which the New York Commission engages. The importance of complaint cases as a source of compliance-promoting activities is indicated by the fact that, of 1,003 employment complaint cases handled by the New York Commission in 1959, it found and adjusted discriminatory practices or policies in 380 instances, or 38 percent of the total.[14]

The second type of pattern-centered activity, called "informal investigation," is directed *primarily* at employment patterns. From time to time, minority-group organizations and other interested civic bodies bring to the agency's attention alleged discriminatory pattern situations. If the information submitted is credible, the

[14] State of New York, State Commission Against Discrimination, *1959 Report of Progress* (Annual Report for 1959), p. 133.

Commission conducts an investigation; and, if the allegation is substantiated, it assigns a commissioner to attempt to correct the discriminatory situation. The weakness of this type of compliance effort lies in the twin facts that organization-initiated allegations do not fall within the definition of "verified complaints" under the New York law [15] and that the Commission itself is not empowered to initiate complaints. Consequently, the Commission does not have "enforceable jurisdiction" in such cases, but must rely entirely on persuasive means in seeking to bring about revision of discriminatory practices.[16] Despite this drawback, however, the Commission initiated about 900 informal investigations between 1945 and 1959.[17]

"Commission-initiated studies" constitute a third type of pattern-centered compliance effort utilized by the New York Commission. Under the statute, the Commission is authorized to issue "such results of investigations and research as in its judgment will tend to . . . minimize or eliminate discrimination because of race, creed, color, or national origin." [18] Most of the studies undertaken have covered groups of companies—usually those comprising a particular industry within the state as a whole or one of its urban areas. In utilizing this device, as in the case of informal investiga-

[15] Since this section was written, the New York State Supreme Court, in deciding a case in which a complainant organization appealed a New York Commission decision against it, has ruled that the Commission does have "enforceable jurisdiction" in organization-initiated complaints, and the Commisson has acted on at least one such complaint. (See New York *Times*, September 28, 1962, p. 1, decision of New York Commission on complaint filed by the American Jewish Congress against the Arabian American Oil Company.) It is not possible at this time to assess the effects of the Court's ruling that the Commission can use its enforcement powers in cases filed by organizations as well as individuals.

[16] Under the New York law, the Attorney General of the State is empowered to file complaints with the New York Commission. Hence, it would be possible for the Commission to obtain "enforceable jurisdiction" in such cases by referring them to the Attorney General. This is a slow and cumbersome procedure, however, and consequently is seldom used. In the entire career of the New York Commission, only two employment cases have been filed by the Attorney General.

[17] State of New York, State Commission Against Discrimination, *1959 Report of Progress* (Annual Report for 1959), p. 14.

[18] New York State Law Against Discrimination, Paragraph 295(9).

tions, the Commission is not empowered to invoke its enforcement sanctions. "Thus, the studies are cooperative and voluntary undertakings, jointly sponsored by [the Commission] and, usually, a firm or an industry. [However,] all have the purpose of establishing the facts and rectifying, if found, the discriminatory conditions." [19]

Despite the lack of enforceable jurisdiction in such matters, the New York Commission has increased the number of employment opportunities open to Negroes through the use of informal investigations and Commission-initiated studies. These achievements will be discussed in more detail below.

In so far as adjusting individual grievances is concerned, the procedures of most of the other state commissions are closely similar to those followed by the New York Commission. The only significant differences are found not in the procedures themselves but in the personnel to whom the conciliation function is assigned. Specifically, the conciliation stage is conducted by commission members in only five other states: California, Massachusetts, Michigan, Ohio, and Rhode Island. In the remaining state agencies and in all of the major municipal agencies, conciliation conferences are conducted by field representatives or other staff personnel—usually the same persons who conduct complaint investigations. With respect to employment-pattern focused efforts, however, there are wide variations in practice among the commissions—particularly regarding the extent to which they engage in this type of activity. In a few states, the commissions concern themselves virtually exclusively with redressing grievances of individual complainants and seldom require from respondents even nominal commitments to revise their over-all practices.

The majority of commissions, in processing complaints, do require such commitments in conciliation agreements when evidence of pervasive discrimination is found; and some, though by no

---

[19] State of New York, State Commission Against Discrimination, *1957 Report of Progress* (Annual Report for 1957), p. 73.

means all, of these commissions include provisions for follow-up reviews of respondents' practices and employment patterns. The New York Commission is, however, the only agency that actually conducts follow-up investigations of employment patterns as a regular practice. In fact, the remaining commissions that nominally conduct such investigations can do so only occasionally, if at all, because of inadequate budgets and small staffs.

In one other respect, also, the New York Commission is unusual. With the single exception of the Philadelphia Commission on Human Relations, no other FEP agency actively engages in pattern-centered compliance efforts that are not integrally connected with individual complaints. The Massachusetts and New Jersey agencies have in the past conducted surveys of employment patterns in a few particular localities or counties similar in nature to New York's Commission-initiated studies, but these surveys did not lead to systematic efforts to eliminate the discriminatory employment patterns they frequently disclosed. Most of the commissions have not surveyed industry employment patterns by race and occupation.

The Philadelphia Commission warrants separate attention, for while it has had less experience with broad-scale pattern compliance efforts than the New York State agency, its powers to undertake such efforts are wider and more explicit, and consequently its approach to the problem can be more direct. Indeed, the Philadelphia Commission possesses the broadest and most explicit powers to undertake such efforts on an enforceable basis of any state or municipal FEP agency. Nearly all the FEP laws, it will be recalled, limit the respective commissions to dealing with complaints in which the complainant alleges that he has himself been the victim of a discriminatory act. Under the Philadelphia law, the Commission is authorized, first, to deal with complaints by persons (or organizations) *other* than those claiming to be personally aggrieved; second, to deal with complaints alleging discriminatory *general practices*—of a company, a union, or an employment agency, or groups or combinations of these—as well as specific discriminatory acts; third, on its own initiative to undertake direct investigations of discriminatory general practices and institute complaints on this basis; and fourth, to hold public hearings in complaint cases directly following the issuance of the complaint without going through the intermediate steps of determining whether probable cause exists and of attempting to obtain voluntary corrective action through conciliation. Following such hearings, the Commission may, if the findings warrant, issue cease-and-desist orders and have them enforced by the courts. Thus, the Philadelphia Commission's powers are unique: only two other FEP agencies—those of Ohio and Rhode Island—are authorized to undertake investigations of general practices situations and institute enforceable action therein, and even these agencies are not permitted to bypass the conciliation stage in dealing with such situations.

The reasons that only the New York State and Philadelphia Commissions, among all the FEP agencies, conduct active programs of pattern-centered compliance activities are fairly apparent. The first and most important reason, as noted earlier, is that these two commissions alone among the agencies have sufficient budgets and professional staffs to enable them to engage in pattern-oriented activities without interfering with their legally imposed primary duty of handling individual complaints. To state it another way, virtually all the other agencies are forced by insufficient budgets and staffs to confine their compliance activities almost entirely to processing complaints. Second, compared with most of the other jurisdictions with long-established FEP laws (Massachusetts, Connecticut, Oregon, Rhode Island, Washington, and New Mexico), New York State and Philadelphia have by far the largest Negro populations. Consequently, their Commissions have been under somewhat greater pressure to "show results" in terms of aggregate gains in Negro employment and employment opportunities. Third, while some of the states with more recently enacted laws have comparatively large Negro populations (Michigan, Ohio, California, Illinois, and Missouri), in most instances their FEP commissions have not been established long enough to plan and execute extensive pattern-centered compliance programs. The commissioners and staff officials interviewed in these states were, however, unanimous in stating that they favored conducting such programs and that inadequate budgets were the overriding obstacle.

6

EXPERIENCE OF ESTABLISHED
FAIR EMPLOYMENT COMMISSIONS

The analysis of Census employment data for the North in Chapter 4 revealed that Negro representation improved substantially in middle-level blue-collar and lower-level white-collar work during the 1940s, largely as a consequence of the critical wartime labor shortages. The rate of nonwhite occupational progress was markedly slower in the 1950s, with the restoration of balance between labor supply and demand and the subsequent appearance of labor surpluses. Negroes are still greatly underrepresented in office, sales, and craft occupations and even more so in the professional and managerial fields. Southern Negroes likewise made progress during the 1940s, as a result of wartime labor stringency, although their advance was confined almost entirely to semiskilled blue-collar work. With the shift from labor shortages to surpluses in the 1950s, their upward movement was slowed almost to a halt. The Negro's occupational status at the present time is even farther below parity with the whites in the South than in the North in all categories above the menial and unskilled level.

In the context of the present study, the most significant feature of the employment experience of Negroes over the past two decades is that they continued to make some occupational progress in the North during the 1950s, although at a slower rate than in the 1940s. Without doubt, their progress in the later decade was due in part to continuing labor stringencies in some sections of the North in the early 1950s, particularly during the Korean War. The FEP laws operative in several Northern industrial states throughout the decade and in several others during the latter half also undoubtedly helped to sustain the progressive trend. This chapter summarizes the experience of the respective FEP commissions in administering these laws and essays an appraisal of their contribution to the continued occupational progress of nonwhites in the North.

Employer-Related Compliance Activities

Our study of FEP legislation has yielded substantial evidence indicating that, in the states and cities having established and enforceable laws, racial discrimination in employment is considerably less prevalent today than it was prior to the enactment of the laws. There are good grounds for believing that the existence of the laws and the efforts of the FEP agencies in administering them have been significant factors in bringing about the change.

The study of commission experience was concentrated largely in eight states: New York, New Jersey, Massachusetts, Connecticut, Ohio, California, Michigan, and Pennsylvania. The four first-named commissions have all had a relatively long experience—fourteen to sixteen years; the latter four have had a much briefer experience, but all these states have relatively large Negro populations. Among the municipal FEP agencies, the principal focus of study was on the Philadelphia Commission on Human Relations, with twelve years of experience in one of the country's largest centers of Negro population. The more recently established commissions in Cleveland and Baltimore were studied in less detail.

As one would expect, the long-established commissions proved to be the most fruitful sources of information relating to compliance activity experience. Each of these commissions, over the total period of its operation, has processed and concluded many hundreds of "probable cause" complaint cases. In investigating these complaints, the commissions have found pervasive discriminatory practices in a large proportion of cases; and in concluding settlements in such cases, they have generally obtained commitments from the respondents to revise their practices to conform with the spirit of the law. The New York Commission, and to a more limited extent the New Jersey and Philadelphia agencies, have gone a step farther by including provisions for follow-up reviews of respondents' employment patterns. The Connecticut and Massachusetts Commissions have given less attention to over-all practices and employment patterns than the other long-established agencies, but have none the less obtained commitments for revision of discriminatory practices in a significant proportion of complaint cases concluded.

Some idea of the aggregate volume of "productive" compliance activity engaged in by the commissions may be obtained from Table 6.1, a cumulative tabulation of complaint cases "satisfactorily adjusted" by each commission over the period since its establishment.

Table 6.1

EMPLOYMENT COMPLAINT CASES "SATISFACTORILY ADJUSTED" BY FEP COMMISSIONS, SINCE ESTABLISHMENT OF EACH COMMISSION

Commission	Total cases	Period covered
New York	3,262	1945–60
New Jersey	701	1945–60
Massachusetts	793	1946–61
Connecticut	506	1947–61
Philadelphia	523	June, 1948–Dec., 1960

Source: Computed from data published by the several commissions in their annual reports.

The total of 3,262 cases listed for the New York Commission includes 1,150 formal "probable cause" complaints adjusted after conciliation, 60 such cases "ordered for public hearing or consent order issued," 1,407 formal cases in which "no probable cause was found but other [more general] discriminatory practices were found and adjusted," and 645 "informal investigations" (informal complaints, in which the New York Commission does not have enforceable jurisdiction). The total of 701 cases listed for the New Jersey Division Against Discrimination also includes cases in each of these categories. The Massachusetts and Philadelphia totals include, in addition to formal "probable cause" and "other discriminatory practice" cases, substantial numbers of "commission-initiated" complaints. (Both these commissions are authorized by their laws to initiate enforceable complaints on their own motion.) The Connecticut total includes only formal "probable cause" and "other discriminatory practice" complaints.

While the number of complaint cases satisfactorily concluded provides no direct measure of the commissions' aggregate achievement in bringing about compliance with FEP laws, certain significant inferences can be drawn from these figures. It should be noted, first of all, that in each of the jurisdictions more than four-fifths of the cases concluded involved complaints against employers —complaints against labor unions and against employment agencies, taken together, accounted for less than one-fifth. Second, the total number of complaints naming employers was only slightly larger than the total number of employing firms dealt with by the commissions, since "repeat" complaints against a given firm are relatively rare. Third, the great preponderance of settlements in employer cases included commitments by the employers to revise their general policies and practices to conform with the spirit of the law. Thus, for example, it is a fairly safe estimate that the New York Commission concluded agreements for revision of employment practices with more than 2,000 separate firms during the fifteen-year period. While this is only a small fraction of all New York State firms with six or more employees (the law does not apply to firms with fewer than six), it is none the less a significant fraction, for it must be borne in mind that these were the firms named in complaints in which the Commission found positive evidence of pervasive discrimination. An even larger number of complaints were dismissed because such evidence was lacking or insufficient. Consequently, assuming that all or most of the 2,000-odd firms with which the New York Commission concluded agreements actually revised their discriminatory policies and practices, the result would be a fairly significant improvement in aggregative employment opportunities for racial and other minorities in the

state. The following summary of follow-up reviews and studies
conducted by the New York Commission indicates that a noteworthy improvement in the employment status of the state's Negroes has in fact occurred. A comparison of the 1960 Census of
Population data on nonwhite employment in New York with corresponding figures for 1950, to be presented later in the chapter,
corroborates the improvement indicated by the Commission's
studies.

The most direct evidence that FEP laws have brought about a
significant reduction in employment discrimination is obtainable
from Commission post-settlement reviews and other follow-up
studies of employment patterns. Our analysis of follow-up review
data obtained from a number of FEP commissions indicates that in
a large proportion of adjusted complaint cases substantial numbers
of Negroes were hired subsequent to the settlement—manifestly as
a direct consequence of the revised employer policies and practices
inspired by the commissions' intervention. In our opinion, one of
the best indicators of progress in overcoming racial employment
discrimination is the extent of admission of Negroes to industries
and occupations from which they have traditionally been entirely
excluded. Accordingly, in examining the follow-up review information obtained from the commissions, we have given particular
attention to cases involving such industries and occupations.

The New York Commission has conducted follow-up reviews
of adjusted complaint cases as a regular practice almost from the
outset. The New Jersey Division Against Discrimination and a few
other agencies have conducted such reviews intermittently or in
special cases; but the majority of commissions, owing to inadequate
budgets, have done so only rarely, if at all. As a result, the New
York Commission has accumulated a much larger volume of "be-
fore-and-after" information on racial employment patterns than
any other agency. As early as 1951, the New York Commission
adduced factual evidence indicating that its compliance efforts had
resulted in substantial changes in racial employment patterns. In

that year the agency undertook a detailed analysis of the 334 follow-up reviews (of previously concluded valid complaint cases) conducted during the year. The results of the analysis were summarized in its annual report as follows:

In 85 percent of the cases studied there was a definite improvement in the employment pattern as compared with the conditions which existed at the time the original complaints against these firms were filed. These changes were reflected in substantial increases in the number of members of different racial, religious and nationality groups employed in professional, technical, skilled, semiskilled, and unskilled job categories. In the other 15 percent of the cases analyzed, although there was no evidence of continued job discrimination, no significant changes in employment patterns were found.[1]

The findings with respect to employment of Negroes in traditionally "white" industries and occupations were especially significant. The study included a sizable number of companies in such industries as banking, insurance, public utilities, and retail trade, where Negroes had traditionally been excluded from all except janitorial and other menial jobs. The reviews revealed that Negroes in significant numbers were now employed in office work at various levels in several large banks and insurance companies; in office, switchboard, and skilled mechanical jobs in major public utility companies; and in sales, clerical, and even supervisory work in retail stores. In nearly all instances, Negroes had been entirely or virtually absent from these positions prior to the Commission's intervention. The study also revealed significant post-intervention entry of Negroes into skilled and supervisory jobs in a variety of manufacturing establishments, where they had previously been limited to unskilled or, at best, to semiskilled production work.

Similar follow-up reviews conducted by the New York Commission in subsequent years have likewise revealed improvement in racial employment patterns over the preintervention situation in most instances. In 1958 the Commission made analyses of all fol-

[1] State of New York, State Commission Against Discrimination, *1951 Report of Progress* (Annual Report for 1951), pp. 7–8.

low-up reviews conducted since its establishment in three "traditionally Negro-excluding" industries, namely, banking, insurance, and department stores.[2] In most instances, the original investigation was conducted either during the latter half of the 1940s or the early 1950s, and the most recent review from two to ten years later. A case-by-case comparison of the later employment patterns with the earlier ones reveals that in the great majority of cases substantial improvements occurred both in the numerical representation of Negroes and in their occupational status. Of the thirteen banking concerns in which follow-up reviews were conducted, seven showed marked increases and three others modest increases in employment of Negroes. None of these banks had more than a few Negro employees above the menial level at the time of the original investigations, and most of them had none. When the follow-up reviews were conducted in the middle 1950s, each of the seven above-mentioned banks—among the largest in the country— had more than 100 Negro employees in a variety of white-collar occupations, and two of them had approximately 300 each. While these figures still represented relatively small proportionate employment of Negroes, the episode must none the less be regarded as a major landmark in the chronology of governmental efforts to eliminate job discrimination, since Negroes were completely debarred from banks in virtually every other state at this time. Some years later the pioneering New York banks became the models for similar breakthroughs in Washington and Baltimore, when bank managements in these cities counseled with several New York managements on approaches and procedures for integrating Negroes into their own work forces. It should be noted that to the average Negro virtually *any* job above the menial level in a bank,

<hr />

[2] State of New York, State Commission Against Discrimination, *The Banking Industry: Verified Complaints and Informal Investigations Handled, 1945–1958; The Insurance Industry: Verified Complaints and Informal Investigations Handled. 1945–1958: Employment in Department Stores: Complaints Against Major New York Department Stores Received, 1945–1958* (New York, 1958, mimeographed).

insurance company, or department store constitutes an improvement in occupational status.

The analysis of follow-up reviews in insurance companies
showed a similar result. Of twenty companies for which follow-up
review data were available, nine firms—six of them among the largest in the country—showed marked increases in employment of
Negroes, and one showed continued employment of Negroes but
no increase. The remaining ten companies still had no Negro employees, but all except one of these were small firms with work
forces averaging fewer than 100 persons, as contrasted with a range
of 1,800 to 13,000 in the large organizations. The record of the
largest company was especially noteworthy. This concern had no
racial minority employees when the New York law was enacted,
but by 1956 it had a total of approximately 750 Negroes working
in a wide variety of occupations, including many supervisory positions, and, in addition, nearly 200 Puerto Ricans in a similar range
of jobs. Puerto Ricans constitute a second large minority group in
New York State, numbering approximately 650,000 in 1960, or
nearly half as many as the total of the State's Negroes. No other
state has more than a small fraction of New York's Puerto Rican
population.

The department store analysis also showed an impressive increase in the aggregate employment and occupational status of
Negroes. While a few of the reviewed stores had Negroes in
above-menial jobs in 1945, the great majority did not. Fourteen of
the fifteen stores analyzed—all of them in New York City and its
suburbs—showed increases in Negro employment, and in most instances the increases were severalfold. While the data presented are
not amenable to exact accounting, it is a safe estimate that by the
middle 1950s Negroes comprised at least 10 percent of the aggregate work force of the major New York City department stores.
The proportion was somewhat less in the sales forces, owing to a
continued reluctance on the part of some store managements to
employ Negroes in "customer contact" positions. Negro sales peo-

ple were much in evidence, however, in virtually all department stores: and in several major establishments Negroes comprised more than 10 percent of the total sales force.

While no corresponding analysis was made of public utilities, another traditionally Negro-excluding industry, it is possible to make a fairly close appraisal of changes in Negro employment in this industry from figures on employment "by color" in the Federal Census statistics. Thus, nonwhite employment in communications utilities (telephone, telegraph, radio, and television) in New York State increased from 1,888 (or 2.2 percent of total employment) in 1950 to 5,320 (or 5.0 percent of total employment) in 1960.[3] Approximately three-fourths of all workers in the communications industry in New York are employed by the dominant company; hence, it is possible to estimate this company's nonwhite employment for both 1950 and 1960. In an earlier study the company reported that in 1944—just prior to the passage of the New York law—it had approximately 200 Negro employees, comprising about ½ of 1 percent of its total work force. By 1950 its Negro employment apparently had increased to approximately 1,500, or over 2 percent of the work force, and by 1960 to approximately 4,000, or about 5 percent of the work force. This company's Negro employees, both men and women, are distributed among a wide range of semiskilled and skilled blue- and white-collar jobs and even in some supervisory and professional positions.

Our researches in the other three states with long-established FEP laws likewise indicate material abatement of employment discrimination since the advent of the laws, although the extent of the indicated progress falls considerably short of that observed in New York. In New Jersey, for example, a series of county racial employment pattern studies conducted by the state's Division Against Discrimination over the period 1947–56, together with a limited

[3] U.S. Bureau of the Census, *U.S. Census of Population, 1950:* Vol. II, *Characteristics of the Population,* Part 32, New York, Table 83. *1960: Detailed Characteristics, New York,* Final Report PC(1)–34D, Table 129.

number of subsequent complaint case reviews, provided evidence of progress in employment of Negroes, primarily in manufacturing industries. A survey of retail stores in 1955 showed that modest headway had been made in a portion of the state's merchandising industry, mainly in department stores. Similarly, a survey of public utility companies in 1960 revealed a sizable improvement in Negro employment in that industry, particularly in the larger companies. As in New York State, Negroes are employed in both skilled blue-collar and in white-collar occupations in New Jersey utility companies. The census data on employment of nonwhites do not, however, entirely corroborate this study. In communications utilities in New Jersey, the proportion of nonwhites in the work force increased from less than 1 percent in 1950 to 2.3 percent in 1960;[4] but in electric and gas utilities the proportion of nonwhites decreased from 2 percent in 1950 to 1.5 percent in 1960, despite an increase in the state's nonwhite population during the decade.[5] The fact that the New York Commission has reviewed company racial employment patterns more systematically than the New Jersey Division Against Discrimination may account in part for greater gains in nonwhite employment in New York State's electric and gas utilities.

A review of the Philadelphia Commission on Human Relations and its experience provides further evidence of tangible reduction in discriminatory employment practices. As noted earlier the Commission on Human Relations, under Philadelphia's Home Rule Charter, possesses broader powers to undertake pattern-based compliance actions than any other fair employment agency. The commission invoked these powers very sparingly during its early career, but has made increasing use of them in recent years. In 1958–60 the Commission conducted a detailed investigation of the city's hotel and restaurant industry, followed by a series of public hear-

[4] U.S. Bureau of the Census, *U.S. Census of Population, 1950:* Vol. II, *Characteristics of the Population*, Part 30, New Jersey, Table 83. *1960: Detailed Characteristics, New Jersey*, Final Report PC(1)–32D, Table 129.
[5] *Ibid.*

ings at which many of the management and union officials connected with the industry testified. On completion of these proceedings, it published a comprehensive report of its findings.[6] This
industry-wide action and the accompanying negotiations with individual managements and unions have resulted in a notable improvement, both quantitatively and qualitatively, in employment opportunities for Negroes in Philadelphia's hotels and restaurants. A
similar broad-scale investigation of the city's banking enterprises,
currently under way, bids fair to bring about a comparable result
in that industry.

When, however, Negro employment trends in New York are
compared with corresponding trends in other industrial states, including both those with and those without FEP laws, it is evident
that New York is now well in the lead among such states in racial
integration in employment. This conclusion is warranted not only
for the "traditionally Negro-excluding industries" cited in the
foregoing pages but with respect to virtually all lines of economic
activity.

The conclusion is corroborated by a comparison of New York
and other Northern states in terms of change in the occupational
status of Negroes between 1950 and 1960, as shown by statistics
from the decennial Censuses of population. As of this writing, it is
not possible to make such a comparison in the most meaningful
way, since the state-by-state 1960 Census volumes giving detailed
occupational data by color are not yet available. The occupational
breakdowns used in the "General Characteristics" state volumes,
however, bring out much of the evidence, although some occupational categories must be omitted because they include both relatively desirable and relatively undesirable occupations. Table 6.2
shows the changes that occurred in New York State between 1950
and 1960 in nonwhite employment as a proportion of total em-

[6] City of Philadelphia, Commission on Human Relations, *Findings of Fact,
Conclusions and Action of the Commission on Human Relations in re: Investiga-
tive Public Hearings into Alleged Discriminatory Practices by the Hotel and
Restaurant Industry in Philadelphia* (Philadelphia, 1961, mimeographed).

ployment in what we may call, for convenience, the "fair employment opportunity" occupational categories. These categories comprise the *employee* occupations (as distinct from self-employment occupations) that afford *potential* employment opportunities for Negroes above the levels of traditional "Negro jobs." Substan-

Table 6.2

PERCENTAGE CHANGES IN NONWHITE EMPLOYMENT IN "FAIR
EMPLOYMENT OPPORTUNITY" OCCUPATIONAL CATEGORIES,
NEW YORK STATE

Occupational category	PERCENTAGE NONWHITE OF TOTAL EMPLOYMENT		1950–60 change in nonwhite proportion
	1950	*1960*	
Male:			
Managers and officials, salaried	1.1	2.9	+ 164
Retail sales workers	2.7	3.8	+ 41
Foremen	1.6	2.8	+ 75
Mechanics and repairmen	4.5	6.6	+ 47
Metal craftsmen	2.1	3.9	+ 86
Construction craftsmen	2.8	4.1	+ 46
Other craftsmen	2.7	3.7	+ 37
Drivers and deliverymen	5.8	10.1	+ 74
Operatives, manufacturing	5.4	8.9	+ 65
Female:			
Professional medical and health workers, salaried	6.5	11.9	+ 82
Secretaries, stenographers, and typists	1.8	3.6	+ 100
Other clerical workers	2.8	5.9	+ 111
Retail sales workers	2.1	4.2	+ 100
Operatives, manufacturing	10.9	12.3	+ 13

Source: *U.S. Census of Population, 1950:* Vol. II, *Characteristics of the Population*, Part 32, New York. *U.S. Census of Population, 1960: General Social and Economic Characteristics, New York*, Final Report PC(1)–34C, Table 58.

tial numbers of Negroes are qualified for employment in these occupations. Certain categories have been purposely omitted—for example, male clerical and kindred workers because the occupation group includes both desirable occupations and such traditional "Negro jobs" as baggagemen, male professional medical and health workers because comparable figures for 1950 and 1960 are not obtainable, and professional engineers because the total number of Negroes who graduated from the nation's engineering colleges during the decade was so small that no significant increase in employment of Negro professional engineers was possible in *any* state.

In discussing the significance of Table 6.2, we should note first that a major increase in New York State's Negro population occurred during the decade: the nonwhite-to-total proportion rose from 6.5 percent in 1950 to 8.9 percent in 1960. This increase in the state's Negro labor force could hardly in itself, however, have been a factor explaining the improved Negro representation in the occupational categories listed, since it was due largely to a major influx of Negroes from the rural South, most of whom could not qualify for any but unskilled and menial jobs. Actually, Table 6.2 considerably understates the gains made by minority groups in "fair employment opportunity" occupations, for three reasons: first, because the period considered begins in 1950, whereas the New York Commission has been functioning since 1945; second, because it takes no account of the state's large Puerto Rican population, which constitutes a separate minority group that is subject to the same kinds of employment discrimination as the Negro group and in much the same degree; and third, because the figures for 1950 as well as 1960 include, for most of the categories listed, an unknown but sizable component based on Negro employment in the segregated Negro community.

The improvement in Negro occupational status indicated by the Census figures must be regarded as significant by almost any standard. Substantial gains in Negro representation occurred over the decade in every category except female operatives in manufacturing, where Negroes were already "overrepresented" in 1950. The gains made by Negro men in managerial positions and in supervisory jobs (foremen) are particularly noteworthy, as are those made by Negro women in professional medical work (nursing, etc.) and in clerical and sales occupations.

The significance of the gains in Negro occupational status in

New York is further borne out if one compares the changes over the decade in that state with the corresponding changes in the states that had no FEP laws or that had non-enforceable laws. Comparison between New York and a *Northern* state without a FEP law is not possible, because all the Northern states with significant Negro populations had some kind of FEP law—either for the state as a whole or in one or more major cities—during part or all of the decade. It is possible, however, to compare New York with Northern states that had only *non-enforceable* laws—either state or municipal. Three states fall in this category: Indiana, Illinois, and Missouri. Indiana had a non-enforceable FEP law from 1945 until 1963, when an enforceable statute was enacted. Illinois and Missouri—both of which now have enforceable laws, passed in 1961—had no FEP laws during 1950–60. Chicago, however, has had a non-enforceable ordinance since 1948; and St. Louis enacted such an ordinance in 1956. Table 6.3 compares the "1950–60 change in nonwhite proportion" percentages for New York developed in Table 6.2 with the corresponding figures for Indiana, Illinois, and Missouri combined.

In interpreting Table 6.3, we should note that Negroes constituted 6.9 percent of the tri-state group's total population in 1950 and 9.1 percent in 1960—as compared with 6.5 and 8.9 percent, respectively, for New York State. Thus, the Negro population characteristics of the two areas were closely similar throughout the decade; and, hence, it is unlikely that any differences between the areas in Negro occupational representation trends were due in any important degree to differences in Negro labor force characteristics.

It is apparent from Table 6.3 that significantly larger gains in Negro representation in "opportunity" occupations occurred in New York than in the states with non-enforceable laws. With the single exception of female professional medical workers, the percentage increases in nonwhite representation were markedly greater in New York throughout; and in nine of the fourteen categories, they were more than double the tri-state increases. The average gain, for all fourteen categories combined, was 75 percent in New York, as compared with 34 percent in the tri-state group. The gains in the three Midwestern states were probably due in

Table 6.3

	PERCENTAGE CHANGES IN NONWHITE PROPORTION OF TOTAL EMPLOYMENT, 1950–60	
Occupational category	*New York State*	*Indiana, Illinois, and Missouri combined*
Male:		
Managers and officials, salaried	+ 164	+ 6
Retail sales workers	+ 41	+ 15
Foremen	+ 75	+ 37
Mechanics and repairmen	+ 47	+ 21
Metal craftsmen	+ 86	+ 50
Construction craftsmen	+ 46	+ 8
Other craftsmen	+ 37	+ 15
Drivers and deliverymen	+ 74	+ 42
Operatives, manufacturing	+ 65	+ 20
Female:		
Professional medical and health workers, salaried	+ 84	+ 82
Secretaries, stenographers, and typists	+ 100	+ 66
Other clerical workers	+ 111	+ 91
Retail sales workers	+ 100	+ 30
Operatives, manufacturing	+ 13	− 1

Sources: New York State: Table 6.2 above. Indiana: U.S. Bureau of the Census, *U.S. Census of Population, 1950:* Vol. II, *Characteristics of the Population,* Part 14, Indiana, Table 77, *1960: General Social and Economic Characteristics,* Final Report PC(1)–16C, Table 58. Illinois and Missouri, 1950 and 1960: Same tables cited above from the separate state volumes for these years.

large part to factors related to the labor market; and it may well be that these factors also account for gains of approximately the same magnitude in New York State. The conclusion seems warranted, however, that the additional gains indicated for New York are in the main attributable to the state's FEP law and the work of the Commission on Human Rights in applying and enforcing it.

Further support for this conclusion is afforded by a comparison of data on Negro employment in establishments holding Federal contracts in the New York City metropolitan area with corresponding figures for the principal metropolitan areas in the three states with non-enforceable laws—namely, Indianapolis, Chicago, and St. Louis. These data, drawn from the 1962 "compliance reports" submitted by Federal contract holders to the President's Committee on Equal Employment Opportunity, are summarized in Table 6.4.

Table 6.4

PERCENTAGE DISTRIBUTION OF NEGRO WORKERS IN ESTABLISHMENTS
HOLDING FEDERAL CONTRACTS WITHIN SELECTED METROPOLITAN
STATISTICAL AREAS, JUNE, 1962

	New York	Indianapolis	Chicago	St. Louis
All occupations	100.0	100.0	100.0	100.0
White-collar occupations	24.9	3.2	4.5	3.6
Officials and managers	1.5	0.3	0.3	0.2
Professional	1.7	0.3	0.5	0.3
Technical	5.1	1.2	1.3	1.3
Sales workers	0.2	0.0	0.1	0.0
Office and clerical	16.4	1.4	2.3	1.8
Blue-collar occupations	75.1	96.8	95.5	96.4
Craftsmen (skilled)	17.3	7.6	7.1	7.2
Operatives (semiskilled)	33.8	46.3	46.3	56.6
Laborers (unskilled)	15.3	26.3	30.4	23.8
Service workers	8.7	16.6	11.7	8.8

Source: U.S. Department of Labor, Bureau of Labor Statistics, *Employment in Establishments Subject to Executive Order 10925: A Preliminary Review of 1962 Compliance Reports* (mimeographed, unpublished), quoted by permission of the President's Committee on Equal Employment Opportunity.

The strikingly higher occupational status of Negro workers in the New York City area is readily apparent from this table. Thus, in the New York City area, one-fourth of the Negro workers were in white-collar occupations—more than five times the proportion in Chicago and more than seven times the proportion in Indianapolis and St. Louis. Similarly, in the New York area approximately one-sixth of the Negro workers were in skilled-craft occupations—more than twice the proportion in each of the three Midwestern areas. It is worth adding that the indicated disparities between the New York area and the two Southern metropolitan areas for which comparable figures are available—Memphis and Dallas—were even greater.

Our review of the activities of other state commissions responsible for the administration of enforceable laws of long standing also yielded indications of improvements in Negro employment patterns. Census data on employment by occupation and color accord with these indications. In most of these states, however, apparent Negro employment gains were smaller than those shown in Table 6.2 for New York. This manifestation of greater progress in New York than in other states with FEP laws cannot be ascribed to any differences in the substantive provisions of the laws themselves, since the other states have followed the New York law very closely in this respect. There is, however, reason to believe that certain distinctive features of the New York Commission's basic approach in administering the New York law, as well as of its organizational set-up, staffing, and procedures, have had a good deal to do with it. These features of the New York Commission's structure and operation are discussed in the concluding section of the chapter. To round out our picture of the FEP commissions' experience, we turn now to a discussion of their relations with employment agencies and, following that, to their efforts to combat discrimination by labor organizations.

Experience of FEP Commissions with Employment Agencies

We noted in Chapter 2 that employer job orders specifying "whites only" are honored by many employment agencies in states with FEP laws despite the statutory prohibition of such transactions. Nearly all the FEP commission officials interviewed during our study conceded that this type of discrimination is still common and that they have been less than successful in their efforts to combat it. Further evidence of its frequent occurrence has come from the employment agencies themselves. Thus, the U.S. Commission on Civil Rights, after surveying the practices of public employment offices in Detroit and Baltimore (subject respectively to a state and a municipal FEP law), reported that "employment office personnel in both cities admitted that they still sent the 'discriminating' firms only those persons who would be hired." [7] And a recent investigation in New York revealed that some public employment office interviewers in that state were accepting and honoring discriminatory job orders.[8]

It is hardly surprising that employers in substantial numbers place discriminatory job orders with employment agencies, even in states with FEP laws. There are, of course, employers in all of these states who are determined to avoid employing Negroes, regardless of the statutory strictures against discriminatory hiring. For such employers, utilizing employment agencies to recruit and screen prospective employees offers a convenient and safe means of evading the law, provided the agencies are willing to cooperate. Since the employer does not recruit directly and since his relations with the agency are conducted on a confidential basis, the excluded job-seeker has no way of identifying the source of the discriminatory treatment in the event he attempts to file a complaint with the FEP commission.

It is somewhat more difficult to explain why employment agencies in states with FEP laws continue to accept and honor job orders on a "whites only" basis. In the case of private agencies, the twin facts that such orders constitute an important source of revenue and that they are readily kept secret are undoubtedly the prin-

[7] U.S. Commission on Civil Rights, *1961 Report: Book 3, Employment* (U.S. Government Printing Office, Washington, D.C.), p. 118.

[8] New York State Commission Against Discrimination (subsequently renamed New York Commission on Human Rights), *Investigation of Charges of Discriminatory Practices in the New York State Employment Services: Report No. 3, Analysis of Interviews with 97 Interviewers and Senior Interviewers of the New York State Employment Service* (New York, 1959, mimeographed), *passim.*

cipal reasons. With regard to public agencies, the USES policy of allocating operating funds to the local employment offices primarily on the basis of their placement record is at least equally significant. Owing to this policy, the local office managers and staff personnel are under constant pressure to maximize their placements and consequently have a strong incentive to comply with "whites only" job orders rather than risk losing this placement business to private agencies. The incentive is further reinforced by the fact that, in most states, promotions of public employment office personnel are also determined largely on the basis of individual placement records.[9]

That recruitment through employment agencies affords discrimination-minded employers good insurance against detection and compliance action is indicated by the relatively small number of complaints involving these agencies filed with FEP commissions. Thus, in New York State, only 6.7 percent of all "probable cause" complaints filed with the state Commission over the period 1946–61 named an employment agency as the respondent; for Massachusetts (1946–59), the corresponding figure was 6.3 percent; and for Connecticut (1949–60), the proportion was 6.1 percent. In view of the fact that more than one-fifth of all hiring in this country is done through employment agencies and of the evidence that processing of discriminatory job orders has been widespread throughout the postwar period, it is apparent that only a small proportion of the discriminatory transactions of employment agencies ever comes to the attention of FEP commissions.

The propensity of public employment agencies to honor "whites only" job orders despite the statutory proscription is not the only conflict between public policy and practice in the states with FEP laws. In most of these states, the officials of the state-controlled employment-service agencies have persistently refused

[9] Interviews with FEP commission officials in California, Connecticut, Michigan, New Jersey, New York, Pennsylvania, and Washington; see also Commission on Civil Rights, *1961 Report,* Book 3.

to cooperate with the FEP commissions in their efforts to uncover and deal with discriminatory referral transactions between employers and public employment agencies. The commissions have repeatedly requested that the employment agencies be required to report cases of discriminatory job orders by employers to them for compliance action; but in all the states except New York and Wisconsin, the employment agency officials have rejected these requests. They have based their refusal in part on an alleged need for retaining and expanding public agency placements in the face of private agency competition, and in part on USES regulations which they interpret as prohibiting such disclosure. Thus, the great majority of FEP commissions have been unable to take effective action against "whites only" orders and referrals, either via the complaint procedure or on their own initiative. Under a revised interpretation of the USES regulations, issued in 1961, the state employment services may reveal information concerning employment transactions to FEP commissions upon specific request by the latter in specified cases; but arrangements for day-to-day reporting of discriminatory job orders to commissions are still not in effect. Hence, the revision has had little practical effect, since the commissions receive very few complaints alleging discrimination by or through employment agencies.

As noted earlier, only two state employment services—those in New York and those in Wisconsin—have consented so far to cooperate with the FEP enforcement agencies in their efforts to deal with discriminatory requests for referrals. In New York State, under an agreement between the employment service and the Commission on Human Rights, public employment agencies are committed to report discriminatory job orders to the Commission in all cases in which the employment offices themselves are unable to secure removal of the discriminatory specifications. A similar arrangement is in effect in Wisconsin, except that here the employment agencies are required to report discriminatory orders to the state's FEP division immediately upon receiving them. While these arrangements are obviously contrary to the aforementioned USES regulations, the Federal agency has not interfered with their implementation.

Although the agreement in New York State has been in effect since the enactment of the State's FEP law in 1945, the staff official most familiar with its history stated frankly that the Commission has never been very effective in bringing discriminatory requests for referrals to light.[10] The pressure on employment office managers and interviewers to maximize placements has provided an ever-present incentive to accept and comply with discriminatory orders and a concomitant deterrent to reporting such orders to the Commission. Indicative of this is the fact that only forty-nine cases were reported to the Commission over the entire period of 1951–56.

In 1957, following a change in the routing procedure within the State Employment Service, the reporting was discontinued entirely, and for two years no discriminatory job order cases were referred to the Commission. In 1959 the Commission, at the behest of the Governor, conducted a state-wide investigation into the referral practices of public employment agencies. The investigation revealed, among other things, that a sizable proportion of interviewers in state employment offices were accepting and complying with discriminatory job orders and that their superiors were condoning or even abetting this practice. Following the issuance of the Commission's findings, the State Industrial Commissioner issued instructions to the Division of Employment ordering the resumption of the reporting system and providing for penalization of employment office personnel found to be participating in discriminatory referral practices.[11]

Subsequent commission experience with the restored reporting system indicates that this action has resulted in some diminution of discriminatory job order processing in New York State's em-

[10] Interview with Milton Rosenberg, Director, Division of Employment Discrimination, New York State Commission on Human Rights, May 11, 1961.

[11] New York State Commission Against Discrimination, *Investigation of Charges of Discriminatory Practices in the New York State Employment Service* (New York, 1959, mimeographed), *passim*.

ployment exchanges, although it has by no means eliminated the practice. There is some evidence, also, that the reporting system in Wisconsin has had a similar modest effect. Meanwhile, however, employment service officials in the remaining states with FEP laws still refuse to cooperate—or at best offer only token cooperation—with the FEP agencies, with the result that compliance with employer requests for "whites only" continues unabated in these states.

The anomaly of persistent discrimination in public employment office operations in states where employment discrimination is prohibited by law is sufficiently obvious. No less anomalous is the USES policy of allocating operating funds to these offices in proportion to workers placed in jobs, which is largely responsible for the persistence of discriminatory practices.

The implication is equally obvious: as an essential move toward eliminating the discriminatory practices, the present formula for allocating Federal funds should be discarded, and a formula that will encourage referral on a nondiscriminatory basis adopted in its place. One possible alternative would be to take the current or prospective total of job-seekers in the local office area as the primary criterion, with somewhat larger than proportionate allotments for areas with an unusually large percentage of minority group job-seekers. To support and strengthen the revised fund-allocation formula, the Federal agency should establish a policy, mandatory on all state employment services, unequivocally prohibiting discrimination in the structure, staffing, and operation of public employment offices and stipulating as a penalty for noncompliance the forfeiture of all Federal operating grants. It would probably also be desirable for the state employment services to issue implementing instructions to the local offices explicitly prohibiting the acceptance and honoring of discriminatory job orders. With the revised Federal policies in effect, this could be done with assurance that the instructions would be observed, not only in states with FEP laws but other states as well.

As a further and possibly even more significant effect of the revised Federal policies, the flagrantly discriminatory practice of keeping public employment offices segregated by race, still followed in most of the Southern states, would have to be discontinued and a system of integrated offices, staffed and operated in a nondiscriminatory manner, established in their place. Since the penalty for failure to comply would be loss of the Federal operating subsidy, it is hardly likely that any but the most obdurate Southern states would insist on continuing to operate their public employment exchanges on a segregated basis.

Experience of FEP Commissions with Unions

Labor organizations have played a prominent role in the legislative effort which has resulted in the passage of enforceable FEP laws in twenty-two states over the past eighteen years. For example, strong support by the state labor federations in California, Michigan, and Pennsylvania was in large measure responsible for the enactment of FEP laws in those states. Indeed, state and city "central" union organizations have backed such legislation in practically every state and municipality where it has been passed. Moreover, union leaders have actively supported the commissions established pursuant to these laws. In Michigan and Pennsylvania, for instance, prominent union officials are currently serving as chairmen of the respective state commissions, and a union attorney heads the state commission in Washington. In keeping with the position of the state organizations and their leaders, the AFL-CIO is on record as strongly favoring a Federal FEP law, which President George Meany has publicly stated is needed to help organized labor eliminate racial discrimination in its own ranks.[12]

In view of this record of support by organized labor, it may seem paradoxical that some of the most intransigent respondents

[12] Statement of George Meany, President, AFL-CIO, in Hearings before the Special Subcommittee on Labor of the Committee on Education and Labor, House of Representatives, Eighty-Seventh Congress, Second Session, January 24, 1962, Part II, pp. 985–95.

before state commissions have been unions. The paradox is more apparent than real, however. The city and state central bodies that have supported FEP legislation are primarily politically oriented organizations, with a large stake in winning Negro support for their political objectives; and the union leaders who are encouraging and participating in the work of the commissions are for the most part officials of industrial unions, which generally make no racial distinctions in their admission practices and for the most part accord Negro members equal status and treatment with whites. On the other hand, the labor organizations involved as respondents before FEP commissions have usually been local craft unions—primarily economic in character—which exclude Negroes from membership or bar them from job opportunities in other ways.

As noted in Chapter 3, there are four main types of union racial practices that adversely affect job opportunities for Negroes; namely, exclusion from membership, discrimination in referring Negroes to employers for jobs, maintenance of racially segregated locals, and segregated seniority arrangements in union contracts. All these union practices fall under the proscription of the FEP laws, both state and municipal. To set our discussion of FEP commission experience with unions in proper perspective, it is necessary to review briefly the extent to which each type of practice exists in the states covered by FEP laws, which include virtually all industrialized areas outside the South. For the sake of brevity, we shall refer to this portion of the country as "the North."

Exclusion of Negroes from membership (and hence from job opportunities) is prevalent in certain craft unions—principally those in printing, railroad transportation, and the higher-skill construction trades (electrical work, plumbing, etc.). It is rarely encountered, however, among unions in manufacturing, mining, trucking, utilities, trade, or any other industry outside the craft-dominated lines of activity. Racial discrimination in job referrals is also confined to certain craft-union locals—i.e., those that function as employment agencies for employers with whom they have contracts and that also customarily admit Negroes to membership. In the North the unions that fall in this category are mainly locals of carpenters, bricklayers, cement-finishers, construction laborers, longshoremen, seamen, brewery workers, and hotel and restaurant workers. Again, while racially segregated locals are fairly common in certain building and "non-operating" railroad crafts in the North, they are rarely found in any other Northern industry. Finally, racially segregated seniority arrangements in union contracts, while quite common in the South, are seldom encountered in other sections of the country.

In sum, union racial discrimination in the North, although by no means a rarity, is limited to a relatively small sector of employing enterprise as a whole. This explains, in large part, why the volume of commission compliance cases involving discrimination by unions has been relatively small—less than 10 percent of all compliance activities on the average. Another factor accounting for the paucity of union-related commission activities is the fact that few Negroes are able to qualify for membership in higher-skill craft unions, since they are largely excluded from apprentice training in these crafts. Still another factor is that most FEP agencies, in processing complaints against discriminatory labor unions, have displayed a marked reluctance to undertake vigorous and sustained compliance efforts in such cases. This reluctance is attributable in large part to the fact that union leaders cannot consummate compliance agreements unless they can first overcome the resistance of union membership and obtain their consent. Thus, achieving compliance is inherently much more difficult in discriminatory union situations than in cases involving employer-related discrimination, where only management's acquiescence is necessary to effect a compliance settlement.

Largely owing to these factors, the aggregative reduction in discriminatory union practices achieved by FEP commissions has been of decidedly minor proportions. The commissions, however—and especially the long-established ones—have obtained corrective action in a number of individual and small-group complaint cases involving, in most instances, particular locals of craft unions. In addition, several commissions have taken action against particular national unions, aimed at eliminating general union policies of a discriminatory nature. The essential facts of the commissions' experience in dealing with union discrimination can be summarized briefly.

In the years immediately following its establishment the New York Commission took action against twelve railroad unions, all of which had racial exclusion provisions in their constitutions. Through intensive conciliation efforts, bolstered by its enforcement powers, the Commission succeeded in getting six of these unions to eliminate their constitutional bars against Negroes. The others refused to do so, although they agreed to make the provisions inoperative in New York State. Later, however, four of these other unions also removed their racial bars on a nation-wide basis.

While the removal of the constitutional barriers did not preclude the individual locals from continuing to practice racial exclusionism, several of the "non-operating" railroad unions subsequently admitted Negro railroad workers in a number of localities, although in most cases further pressure from state commissions was required before they would do so. Even the Brotherhood of Railroad Trainmen, the largest of the "operating" unions, admitted a number of Negroes to membership in several Jersey City lodges following complaint action by the New Jersey Division Against Discrimination. The Firemen's, Engineers', and Conductors' unions have, however, continued their practice of complete exclusionism—even in New York and other states where they have agreed to make their constitutional provisions inoperative.

Another potentially significant development is the series of complaint-based actions taken by state and municipal commissions against local craft unions in the construction industry to get them to admit Negroes to membership. At least seven different commissions have successfully consummated such actions. Table 6.5, though not exhaustive, will serve to illustrate the variety of craft unions and FEP commissions involved in building trades exclusion cases.

In the Hartford electricians case, the earliest of these actions (1952), the union at first defied the Connecticut Commission's

Table 6.5

BUILDING TRADES LOCAL UNIONS THAT HAVE ADMITTED NEGROES TO
MEMBERSHIP AS A RESULT OF FEP COMMISSION ACTIONS

Craft	Commission	Location of local union	Number of Negroes admitted	Admitted to journeyman or apprentice status
Electricians	Connecticut	Hartford	2	journeyman
Electricians	Cleveland	Cleveland	3	journeyman
Electricians	Michigan	Detroit	8	journeyman
Plumbers	Michigan	Saginaw	1	journeyman
Plumbers	California	San Francisco	1	apprentice
Plasterers	Wisconsin	Milwaukee	1	journeyman
Bricklayers	Wisconsin	Milwaukee	2	journeyman
Painters	Pittsburgh	Pittsburgh	1[a]	journeyman
Glaziers	Oregon	Portland	1	apprentice

[a] More than 20 others subsequently admitted.

cease-and-desist order and appealed to the state courts, but quickly admitted the Negro electricians to membership when the Superior court upheld the commission and imposed a fine of $2,000 for contempt as well as a contingent fine of $500 per week for continued noncompliance.[13] This case soon became widely known in union circles, which undoubtedly helps to explain why, in all of the subsequent cases cited, the commissions involved won admission for the Negro craftsmen through conciliation agreements with the unions and hence did not need to resort to court action.

A third class of union-connected cases dealt with by the commissions has been concerned with discrimination against Negroes in referring union members to jobs. Of necessity, these cases have

[13] Superior Court, Hartford County, Connecticut, File No. 90351–2, March, 1954.

been confined to local unions that both admit Negroes to membership and function as employment or referral agencies for employers. Thus they have often arisen in the bricklayers', cement-finishers', and building laborers' locals in the construction industry and also in various types of locals in the hotel and restaurant industry. Frequently, in such cases, the unions have disavowed responsibility for the discriminatory action on the ground that the employers have specifically requested referral of white members. Consequently, the commissions that have dealt with this problem have usually found it necessary to conduct conciliation sessions jointly with union and employer representatives in order to ascertain the true source of the discrimination and to devise a viable basis for eliminating it. The New York, New Jersey, Connecticut, and Michigan commissions have successfully dealt with job referral cases involving construction trades locals, as have the California, Michigan, and Philadelphia commissions in hotel and restaurant industry cases.

Finally, a number of state commissions have had to deal with situations involving segregated local unions. Segregated or semi-segregated locals of carpenters, cement-finishers, and building laborers exist in a number of Northern cities. In only two particular unions, however—the Brotherhood of Railway and Steamship Clerks and the American Federation of Musicians—are separate Negro locals still found in any substantial numbers in the North; and the experience of state commissions in dealing with this type of union discrimination has centered, in the main, on these two unions. The commissions that have attempted to bring about mergers of white and Negro locals have encountered two main obstacles: the refusal of white rank-and-file union members to vote for mergers and the opposition of the leaders of some Negro locals to merging with white locals, based on fears of losing their leadership status. For example, the New York commission, after five years of effort, has been unable to effect a merger of the white and Negro locals of the Railway Clerks in New York City, owing to the persistent refusal of the white local's membership to vote for the change and the unwillingness of the union's national leaders to circumvent the rule of local union autonomy. Similar situations exist in numerous other cities where separate locals of this union still exist. On the other hand, considerable progress has been made in eliminating segregated locals of musicians. Partly owing to the policy of the national leaders of the Musicians' Union to encourage mergers and partly as a result of FEP commission efforts, a majority of the Northern locals of this union are now integrated. A sizable number of separate locals still exist, however, owing largely to opposition on the part of the Negro local union leaders involved.

In concluding our discussion of FEP commission experience with unions, it is worth re-emphasizing that the volume of commissions' compliance actions involving unions has been only a small proportion—less than 10 percent—of all commission actions. It should also be noted, however, that, in terms of eliminating discriminatory practices, the results achieved by commissions in union-connected actions have been even smaller than the relative volume of such actions would indicate. This is particularly evident with respect to the two most prevalent union practices—exclusion from membership and discriminatory job referrals. The total of exclusionist craft locals that have admitted Negroes to membership as a result of commission intervention is only a small fraction of all such locals, and the same is true with regard to locals that discriminate in referring Negro members to jobs.

The reasons for this meager achievement are also worth re-emphasizing. With regard to unions excluding Negroes from membership, it is attributable in considerable part to the fact that, since this also means exclusion from apprentice training, few Negroes are able to qualify for membership. Equally important is the fact that the leaders of exclusionist craft locals are usually extremely resistant to commission conciliation efforts, since admission to craft-union membership is almost invariably decided by vote and since the memberships they represent are in most cases opposed to admitting Negroes. The difficulty of the conciliator's problem is obvious—in order to fulfill his mission, he must persuade the union membership as well as the leaders to remove the racial barrier.

The problem of resistance by union leaders is also often a factor in cases involving discriminatory job referrals. Even when craft locals admit Negroes to membership, they usually constitute only a small minority and hence have little voice in decisions regarding union policies and practices. A further problem is created when unions involved in job referral cases insist they are merely complying with employers' requests for "whites only"—the commission must then determine which party is responsible for the discriminatory act.

Still another retardant to progress in abating union discriminatory practices is the fact that most commissions are exclusively preoccupied with processing individual complaints—or nearly so. For reasons already noted, individual complaints against unions take a much longer time to process to conclusion than do complaints involving employer practices. Moreover, it is far more difficult for commissions to seek pattern adjustments in union-connected complaint cases, owing to the strong exclusionist sentiments prevailing among most craft-union members. For these and other reasons, the FEP commissions, without exception, have confined their compliance efforts with unions almost exclusively to individual complaints. Even the New York State Commission, which leads all others in effecting employer compliance on a pattern basis, has rarely attempted to obtain pattern compliance in cases involving unions.

Conclusions

The analysis of the effects of FEP commissions and their work presented in this chapter has adduced strong evidence that FEP legislation of the type now in effect in more than a third of the states can, if effectively administered, be a potent instrument for combating discrimination in employment. Follow-up reviews of compliance actions conducted by the long-established commissions in New York, New Jersey, Philadelphia, and other jurisdictions provided the most direct indications of progress in overcoming racial bias in the allocation of jobs. The reviews and other studies conducted by the New York State Commission, in particular, revealed major breakthroughs and subsequent sustained improvement in employment of Negroes in banking, insurance, retail trade, and public utilities and in numerous traditionally "all white" occupations in other industries. These evidences of substantial positive results from commission compliance efforts are borne out by the Census statistics on employment by occupation and color for 1950 and 1960. A 1950–60 comparison of nonwhite representation in fourteen middle- and upper-level occupational categories in New York State revealed striking increases in nine categories and significant improvements in the other five. Moreover, on the average the gains in nonwhite representation in New York were more than double, and in several instances more than triple, the corresponding increases in the total for three Midwestern states that had non-enforceable laws during 1950–60.

Both the direct evidence and the Census data indicate further that a considerably greater improvement in the occupational status of Negroes has occurred in New York than in the other states with enforceable FEP laws. As noted earlier, greater headway against employment discrimination in New York cannot be due to differences in the substantive provisions of the laws themselves, since nearly all the other enforceable statutes have been modeled closely on the New York law. Indeed several later laws, including those in Ohio and Philadelphia, grant the respective commissions more explicit powers to take broad-based compliance action than the New York statute. The explanation is to be found, rather, in the distinctive features of the New York Commission's organization and composition and in its general approach and specific procedures in administering the law, which taken together distinguish it from other FEP agencies. Some of these features have already been referred to in the earlier exposition. In the first place, the New York Commission has always had, and still has, by long odds the largest operating funds of any state or municipal FEP agency. Thus, it is able to employ a much larger compliance and enforcement staff than other agencies. Of major importance in this connection is the New York Commission's complement of five full-time adequately salaried commissioners (increased to seven in 1961), as contrasted with only part-time (and greatly underpaid) commissioners in five other states and nonworking unpaid commissioners in the remainder.

In the matter of organizational structure, the New York Commission is also in a class by itself—again largely as a result of comparatively generous annual budgets. The basic structure consisting of functional divisions—regulatory, research and statistics, legal, education and publications, etc.—permits the agency to employ personnel specially qualified and trained for these functions and to utilize them primarily in their specialties. Probably the most significant division of functions is that between the Regulatory Division and the Commission itself, whereby the Division assigns trained field representatives to conduct investigations under the direction of individual "operating" commissioners, leaving the latter free to concentrate on the crucially important conciliation and follow-up functions. This feature, together with the New York Commission's record of notably high-caliber commissioners, has unquestionably contributed much to the agency's effectiveness.

The New York Commission is also well in the lead with respect to geographic specialization, with seven regional offices strategically located throughout the state. (Only one other commission state—Ohio—has as many as five offices, three states have two each, and the remainder have only a single office.) This feature greatly facilitates the filing of complaints by aggrieved individuals and groups, and it also enhances the agency's effectiveness in conducting follow-up reviews and other compliance-connected studies.

In its general approach to the problem of employer compliance,

the New York Commission has given greater emphasis to employment patterns than any other agency. In processing individual
complaints, it has consistently required commitments from employers for revision of over-all policies and practices, where found to
be discriminatory; and alone among agencies it has conducted
follow-up reviews of respondents' employment practices as a regular practice. Moreover, it is almost the only commission (the
Philadelphia Commission on Human Relations being the only other
one) that has conducted compliance efforts directed originally and
solely at employment patterns—frequently on the commission's
own initiative. While most of these actions have dealt with the
patterns of particular companies, a significant proportion have em-
braced entire local or even state-wide industries. In this sphere of
activity, as in complaint cases, the commission keeps a check on
the progress of compliance through periodic follow-up reviews.

In its pattern-based compliance efforts, the New York Commission often follows what has come to be known as the "affirmative action" approach. Under a literal interpretation of the FEP
law, employers are required to hire and upgrade the best qualified
applicants regardless of race, creed, or national origin; but they
are not required to go beyond this in providing equal opportunity.
Under the hiring standards in effect in most employing establishments, however, Negroes applying for positions are likely to be
less well qualified, on the average, than white applicants. One reason is that the average level of educational attainment and achievement is lower among Negroes than among whites; but a corollary
reason is that the educational standards established by employers,
especially for semiskilled blue-collar and lower-level white-collar
jobs, are often unnecessarily high. Consequently, under usual hiring standards and methods, few, if any, Negroes would be hired
even in these categories.

In recognition of this doubly disadvantaged position of Negroes
in the job market, the New York Commission and (to a lesser
extent) several other FEP agencies, in seeking conciliation agree-

ments with noncomplying employers, endeavor to obtain commitments from them that they will go beyond the mere literal observance of the statutory requirements and make an affirmative effort to recruit and employ Negroes above the menial and unskilled levels. In implementing this approach, the commissions do not suggest that employers hire Negroes who are less well qualified than white applicants; rather, they may suggest that the employer broaden his recruitment efforts with the aim of attracting larger numbers of Negro applicants or—where conditions warrant—that he modify the formal educational requirements for hiring eligibility. Virtually all commissioners and staff officials interviewed during the course of the study were agreed that the affirmative action approach is essential if FEP agencies are to succeed in promoting real equality of employment opportunity.

The New York State agency has also given major attention to planning and programing its employer compliance and follow-up activities, whereas most of the other agencies—owing primarily to inadequate budgets and staffs—have had to confine their efforts mainly or exclusively to processing individual complaints. The New York Commission's programed efforts have taken such forms as analytical studies of follow-up reviews in key "progress" industries and commission-initiated compliance efforts on a city-wide basis in specific fair employment problem areas, such as hotels and local delivery services.

Discrimination in the functioning of employment agencies presents a peculiarly difficult problem for FEP commissions, primarily because it entails collaboration between the employer-client and the agency. The achievement record of the state commissions in this problem area is far from impressive—especially with regard to the state-controlled, Federally-financed public employment offices. In dealing with this problem, the New York and Wisconsin commissions have made somewhat better progress than their counterparts in other states by enlisting the cooperation of their respective state employment services in reporting discriminatory employer orders for workers to the commissions. Even in these two states, however, some discriminatory referring of workers for employment still continues. It is unlikely that the problem can be adequately dealt with until the over-all *Federal* policies governing the operation of all public employment offices are drastically revised.

Racial discrimination by labor unions also poses a difficult problem for FEP commissions, particularly with regard to the two most prevalent types of such discrimination, namely, exclusion of Negroes from membership by local unions in certain skilled crafts and discrimination in job referrals by locals in other crafts. In this problem area, as in the case of discrimination by employment agencies, the achievement record of the commissions leaves much to be desired. The difficulty of dealing with discriminatory craft unions stems principally from the strongly exclusionist sentiments prevailing among the rank-and-file membership of many of these unions. Largely for this reason, the commissions have been reluctant to undertake vigorous compliance efforts with such unions; and when they have done so, the outcome has often been only token compliance. Even the New York State Commission, with its notable record of promoting compliance by employers, has made little progress in dealing with discriminatory craft unions.

With regard to over-all achievement in reducing employment discrimination, however, the New York State Commission is demonstrably in the forefront among state and municipal FEP agencies. There can be little doubt that this commission's distinctively better financing and staffing, its more efficient organizational set-up, and its unusual pattern-centered approach to the problem of securing affirmative employer compliance with the FEP statute account in large measure for the results it has achieved. The implications of these characteristics of the New York Commission for improving the effectiveness of FEP legislation and administration in all jurisdictions are discussed in the concluding chapters of this book.

7

PRESIDENTIAL FAIR EMPLOYMENT
COMMITTEES—1941–1963

Fair employment practice activities at the Federal government level have been of two kinds: those concerned with the executive policy prohibiting discrimination in private firms holding Federal procurement contracts and those concerned with the corresponding policy regarding employment in the Federal government itself. Five different agencies charged primarily with the former duty have functioned for varying periods over the past two decades. All of these agencies have taken the form of committees created by executive order of the President, every attempt to obtain passage of FEP legislation by Congress having failed. The experience of these committees with respect to discrimination in Federal contract establishments is reviewed in the present chapter. The efforts of Presidentially appointed bodies (including three of these committees) to enforce the antidiscrimination policy in Federal government employment are dealt with in Chapter 8.

The first Presidential committee, called the Committee on Fair Employment Practice (FEPC) functioned during the early years of World War II. It was succeeded by another agency bearing the same name, which operated until the end of the war. The third agency, called the President's Committee on Government Contract Compliance, was established by President Truman and functioned for less than a year. The fourth committee, titled the President's Committee on Government Contracts, was appointed by President Eisenhower and operated for more than seven years. Finally, the President's Committee on Equal Employment Opportunity was established by President Kennedy in 1961 and is still in existence. The chronology of these five committees is summarized in Table 7.1.

Table 7.1

FEDERAL FAIR EMPLOYMENT COMMITTEES, 1941–1963

	Term of office	Number of members
First Committee on Fair Employment Practice[a]	8/41–1/43	5–7
Second Committee on Fair Employment Practice[a]	5/43–6/46	7
Committee on Government Contract Compliance[b]	4/52–1/53	11
Committee on Government Contracts[b]	9/53–1/61	15
Committee on Equal Employment Opportunity[c]	4/61–	28

Source: Reports of the several committees.

[a] These committees were responsible for the observance of fair employment practices in the Federal civil service, in essential industries, and in plants engaged in work on Federal contracts.

[b] These committees were responsible only for the observance of fair employment practices in plants engaged in work on Federal procurement contracts. During both the Truman and Eisenhower administrations, separate committees were responsible for fair employment practices in the Federal civil service.

[c] The committee appointed by President Kennedy is responsible for fair employment practices in the plants of Federal contractors *and* in the Federal civil service.

Membership and Meetings

Committee members have been appointed by the President and have served without compensation on a part-time basis. The sole exception was the chairman of the second Committee on Fair Employment Practice, who received a salary and devoted full time to his position. Presidents have attempted to give prestige to the committees by the appointment of prominent persons as members. During the Eisenhower and Kennedy administrations, the Vice President of the United States served as chairman of the committees. The Truman, Eisenhower, and Kennedy committees were ostensibly interdepartmental bodies composed of government officials, although members of the public served on all three committees.

Because of additional private or official responsibilities, members have usually devoted but little time to committee affairs, except for formal committee meetings. The Roosevelt committees met for one or two days monthly. The Eisenhower committee held some sixty meetings of one and one-half to two hours each during a period of seven and one-half years. The Kennedy committee has held but seven meetings, each of three to four hours duration, since the date of its organization. As of this writing (March, 1963), the committee had not met since November, 1962, nor is a meeting scheduled for any date in the future.[1]

We have been unable to determine with what regularity members attended meetings of the Roosevelt and Truman committees, but some information on this point is available for the Eisenhower and Kennedy committees. Between September, 1953, and June, 1957, the Eisenhower committee held thirty-seven meetings. During this time, Vice President Nixon, who was Chairman of the committee, attended eighteen meetings; and its Vice Chairman, Secretary of Labor James P. Mitchell, attended twenty-five meetings. Three of the remaining twelve members attended about thirty meetings each; the others were present much less frequently. The two committee members from the labor movement, George Meany and Walter Reuther, were present at but one meeting.[2] Thus far during the Kennedy administration, the attendance record of committee members has been much the same.[3]

During both the Eisenhower and Kennedy administrations, members have been frequently represented at committee meetings by alternates. Inspection of the minutes of the Eisenhower committee shows that alternate members frequently hesitated to commit their principals on important matters before the committee. Apparently, the effectiveness of the committees was impaired by the irregular attendance of their members and the frequent use of alternate members.

Jurisdiction

The jurisdiction of presidential committees has been defined by executive orders, subject to limitations imposed by Congress. Invariably, jurisdiction has been narrower than the entire field of

[1] Committee reports and minutes and interviews with Committee members and staff personnel.

[2] Committee on Government Contracts, tabulation of attendance of committee members, 1953–57 (unpublished).

[3] Interviews with staff members, the President's Committee on Equal Employment Opportunity.

interstate commerce, the normal jurisdiction of Federal regulatory agencies. The Roosevelt committees had the widest jurisdiction of any of the presidential committees. The order establishing the second Committee on Fair Employment Practice stated that it was

the policy of the United States that there shall be no discrimination in the employment of any person in war industries or in Government by reason of race, creed, color or national origin, and . . . it is the duty of all employers, including the several Federal departments and agencies, and all labor organizations . . . to eliminate discrimination in regard to hire, tenure, terms or conditions of employment, or union membership.[4]

Agencies of the United States were directed to include in all contracts negotiated or renegotiated by them a provision obligating contractors not to engage in discriminatory practices. The order gave the Committee responsibility for eliminating discriminatory employment practices from the Federal civil service, defense industries, plants holding government contracts, and labor unions representing workers in such activities. Plants engaged in interstate commerce were not within the Committee's jurisdiction unless they held Federal contracts or were part of an industry essential to the national defense. The committee construed its jurisdiction liberally and tried to move against discriminatory practices on a broad front.

Committee activities were opposed vehemently by certain members of the Congress from Southern states. In 1944, Senator Richard Russell of Georgia introduced an amendment to an appropriation bill for the purpose of preventing a President from using funds available to him or appropriated for use by one of the departments and agencies of the United States to pay the expenses of any agency, including those established by executive order, unless the Congress appropriated funds for such use.[5] To state the

[4] Executive Order No. 9346, May 27, 1943.
[5] Act of June 27, 1944, 58 Stat. 387, Independent Offices Appropriation Act of 1945, 31 U.S.C. 696.

matter more plainly, the purpose of Russell's amendment was to put an end to the Committee on Fair Employment Practice by depriving it of funds. The Committee came to an end about a year after the amendment became effective because the Congress refused to approve additional appropriations for its use. The amendment has never been rescinded.

Since passage of the Russell amendment, the jurisdiction of presidential committees in the sphere of private employment has been limited to establishments engaged in performing work under contracts with Federal agencies, a far narrower jurisdiction than that of the Roosevelt committees, which had jurisdiction over all essential industries. Although the number of establishments engaged in work under Federal contracts is large, it is obviously much smaller than the number of establishments engaged in interstate commerce. In fact, a very rough estimate of the number of persons employed in establishments subject to committee jurisdiction indicates that Federal contractors employ no more than 20 to 25 percent of all persons at work in nonagricultural industries, excluding persons employed by the Federal government itself.[6]

The Russell amendment also made it more difficult for the committees to deal with labor unions because unions are rarely parties to government contracts. After the amendment became effective in 1945, the proportion of cases dismissed on jurisdictional grounds rose sharply. Table 7.2 suggests the extent to which committee jurisdiction was curtailed by the Russell amendment.

The Eisenhower committee construed narrowly its jurisdiction

6 The Kennedy committee has established two programs for securing employment data from Federal contractors. Preliminary reports show that these two programs may have covered establishments employing 9 to 10 million persons in 1961. Employment in small establishments that are not required to submit employment data is not known, but may total as many as 3 to 5 million persons. Thus, total employment in contractor plants may amount to 12 to 15 million employees, or 20 to 25 percent of the 58,122,000 persons employed in nonagricultural industries in 1960, excluding Federal employees. U.S. Department of Labor, *Employment in Establishments Subject to Executive Order No. 10925: A Preliminary Review of 1962 Compliance Reports* (unpublished), and U.S. Bureau of the Census, *U.S. Census of Population, 1960: General Social and Economic Characteristics, U.S. Summary*, Final Report PC(1)–1C, Table 86.

over government contractors. Any technical impediment to asser-
tion of jurisdiction delayed or prevented action. Early in its career,
for example, the Eisenhower committee received complaints of
discrimination in employment on certain railroads. An investigation established that the standard form of contract between the

Table 7.2

COMPLAINT CASES DISMISSED FOR LACK OF JURISDICTION

	Time period	Percentage of cases dismissed
Second Committee on Fair Employment Practice	7/1/32–12/31/44	4
Committee on Government Contracts	9/53–1/61	46
Committee on Equal Employment Opportunity	4/61–2/63	15

Source: Published and unpublished tabulations showing the disposition of cases
received by the several committees.

United States and the carriers did not include the usual nondiscrimination clause supposedly present in all government contracts.
The committee decided not to proceed with the cases until the
omission was corrected and held them in abeyance for six years
until government contract forms were revised. In the end, the
committee closed the cases without action and did not notify complainants of its decision.[7] In union cases, the Eisenhower committee
usually asserted that it lacked jurisdiction, on the ground that labor
unions were not parties to government contracts; but in a few instances it attempted to take action against unions by proceeding
against employers.[8]

The jurisdiction of the Kennedy committee over private employers is substantially the same as that of the Eisenhower committee; that is, jurisdiction is limited to government contractors, and
their immediate subcontractors. The Kennedy executive order
gives the committee a tenuous jurisdiction over labor unions. The
committee is authorized to require contractors to file reports containing information as to the practices of unions with which they

[7] Committee on Government Contracts—case files (unpublished).
[8] *Ibid.*

deal. It may also hold hearings, public or private, concerning the practices of such unions and report its findings to the President and to Federal, state, and local agencies.[9] Such an approach relies upon the threat of publicity or upon referral of findings of discrimination to state and local commissions with enforcement powers to secure compliance on the part of unions. In the absence of a Federal FEP statute, the Kennedy committee in reality possesses no greater power to compel labor unions to abandon discriminatory practices than did its predecessors. It cannot, for example, compel union officers to attend hearings it may hold concerning union practices.

Expenditures

The committees have always operated under severe budgetary limitations. Table 7.3 shows in approximate terms the funds that have been available to the several committees.

Table 7.3

EXPENDITURES OF PRESIDENTIAL FEP COMMITTEES

	Year	Expenditure per year
First Committee on Fair Employment Practice	1942–42	$ 80,000
Second Committee on Fair Employment Practice	1943–45	147,000–500,000
Committee on Government Contract Compliance	1948	125,000
Committee on Government Contracts	1953–61	125,000–375,000
Committee on Equal Employment Opportunity	1961–62	425,000

Source: Published and unpublished materials relating to the expenditures of the several committees.

Prior to July 1, 1944, funds for committee expenses were appropriated from unallocated funds available to the President. In 1944, the Congress approved a budget request of $500,000 for the fiscal year 1945, the largest sum ever made available for a Federal

[9] Executive Order No. 10925, 26 Fed. Reg. 1977 (1961).

FEP committee. For the fiscal year 1946, Congress appropriated $250,000 to liquidate the affairs of the Committee. Passage of the Russell amendment made it impossible to continue to meet committee expenses from the President's unallocated funds. Opposition from Southern Congressmen made approval of a specific budget request most unlikely. The apparent impossibility of financing committee activities was not overcome until 1948, when it was determined that the Russell amendment of 1945 did not apply to interdepartmental committees. The Truman, Eisenhower, and Kennedy committees were therefore designated "interdepartmental" committees in order to circumvent the provisions of the Russell amendment; and their expenses were paid from unallocated funds available to the principal contracting agencies. Agencies are usually reluctant to divert monies from their relatively small unallocated funds. They have been particularly reluctant to turn over funds to the committees on any but a modest scale, for fear of jeopardizing Congressional approval of their regular appropriations.

The Kennedy committee approved a proposed budget request in the amount of $1 million for its first year of operation; but this amount was reduced to $425,000 by the Chairman, Vice Chairman, and Executive Vice chairman of the committee, who constituted themselves a budget review committee. They reduced the proposed budget by almost 60 percent on the ground that committee expenditures should not exceed the combined expenditures of the Committee on Government Contracts and the Committee on Government Employment Policy, whose functions were combined in the Committee on Equal Employment Opportunity by the Kennedy administration.[10]

Staff and Offices

The number of professional and clerical personnel employed by the committees is shown in Table 7.4, together with the num-

10 Interviews with members of the staff of the President's Committee on Equal Employment Opportunity, February, 1963.

ber of offices maintained by each. The second Roosevelt committee opened twelve regional offices and a number of suboffices, as well as a headquarters office in Washington. The remaining committees operated entirely from Washington, with the exception of small regional offices maintained for several years by the Eisenhower

Table 7.4

PERSONNEL AND OFFICES OF PRESIDENTIAL
FAIR EMPLOYMENT COMMITTEES

	PERSONNEL			Number of offices
	Professional	Clerical	Total	
First Committee on Fair Employment Practice	7–27	5–16	12–43	2
Second Committee on Fair Employment Practice	56	63	119	18
Committee on Government Contract Compliance	6	4	10	1
Committee on Government Contracts	5–15	4–15	9–30	3
Committee on Equal Employment Opportunity	20	12[a]	32	1

Source: Reports of the several committees.

[a] The Committee on Equal Employment Opportunity also employed twelve temporary part-time clerical employees in addition to those shown here.

committee in Chicago and Los Angeles. Since passage of the Russell amendment, committee staff has never exceeded thirty-two full-time employees.

Penalties and Sanctions

The Roosevelt committees were authorized to "take appropriate steps" to redress valid grievances and eliminate discrimination, but the steps were not defined in the executive orders establishing the committees. The second Roosevelt committee listed cancellation of contracts, refusal to renew contracts, and loss of manpower priorities among the penalties available to it. As a practical matter, sanctions could be used only with the consent and cooperation of other government agencies or by the President. In fact, the Roosevelt committees never sought to enforce their decisions through contract cancellation.[11] The only case in which extraordinary war powers of the President were used to enforce a committee decision resulted from a strike of local transit workers in Philadelphia.

During the Truman and Eisenhower administrations, all responsibility for enforcement was placed in the hands of the contracting agencies. The agencies were directed to take "appropriate measures" to secure compliance with the nondiscrimination clause in government contracts. The Truman and Eisenhower executive orders contained no mention of specific sanctions or enforcement techniques and seem to have been drafted on the assumption that the agencies would move to eliminate discriminatory employment practices from the plants of their contractors even though the measures agencies might take were nowhere defined. The agencies never used the powers of contract cancellation or debarment available to them by implication under the executive orders. The committees were equally reluctant to recommend penalties to the agencies, with the result that not a single contract was canceled for failure to observe the nondiscrimination provisions of government contracts during the Truman or Eisenhower administrations. We have reviewed the records of the Eisenhower committee and have found only four cases in which even the threat of cancellation or debarment was recommended to contracting agencies by the committee. Each case was a difficult one, but the mere threat of enforcement action was sufficient to cause at least limited improvement in employment practices in three of the four cases. In the remaining case, the contracting agency refused to act on the committee's recommendation. No improvement in employment practices occurred in this case.

The executive order establishing the Kennedy committee is the first to spell out penalties and sanctions. The authority of the committee is strengthened by providing that the committee or the con-

[11] Interview with Will Maslow, formerly Director, Division of Field Operations, Second Committee on Fair Employment Practice.

tracting agencies may take the following measures to secure compliance:

1. Publish the names of contractors or unions which have complied or failed to comply with the provisions of the order.

2. Recommend to the Department of Justice that proceedings be brought to enforce the nondiscrimination provisions of government contracts in cases where there is "substantial or material" violation of the provisions or the threat thereof.

3. Recommend to the Department of Justice that criminal proceedings be brought for the furnishing of false information to the committee or a contracting agency.

4. Terminate all or any portion of a contract for failure to comply with its nondiscrimination provisions or make continuance of a contract contingent upon the contractor's adoption of a program for future compliance.

5. Cause contracting agencies to refrain from entering into further contracts with any noncomplying contractor until the contractor has satisfied the committee that he will observe the provisions of the order.[12]

It is obvious that each of these powers was available, at least by implication, in the earlier executive orders. At this writing, twenty-three months after the effective date of the order, no contracts have been canceled for noncompliance, nor has any contractor been debarred from receiving additional contracts. In an action similar to debarment, however, the committee notified government agencies that four contractors could receive no further Federal contracts until they had submitted special compliance reports to the committee. Threats of similar action are reported to have been made in a number of other cases.[13]

---

[12] Executive Order No. 10925, Sec. 312 (a–d), paraphrased except for material in quotes.

[13] Interviews with members of the staff of the President's Committee on Equal Employment Opportunity.

Concepts of Administration

There have been almost as many different concepts as to how a Federal fair employment program established by executive order should be administered as there have been committees. The Roosevelt committees conducted their affairs in the manner of administrative agencies with enforcement responsibilities. They conducted investigations, held hearings, made findings of fact, and issued decisions in the cases coming before them. The committees were handicapped by their inability to use the subpoena power to compel attendance of witnesses or the production of books and records for examination, nor could they appeal to the courts for enforcement of their orders. The Russell amendment so severely limited the power of the President to establish agencies by executive order that all the more recent committees have been established as "interdepartmental" committees. The executive order creating the first of these "interdepartmental" committees, the Truman Committee on Government Contract Compliance, made contracting agencies primarily responsible for obtaining contractor compliance with the nondiscrimination clause in government contracts. The Truman committee played no part in compliance activities and functioned only as a study group. The Eisenhower committee was given somewhat broader functions than the Truman committee. It was authorized to make recommendations to the contracting agencies for improving and making more effective the nondiscrimination provisions of government contracts and to receive complaints of violations of the nondiscrimination clause of government contracts and refer them to the appropriate agencies for consideration.[14] Under this concept, the committee could not deal directly with contractors on complaint cases or compliance matters and had to rely upon contracting agency personnel to investigate and resolve complaints and make surveys of contractor racial employment patterns.

In the executive order establishing the Kennedy committee, an

[14] Executive Order No. 10479, 18 Fed. Reg. 4899 (1953), Secs. 4 and 5.

attempt has been made to combine the approaches of the Roosevelt and Eisenhower orders. The contracting agencies remain primarily responsible for obtaining compliance, but the committee itself is authorized to investigate employment practices of contractors or to direct that they be investigated by contracting agencies or by the Secretary of Labor. The committee and the contracting agencies are also authorized to hold hearings, public or private, for compliance, enforcement, or educational purposes. There has not been sufficient experience under the Kennedy executive order to assess the effectiveness of such an amalgamation of the administrative methods prescribed by the Roosevelt and Eisenhower executive orders.

HEARINGS

Hearings, public or private, have been used by state and city FEP commissions for fact-finding purposes or as a preliminary to enforcement proceedings. Table 7.5 indicates the extent to which presidential committees have utilized hearings in the course of their work.

Table 7.5

NUMBER OF COMMITTEE HEARINGS AND RESPONDENTS

	NUMBER OF HEARINGS			NUMBER OF RESPONDENTS		
	Public	*Private*	*Total*	*Em-ployers*	*Unions*	*Total*
First Committee on Fair Employment Practice	5	2	7	41	10	51
Second Committee on Fair Employment Practice	14	1	15	52	24	76
Committee on Government Contract Compliance	0	0	0	0	0	0
Committee on Government Contracts	0	1	1	1	1	2
Committee on Equal Employment Opportunity	0	0	0	0	0	0
Total	19	4	23	94	35	129

Source: Reports of the several committees.

In the absence of Federal FEP legislation, none of the committees has had power to issue subpoenas. Given this limitation, and in the absence of clearly defined enforcement procedures, the hearing device has not been particularly useful to the committees. All but one of the hearings were conducted by the Roosevelt committees. The first Committee on Fair Employment Practice devoted most of its time to hearings in Birmingham, Chicago, Los Angeles, and New York. The committee sought by means of the hearings to make known its existence and the policies expressed in the executive order. Following the hearings, the committee issued findings of fact and orders to individual respondents, directing them to take certain actions to place themselves in compliance. The second Committee on Fair Employment Practice began its career with hearings on the employment practices of Southern railroads and the policies of labor organizations representing their employees. The hearings did not lead to changes in employment practices on the Southern railroads. Respondent labor organizations did not appear at the hearings. The railroads refused to obey directions issued by the committee. The cases were referred to the President, but compliance was not obtained.

The second Committee on Fair Employment Practice reported on compliance with its orders in fifty-two "difficult cases" in which hearings were held. Complete or partial compliance was obtained in only seventeen cases.[15] Since passage of the Russell amendment, only one hearing has been held—a private hearing by a subcommittee of the Eisenhower committee concerning racial employment practices on the New York waterfront.

COMPLAINTS

Each of the committees has received complaints of discrimination prohibited by the executive orders. Table 7.6 gives the approximate number of complaints received annually by each of the com-

[15] Committee on Fair Employment Practice, *Final Report, June 28, 1946* (Washington, D.C., 1947), pp. 11–23.

mittees. The second Committee on Fair Employment Practice received by far the largest number of complaints of any of the presidential committees and devoted most of its time to complaint processing. The committee received, investigated, and attempted to resolve complaints of discrimination filed with it. Committee

Table 7.6

COMPLAINTS RECEIVED AND ADJUSTED

	Number of complaints received per year	*Percentage of closed cases satisfactorily adjusted*
First Committee on Fair Employment Practice	1,500	a
Second Committee on Fair Employment Practice	4,000	36
Committee on Government Contract Compliance	400	a
Committee on Government Contracts	150	45
Committee on Equal Employment Opportunity	750b	62

Source: Reports of the several committees and unpublished tabulations of the disposition of complaints received by the committees.

a Information not available.

b Based on the average number of complaints received per month by the Committee on Equal Employment Opportunity between April, 1961, and February, 1963.

staff members were responsible for each of these functions and sought to resolve cases through the techniques of mediation, conciliation, or persuasion.

Since passage of the Russell amendment, complaint investigations and adjustments have been undertaken primarily by personnel of contracting agencies rather than by committee staff. A review of the complaint procedures of the Eisenhower committee indicates some of the difficulties involved in administering a fair employment program through outside agencies.[16] Complaints were filed with the Eisenhower committee in Washington. The com-

16 Interviews with contracting agency personnel and members of the staff of the Committee on Government Contracts. Review of complaint case files.

mittee staff then determined whether the committee had jurisdiction, i.e., whether the complaint was directed against a plant currently engaged in work on a government contract. Once committee jurisdiction was established, complaints were sent to "compliance officers" in the headquarters offices of contracting agencies for referral to local agency representatives, usually procurement officers unfamiliar with racial employment problems. Complaints against Department of Defense contractors passed through as many as five or six bureaucratic layers before reaching those responsible for investigations. The latter conducted investigations and prepared reports of their findings, which were returned to agency compliance officers. These officials reviewed the reports of their investigators and sent them to the committee, where they were again reviewed by the committee's staff. Committee staff reviews and recommendations were considered by the committee's subcommittee on review and enforcement. The subcommittee either asked for further investigation by the contracting agency or recommended to the full committee that it approve the disposition of cases suggested by the contracting agency. The recommendations of the subcommittee were then considered by the full committee. Many cases went the rounds five or six times before they were closed. The average time required to complete action on a "valid" complaint was about one year. Many cases dragged on for three or four years. Complex and tedious as it may appear from this description, the complaint investigation process was even more tortuous in practice.

The procedures outlined above have been continued by the Kennedy committee with modifications intended to minimize delay. Several procurement agencies have employed persons familiar with racial employment problems to assist in the adjustment of complaints and in the investigation of contractor racial employment patterns and practices. These persons usually serve as advisers to agency procurement officials. The contracting agencies themselves remain primarily responsible for investigation and adjustment of complaints. Under regulations issued by the committee, its Executive Vice Chairman may take jurisdiction over the processing of cases, although the Kennedy executive order makes no provision for such action. The Executive Vice Chairman can take final action on complaint cases without securing committee approval, so that at least one cause of the delays occasioned by the procedures of the Eisenhower committee has been eliminated.

REVIEW OF RACIAL EMPLOYMENT PATTERNS

None of the presidential committees has conducted a systematic compliance program based upon evidences of discrimination disclosed by surveys of racial employment patterns. The hearings of the first Roosevelt committee produced some information on racial employment practices in four cities, but were not followed by sustained efforts to eliminate the discriminatory patterns they disclosed. The second Roosevelt committee devoted itself almost exclusively to processing complaints and never undertook investigations in the absence of complaints. The Eisenhower committee followed a similar policy during the first three and one-half years of its life. In 1956, however, the committee decided to conduct "compliance surveys" in contractor plants. The surveys obtained information on employment, by race and occupation group, in a small sample of relatively large plants located in twenty-five metropolitan areas with Negro populations of 50,000 or more. Some 450 plants were surveyed in each of the years 1957–1960. Committee members visited a few plants with no Negro employees, for the purpose of persuading the managements to change their practices. Similar appeals were made to a number of companies employing few, if any, Negroes in clerical positions. The number of companies reached by these efforts was too small to cause any significant change in racial employment patterns in plants performing work on government contracts. With these exceptions, the committee did not use the information obtained through the survey program as a basis for compliance programs. The employment data were merely tabulated and placed in the files of the committee.

The Kennedy executive order requires contractors and subcontractors to file "compliance reports" containing information as to their "practices, policies, programs and employment statistics." [17] Contractors were required to submit initial compliance reports to the committee in March, 1962, showing employment by sex and race in nine groups of occupations, and are to be required to submit similar information annually. First-tier subcontractors must also file such reports. Multiestablishment employers must submit separate reports for each plant where work is performed on government contracts and for their home offices. Tabulations of the data by industry and geographic area are to be prepared for use by the committee and by contracting agency compliance personnel. About 8,000 prime contractors submitted reports during 1962. The committee will have a more comprehensive picture of racial employment patterns in contractor plants than any of its predecessors, but the program has not been in effect long enough to determine whether the committee will use the data available from it in a broad-scale compliance program.

A second pattern-oriented approach of the Kennedy committee is called "Plans for Progress." Under the program, a number of the largest Federal contractors have agreed to review their employment practices, submit facts on employment by race and occupation, and prepare programs to improve their employment practices. Participation in the Plans is voluntary. There is some danger that "Plans for Progress" employers may think of themselves as exempt from the normal compliance procedures of the committee because of the emphasis given to voluntarism in "Plans for Progress." A recent report concerning employment practices in the Atlanta, Georgia, establishments of twenty-four large companies participating in the "Plans for Progress" reached the following conclusion:

[17] Executive Order No. 10925, Sec. 302(a).

Only seven of the firms interviewed produced evidence of affirmative compliance with their pledges. Of the seven, three—Lockheed, Western Electric, and Goodyear—demonstrated what appeared to be a vigorous desire to create job opportunities. The remaining seventeen firms have paid varying degrees of attention to Plans for Progress, ranging from ignorance to indifference.[18]

This report indicates that the Kennedy committee will encounter difficulty in obtaining contractor compliance with the nondiscrimination clause in government contracts as long as it emphasizes "voluntarism" with one group of contractors and "affirmative compliance" with another group.

Effectiveness of Committee Programs

The results of committee complaint settlements, pattern-centered activities, and hearings can be summarized briefly.

The second Roosevelt committee had the most extensive experience with complaints. It completed action on 4,801 complaints between July 1, 1943, and December 31, 1944, and closed 1,723 cases as "satisfactorily adjusted." [19] The materials published by the committee give no indication of the number of complainants employed as a result of these closings. The Eisenhower committee received 1,042 complaints during its life of seven and one-half years, but was able to give final approval to procurement agency actions in only 372 cases, or 35 percent of the total.[20] The remaining cases were dismissed for lack of jurisdiction or were still under investigation when the committee came to an end. We have reviewed about one-third of all complaints received by the Eisenhower committee and have concluded that fewer than twenty persons obtained employment or promotion as a result of filing complaints.

[18] Southern Regional Council, *Plans for Progress: Atlanta Survey* (Atlanta, January, 1963), mimeographed, pp. 8–9.
[19] Committee on Fair Employment Practice, *First Report*, Table 1-G, p. 116.
[20] Committee on Government Contracts, *Pattern for Progress, Seventh* [Annual] *Report* (Washington, D.C., 1960), pp. 20–21.

The second Roosevelt committee surveyed changes in Negro employment in companies that appeared at hearings conducted by the first Committee on Fair Employment Practice. The survey findings are summarized in Table 7.7.

Table 7.7

TOTAL AND NONWHITE EMPLOYMENT, THIRTY-ONE PLANTS
INVOLVED IN FOUR COMMITTEE HEARINGS

Year	Total employment	Nonwhites	Nonwhite as percentage of total
1941–42	277,681	4,262	1.5
1943–44	468,517	23,759	5.1

Source: Committee on Fair Employment Practice, *First Report, July, 1943–December, 1944* (Washington, D.C., 1945), p. 66.

Nonwhites increased as a percentage of total employment in surveyed plants between 1941 and 1944. Many of the plants were engaged in shipbuilding or aircraft production and were located in cities that experienced increasingly acute labor shortages during the war years. War industries in general reported similar increases in the proportion of nonwhites in their employ during these years. Shortage of manpower rather than committee action seems to have been primarily responsible for the rise in Negro employment found by committee surveys.

As noted earlier, the Eisenhower committee obtained information on employment, by race and occupation group, in a sample of contractor establishments each year beginning in 1957. While these covered only a small proportion of all contract holders, the results give some indication of the racial employment pattern in government contract plants during the latter half of the committee's tenure. The figures for the plants that submitted information in each of the survey years are summarized in Table 7.8. (Figures from the 1960 survey were not available in a comparable form.)

Between 1957 and 1959, the proportion of Negroes to all employees in the technical, supervisory, clerical, and skilled blue-collar categories showed slight increases. These slight gains were more than offset, however, by a sizable drop in the percentage of Negroes in the semiskilled category, with the result that the proportion of Negroes in the total work force decreased from 8.6 percent in 1957 to 7.5 percent in 1959. Moreover, even in 1959 the Negro proportion was only 1 percent in the clerical occupations

Table 7.8

NEGROES AS PERCENTAGE OF TOTAL EMPLOYMENT
IN SELECTED CONTRACTOR PLANTS

Occupation group	Number of identical plants reporting	PERCENTAGE OF NEGROES		
		1957	1958	1959
Professional and technical	85	0.6	0.5	0.9
Supervisory	87	0.8	0.5	0.9
Clerical and stenographic	93	0.6	1.8	1.0
Skilled	79	3.5	4.3	4.0
Semiskilled	72	12.7	11.5	11.6
Unskilled	74	18.2	17.1	18.7
All others	26	2.0	2.2	2.5
Total employment	130	8.6	7.1	7.5

Source: Committee on Government Contracts, *Tabulations of Employment by Race and Occupation Group in Plants of Federal Contractors, 1957–1959* (unpublished). Employment data were obtained almost exclusively from fairly large manufacturing establishments located in about twenty-five large metropolitan areas with substantial Negro populations. In this table, the number of plants reporting employment data by occupation group varies from group to group because many of the individual establishment reports were incomplete. For this reason, racial employment trends in a given occupation group should not be compared with trends in any other occupation group.

and less than 1 percent in the two highest categories. In sum, the survey results—in so far as they are representative of all government-contract establishments—indicate that the activities of the Eisenhower committee failed to bring about any improvement either in aggregate employment or in the occupational status of Negroes over the period covered.

One can only conclude that the twenty years of intermittent activity by presidential committees has had little effect on traditional patterns of Negro employment. This conclusion is further supported by the results of a study of Federal-contract employment conducted in 1960–61 by the United States Commission on

Civil Rights. The Commission's findings are summarized, in part, in its 1961 report as follows:

This Commission's investigations in three cities—Atlanta, Baltimore, and Detroit—and a Commission hearing in Detroit revealed that in most industries studied patterns of Negro employment by Federal contractors conformed to local industrial employment patterns. In the automotive industry, for example, even though each of the three manufacturers contacted had adopted a company-wide policy of nondiscrimination, employment patterns varied from city to city. In Detroit, Negroes constituted a substantial proportion—from 20 to 30 percent—of the total work force. Although their representation in "nontraditional" jobs was slight, all companies employed them in all classifications other than management positions, and one company employed Negroes in administrative and management jobs as well. In Baltimore, each of the companies employed Negroes only in production work and not above the semiskilled level as assemblers, repairmen, inspectors, and material handlers. In Atlanta the two automobile assembly plants contacted employed no Negroes in assembly operations. Except for one driver of an inside power truck, all Negro employees observed were engaged in janitorial work—sweeping, mopping, carrying away trash. Lack of qualified applicants cannot account for the absence of Negroes from automotive assembly jobs in Atlanta. Wage rates are relatively high for the locality and the jobs are in great demand. The work is at most semiskilled and educational requirements are extremely low (present employees averaging a third-grade education). . . . There are indications too that, in the same geographic location, patterns of Negro employment are substantially the same in plants of government contractors as in plants of noncontractors. The commission mailed questionnaires to a 5 percent sample of all manufacturing and assembly plants in Atlanta, Baltimore, and Detroit. While the returns were limited, they showed no appreciable difference between Federal contractors and noncontractors in the proportion of Negroes employed or in the types of positions in which Negroes were working. A similar conclusion was drawn on the basis of questionnaire surveys of Federal government contractors by the Commission's State Advisory Committees in six Southern States—Kentucky, Louisiana, North Carolina, South Carolina, Tennessee, and West Virginia.[21]

[21] U.S. Commission on Civil Rights, *1961 Report:* Book 3, *Employment* (Washington, D.C., undated), pp. 65–66.

Almost 90 percent of the Federal contractors in these same states reported that procurement agency representatives had never talked with them about their racial employment practices. Fewer than 4 percent of the contractors reported any difficulty in complying with the nondiscrimination provisions of their government contracts, yet about one-quarter of them employed no Negroes whatever. When Negroes were employed, there was substantially no departure from the racial employment patterns traditional in Southern and Border states.[22] It is evident that the nondiscrimination clause in government contracts was virtually unenforced by the contracting agencies during the years preceding 1961.

The Committees and Racial Practices of Labor Unions

Persons from national labor organizations have served on each of the committees and have supported, at least in principle, nondiscriminatory union racial practices. At the same time, labor organizations, most frequently local unions, have presented some of the most difficult problems faced by the committees.

The executive orders establishing the Roosevelt committees asserted that it was the "duty" of labor organizations to eliminate discrimination in union membership. The executive orders gave the committees no direct means of enforcing orders concerning union practices, although unsolved cases could be referred to the President or to the contracting agencies. The first Roosevelt committee came to an end when several members resigned during a dispute over the conduct of hearings on the practices of Southern railroads and unions representing their employees. The second Roosevelt committee held hearings and issued orders in the railroad cases. The unions did not attend the hearings and disregarded cease-and-desist orders issued by the committees. The cases were

[22] U.S. Commission on Civil Rights, *Negro Employment Practices in Private Firms with Federal Government Contracts Operating in Six Southern States— Kentucky, Louisiana, North Carolina, South Carolina, Tennessee, and West Virginia* (unpublished manuscript, 1961), pp. 1, 30.

referred to the President but remained unresolved when hostilities ended. A strike of local transit workers in Philadelphia against employment of Negroes as platform men and operators led to the most dramatic use of Federal power in support of fair employment practices during the war. Acting under orders of the President, the Army seized the transit lines. The Army let it be known that it was prepared to operate the lines with troops and that those who remained on strike would be dismissed, subject to immediate induction into the armed forces, loss of unemployment benefits, and prosecution under the War Labor Disputes Act. The strike was broken.[23] These dramatic incidents show that it is difficult to use the powers of the President and the contracting agencies to enforce committee decisions in union cases. Between the middle of 1943 and the end of 1944, the second Roosevelt committee received 250 complaints of discrimination by unions, but was able to close only seventeen of them as satisfactorily adjusted—a poorer record of compliance than was established in the case of employers.[24]

The executive order creating the Eisenhower committee made no mention of labor unions. Committee jurisdiction was based on contracts between suppliers and agencies of the United States, to which labor unions are not parties. Nevertheless, more than 10 percent of the cases received by the committee between 1953 and the end of 1956 alleged discrimination by labor unions or by unions and employers acting in concert.[25] If the act complained of was attributable solely to unions, the Committee usually declined to take jurisdiction, but sometimes referred the matter to one of its labor members for informal disposition. If unions and employers

[23] Ruchames *Race, Jobs, and Politics*, pp. 110–17.
[24] Committee on Fair Employment Practice, *First Report, July, 1943–December, 1944*, Table 7, p. 128.
[25] Tabulation by the authors of complaints received by the Committee on Government Contracts between September, 1953, and May, 1956. During this time the committee received 200 complaints, of which twenty-four alleged exclusion from union membership by reason of race or exclusion from employment by means of discriminatory union referral practices.

were jointly responsible, the Committee sometimes took jurisdiction and proceeded against employers. In a number of union-employer cases, the Committee advised employers that discriminatory practices of labor unions did not relieve contractors of their obligations under the nondiscrimination clause in government contracts. Action to secure compliance was taken in only two such cases. Given the Committee's limited power and jurisdiction, it was usually possible, in cases where unions and employers were jointly responsible for discriminatory practices, for the parties to shift the responsibility for the practices back and forth in such a way that effective action was impossible.

Union and union-employer cases received by the Committee came primarily from the railroad, construction, and petroleum-refining industries. The practices most commonly complained of were exclusion from membership, discrimination in the operation of union job referral programs, and restriction of Negroes to departments of industrial establishments composed exclusively of laborers or menials. In the last-mentioned cases, exclusion occurred by custom or by the operation of provisions included in labor agreements. The committee took no action on the railroad cases because of jurisdictional problems. Construction contractors were successful in using union referral practices as their defense against complaints. In the petroleum-refining cases a member of the committee persuaded a number of companies and unions to amend their labor agreements in such a way as to eliminate formal contract barriers to the promotion of Negroes employed in company labor departments, but the contract amendments did not enable an appreciable number of Negroes to gain promotion.[26] Little change in petroleum industry racial employment patterns occurred between 1953 and 1960. The filing of lawsuits in the Federal courts by aggrieved Negro members of the Oil Workers International Union was a more important cause of changes in the formal provisions

[26] See Chapter 2.

of petroleum industry labor agreements than was action by the Committee on Government Contracts.[27]

The order establishing the Kennedy committee takes a more direct approach to union racial problems than the earlier orders; but again the committee must operate without benefit of direct enforcement powers in union cases. The committee is directed to "use its best efforts . . . to cause any labor union . . . representative of workers who [are] or may be engaged in work under government contracts to cooperate with . . . the purposes of this order." [28] The committee is authorized to hold hearings, submit reports to the President, recommend remedial action in connection with union practices, and notify Federal, state, and local agencies "of its conclusions and recommendations with respect to any . . . labor organization which in its judgment has failed to cooperate with the Committee, contracting agencies, contractors or subcontractors in carrying out the purposes of [the] order." [29]

The committee is also authorized to require bidders on government contracts to provide it with statements in writing from officers of labor unions

together with supporting information, to the effect that the said labor union's . . . practices and policies do not discriminate on the grounds of race, color, creed, or national origin, and that the labor union . . . will affirmatively cooperate, within the limits of [its] legal and contractual authority, in the implementation of the policy and provisions of this order or that it consents and agrees that recruitment, employment, and the terms and conditions of employment under the proposed contract shall be in accordance with the purposes and provisions of the order.[30]

---

[27] See *Holt vs. Oil Workers Union, Labor Relations Reporter Manual,* XXXVI, 2702 (Harris County, Texas, District Court, 1955), and an earlier case, *Syres vs. Oil Workers International Union,* 350 U.S. 892 (1955).
[28] Executive Order No. 10925, Sec. 304.
[29] *Ibid.,* Sec. 305.
[30] *Ibid.,* Sec. 302(d).

As of this writing (March, 1963), the Committee has not used openly the various devices authorized by the order to bring pressure to bear upon discriminatory unions.

In the summer of 1962 the Kennedy Committee developed a program of nondiscriminatory policies for unions, similar to the "Plans for Progress" program for Federal-contract employers, announced some months earlier. The Committee asked the leaders of all national unions to sign pledges committing their organizations to follow the policies specified in the program, including acceptance of all eligible applicants for membership regardless of race or color, abolition of racially segregated locals, and nondiscriminatory conduct of apprentice training plans. In November, 1962, eighty-seven national labor organizations, all affiliates of the AFL-CIO, formally adopted the program; and at the time of writing the number of signatory unions had increased to more than one hundred. However, some seventeen national AFL-CIO affiliates and a number of unaffiliated national organizations had either refused or failed to sign the pledge.[31] Experience under the program is still too brief to permit any assessment of its effectiveness in abating discriminatory practices at the local union level.

Conclusions

The foregoing review of the activities of the presidential committees leads us to conclude that they have failed to effect a significant improvement in the number or quality of job opportunities open to members of minority groups. In the case of the Kennedy committee, the conclusion must be tentative because of its limited experience; but so many of the factors that hampered the earlier committees are still present that the Kennedy committee may be equally ineffective. The causes of committee ineffectiveness fall

[31] Interview with staff official, President's Committee on Equal Employment Opportunity, March, 1963.

into two groups: those external to the committees and therefore largely beyond committee control and those internal to the committees in the sense that they resulted from committee procedures.

EXTERNAL CAUSES OF COMMITTEE INEFFECTIVENESS

1. Each of the committees has been created by executive order and has thus been unable to organize its affairs on the same basis as Federal regulatory agencies responsible for the administration of Federal programs embodied in statutes. Consequently, the committees have never been wholly accepted by employers, unions, or agencies of the Federal government. Committees have been attacked on numerous occasions by hostile critics on the ground that their activities were improper because they lacked explicit Congressional approval. In such an atmosphere committees have tended to act slowly and cautiously.

2. Committees have never been provided with sufficient funds or staff to discharge their obligations adequately. All committee members, save one, have served without compensation on a part-time basis, so that the committees have appeared to the public as little more than temporary, expedient responses to minority group protests against discrimination.

3. Jurisdiction of the committees has been too narrow to embrace the entire range of firms engaged in interstate commerce, but may cover from 20 to 25 percent of employment in nonagricultural industries. In addition, it has been particularly difficult to exercise jurisdiction over labor unions, because they are not parties to government contracts and therefore are not subject to the penalties nominally usable in support of committee programs. Discrimination against Negroes and other minorities is frequently supported by the actions of public and private employment services and by the manner in which vocational education programs are administered. The committees have made sporadic efforts to deal with these problems, but their jurisdictional limitations have prevented them from acting effectively.

4. One important result of the Russell amendment was to make it impossible for committees to deal directly with employers. Committees established after passage of the Russell amendment have been forced to deal with respondents primarily through personnel of contracting agencies instead of through their own staffs. During the Eisenhower administration, procurement officers of the contracting agencies conducted complaint investigations and compliance surveys. Procurement officers almost invariably defended the actions of agency contractors no matter what facts were disclosed by their investigations. The Eisenhower committee occasionally assigned important matters to individual committee members in an attempt to avoid the difficulties inherent in dealing with problems at second-hand. In a very few cases, committee members were successful in their endeavors, but the number of cases settled by such means was insignificant.

The Kennedy committee also deals with respondents primarily through contracting agencies. The Committee has requested contracting agencies to add to their procurement staffs persons familiar with the employment problems of minority groups and hopes to avoid thereby some of the difficulties encountered by its predecessors. In January, 1963, procurement agencies employed a total of thirty-seven such persons and expected to add another twenty-five to thirty-five to their staffs within the next six months.[32] This total of sixty to seventy persons will be somewhat smaller than the investigative and compliance staff of the New York State commission.[33] Thus, it is apparent that the Kennedy committee and the Federal procurement agencies are inadequately staffed to deal with discriminatory employment practices in the plants of Federal contractors throughout the nation, even though staff resources are more adequate for the task than they were during the Truman and Eisenhower administrations.

[32] Interviews with members of the staffs of Federal procurement agencies and the Committee on Equal Employment Opportunity.
[33] See Chapter 5.

The policies and practices adopted by the committees have contributed to their lack of success. In retrospect three matters seem to have been particularly important.

1. Perhaps the most serious weakness of the committees was their failure to negotiate comprehensive programs for the elimination of discrimination in entire companies, industries, or labor unions or to base their compliance activities upon reviews of racial employment patterns. The first Committee on Fair Employment Practice made a modest beginning in this direction when it held hearings in four cities on employer and union practices. Thereafter, however, such approaches were abandoned, and the committees became little more than processors of complaints. Taking into account the pervasiveness of discriminatory employment practices, the number of complaints was so small, even during the war years, that little could be accomplished by such an attack on the problem.

2. The committees have gone to great lengths to try to bring employers and unions into compliance on a voluntary basis. The use of penalities, or the threat of their use, has been carefully avoided. To some extent voluntarism became the policy of the committees simply because it was realized that penalties nominally available for enforcement purposes could not be used in fact, but for the most part committees preferred to avoid compulsory approaches as a matter of principle. The Eisenhower committee's preference for voluntarism became so well known to contracting agencies, employers, and unions that little heed was paid to its activities throughout most of its career.

The program of the latest of the five presidential committees, President Kennedy's Committee on Equal Employment Opportunity, also emphasizes voluntarism to a considerable extent. In effect, the committee has sponsored two programs: a "voluntary" program, called "Plans for Progress," and a "compliance" program applicable to Federal contractors who have not signed "Plans for Progress." Each of the two programs covers roughly the same number of workers. The motives that led the Committee to adopt such contradictory approaches are not entirely clear, but it is obvious that the Committee is not likely to succeed with a "compliance" program as long as it emphasizes "voluntarism" with a number of large contractors.

3. The administrative procedures adopted by the committees were so complex and awkward that they operated with glacial speed. During the Eisenhower administration it required about a year to complete action on a "valid" complaint. Speed is essential if a complaint-centered fair employment program is to have the slightest prospect of success. If complaints cannot be quickly and equitably resolved, those who experience discrimination become convinced that it is futile to file complaints, and the complaint adjustment machinery becomes ineffective through disuse.

Even more important than these immediate causes of failure has been the lack of adequate political support for Federal fair employment programs. Enforceable FEP legislation has been introduced during each session of the Congress for almost twenty years but has never passed either house. In the face of this fact, Presidents have been reluctant to give more than token support to committees established by executive action, in all likelihood because they did not wish to be accused of attempting to enforce by executive edict policies the Congress has refused to embody in legislation.

8

NEGROES IN THE ARMED FORCES AND IN
FEDERAL CIVILIAN AGENCIES

The Federal government is the largest employer in the nation, and its employment practices are therefore bound to be important to minority groups. As Chief Executive and Commander-in-Chief of the armed forces, the President is directly responsible for employment policy and practice in the entire Federal establishment. In these areas he has been able to take direct action, instead of relying upon the roundabout indirect approaches to which he has been limited when dealing with the employment practices of private employers engaged in work on Federal contracts. Each of the Presidents from Franklin Roosevelt to Kennedy has acted to assure equality of opportunity in Federal employment. The resulting changes in the status of Negroes in the military and civilian services are reviewed separately.

Utilization of Negroes in the Armed Forces

Negroes served in the armed forces from the time of the Revolution until the end of the Civil War. The services had no explicit racial employment policies during these years and used Negroes in whatever ways semed expedient. In 1866, Congress passed a statute providing for four permanent Negro regiments in the reorganized post-Civil War army. Enlisted personnel of the regiments were Negroes; officers were whites. Until the United States prepared to enter World War I, Negroes were excluded from service in any other combat units of the Army. Negroes not attached to these regiments were assigned only to segregated labor battalions and similar duties. The Navy restricted Negroes to enlisted ratings.

During World War I, the only Negro units committed to combat were four Negro regiments of the Ninety-Third Division and the Ninety-Second Division composed entirely of Negro soldiers. The Negro regiments of the Ninety-Third Division fought well under French command; but the Ninety-Second Division was not well prepared for combat, and one of its regiments retreated in panic during an attack on enemy positions. During the war, segregated Negro units presented disciplinary problems more frequently than white units and occasionally figured in unfortunate incidents growing out of racial antagonisms with white civilians and white military units. Negro troops were more frequently involved in drunkenness, absence without leave, pilfering of stores, and other infractions of military regulations than were whites. Such experiences seemed to confirm the opinion that Negroes were unreliable in combat and a source of serious disciplinary problems. Between the World Wars few changes occurred in the Negro personnel practices of the services.

World War II occasioned a massive mobilization of manpower for military service—more than 12 million persons were in uniform at the height of the war. Necessity required modification of many military doctrines concerning the use of manpower, but traditional views on racial practices were so strongly held by the services that little change occurred in that area of manpower policy. When President Roosevelt asked the War Department in 1940 for its recommendations on the question of ending segregation in the Army, the Department replied that segregation "has been proven satisfactory over a long period of years and to make changes would produce situations destructive to morale and detrimental to the preparations for national defense." Throughout the War most of the Negro officers and enlisted personnel of the Army served in segregated noncombat units engaged in supply, transportation, and labor duties. In other words, Army utilization of Negro manpower largely duplicated patterns of Negro employment customary in civilian life during the war years. As in World War I, the Army formed two Negro divisions. One division was used in the South Pacific and was assigned primarily to noncombat duties because of lack of confidence in its combat capabilities. The second Negro division was used in Italy with mediocre results. Once more, segregated Negro infantry units failed to display the aggressiveness and initiative of white units. The Army Air Corps followed Army practice and used Negroes in noncombat assignments, except for two all-Negro fighter groups. In contrast with the poor performances of Negro infantry units, the fighter groups gave a good account of themselves in combat. Higher standards of selection and training could be observed in the relatively small fighter groups than in units of division size.

The Navy did not deviate from prewar racial personnel practices until the middle of 1942, when, at President Roosevelt's insistence, it announced that Negroes could enlist in branches of the service other than the traditionally colored Stewards' Branch. Negroes were not used in the general naval service, however, but were assigned to duty in segregated Negro units and excluded from the crews of ocean-going vessels. Under a quota system adopted in 1944, Negroes were assigned to the crews of auxiliary vessels such as tankers and supply ships. Two small combat ships were manned by Negro sailors commanded by white officers. Navy experience with Negroes integrated in ships' companies was favorable. Segregated Negro units presented the same problems of inefficiency and lack of discipline found in similar Army units. There were riots and mutinies in a number of the Navy's segregated service units.[1]

INTEGRATION OF THE ARMED FORCES, 1948–54

In the period since World War II, both policy and practice with respect to Negroes in the military services have changed radi-

[1] This synoptic account of the utilization of Negroes in the armed forces prior to 1948 is based on the following sources: Jean Byers, *A Study of the Negro in Military Service* (Department of Defense, 1950, Washington, D.C., mimeographed); Dennis D. Nelson, *The Integration of the Negro into the United States Navy, 1776–1947* (Navy Department, Washington, D.C., 1948, mimeographed); Nichols, *Breakthrough;* President's Committee on Equality of Treatment and Opportunity in the Armed Services, *Freedom to Serve—A Report by the President's Committee* (Washington, D.C., 1950).

cally. In July, 1948, President Truman issued an executive order directing the armed forces to abandon the practice of segregation and discrimination. The order stated that:

It is hereby declared to be the policy of the President that there shall be equality of treatment and opportunity for all persons in the armed services without regard to race, color, religion or national origin. This policy shall be put into effect as rapidly as possible, having due regard to the time required to effectuate any necessary changes without impairing efficiency or morale.[2]

The order created a Presidential Committee on Equality of Treatment and Opportunity in the Armed Services to review service practices and determine what changes should be made in them to achieve the President's policy. Thereafter there was relatively rapid progress toward genuine equality of opportunity and elimination of segregation. Basic military personnel policy on these matters was never afterward subject to debate, although there were controversies as to the rapidity with which the new policy could be made effective. In June, 1954, the Department of Defense reported, "There are no longer any all-Negro units in the services." By this date all segregated facilities maintained for use by service personnel on posts, camps, and stations had been abandoned in favor of integrated facilities.[3]

The Navy accepted the new policy in principle, but was slow to eliminate all vestiges of discriminatory practices. In 1949, the President's Committee reported that the Navy had "moved from a policy of complete exclusion of Negroes from general service to a policy of complete integration in general service," but found that there were relatively few Negroes or Negro officers in the Navy and made a number of recommendations designed to increase Negro participation in the Navy outside the traditionally colored Stewards' Branch.[4] Although the Navy accepted the recommenda-

---

[2] Executive Order No. 9981, July, 1948, Sec. 1.

[3] Department of Defense, Office of the Assistant Secretary of Defense (Manpower and Personnel), *Integration in the Armed Services—A Progress Report* (Washington, D.C., January, 1955), p. 3.

[4] *Freedom to Serve*, pp. 23–29.

tions, it apparently did little to make them effective. Not until March, 1954, was a separate recruitment program for stewards abandoned.[5] There can be little doubt that the purpose of the program was to perpetuate the racial composition of the Stewards' Branch. Negroes declined as a percentage of Navy enlisted personnel between 1949 and 1954.[6]

The Air Force Chief of Personnel issued a memorandum early in 1948, stating that "the ultimate . . . objective [should be] to eliminate racial discrimination and segregation among . . . personnel by unrestricted assignment of Negro personnel in free competition with white personnel to any duty . . . for which they qualify." In a program adopted in May, 1949, a board of officers screened personnel at the only all-Negro Air Force base. Negroes found to be unsuited for reassignment to white units or to training schools were dismissed from the service. Similar methods were used to screen personnel of segregated Negro service units attached to other commands. The screening process was completed in about three and one-half years, so that by the end of 1952 there were no all-Negro units in the Air Force. The Air Force took a number of measures to assure the success of its integration program. Commanding officers were advised that failure to make the program effective promptly would be considered a command failure. An order was issued requiring "prompt disciplinary action" in the event of disobedience. A number of commanding officers made careful, detailed plans for integration of Negroes in their units, including briefings of their white officers and enlisted personnel; others made no special preparations for the change. Despite these differences in approach on the part of individual commanders, the results were everywhere the same. In the months following integration, commanders reported few difficulties in their organizations or in adjacent civilian communities. Disciplinary action

[5] Interviews with members of the staff, Bureau of Personnel, Department of the Navy, Washington, D.C., June, 1962.
[6] See Table 8.4.

was taken promptly in cases of overt opposition to integration on the part of officers or enlisted men.[7]

The Army resisted integration more strongly than the other services. Not until January, 1950, did the Army adopt a policy of assigning Negroes with special skills without regard to race, i.e., to previously all-white units. The order probably had limited effects, because only a small number of Negroes could qualify for such assignments. After the outbreak of the Korean War in June, 1950, integration soon became effective in Army training bases in the United States. Informal integration of segregated Negro units occurred in Korea under the stress of manpower shortages in white combat units. By the end of 1952, integration was largely completed in the United States and in American forces in Europe. Negro units were disbanded and their members reassigned to white units or discharged.[8]

ARMY STUDY OF ATTITUDES TOWARD INTEGRATION

Negroes have always formed a larger part of the Army than of the Navy or Air Force. For this reason, the Army wished to review carefully its experiments in integration before completing the process. In the middle of 1951, opinion surveys were conducted among selected groups of officers and enlisted men. The material that follows is based on that study.[9]

For our purposes, the most interesting of the survey findings are those concerning the effectiveness of integrated versus white combat units and the acceptance of Negroes in previously all-white units. In the past, Army authorities had resisted integration on the ground that it would impair combat effectiveness and increase racial conflict in military units. There was reason to fear that integrated units would be less effective in combat than white units because of the distribution of whites and Negroes among Army

[7] Nichols, *Breakthrough*, pp. 73–81, 98–106.
[8] *Ibid.*, pp. 96, 107–117, 130.
[9] U.S. Department of Defense, Department of the Army (unpublished manuscript, 1951), quoted by permission.

General Classification Test (AGCT) groups at the beginning of the Korean War (see Table 8.1).

Table 8.1

PERCENTAGE DISTRIBUTION OF ARMY ENLISTED PERSONNEL
BY AGCT GROUP AND RACE, JUNE, 1950

AGCT group	White	Negro
I	4	1
II	27	8
III	40	31
IV	28	54
V	1	6
Total	100	100

The AGCT is not an intelligence test. It is designed to classify soldiers into categories according to their ability to learn and to apply military skills. In 1950 Negro soldiers appeared twice as fre-

Table 8.2

PERCENTAGE OF OFFICERS INDICATING THAT INTEGRATED UNITS PERFORMED
"ABOUT ON A PAR WITH" WHITE UNITS

	STATIONED IN UNITED STATES		STATIONED IN KOREA WITH INTEGRATED COMBAT UNITS
	No experience with integrated units	Limited experience with integrated units	
Becoming seasoned to combat and acquiring military skills	29	58	67
Maintenance of weapons	49	83	90
Using ammunition and weapons effectively	31	57	81
Carrying out orders to the letter	35	53	73
Being observant and alert when on patrol	42	52	67
Having good judgment in difficult combat situations	32	47	72
Holding ground in hand-to-hand combat	29	42	69
Standing up under mass attack	35	67	85

Table 8.3

White soldiers in Korea:

	COMBAT INFANTRY		QUARTERMASTER CORPS	
Attitude	*Integrated*	*All white*	*Integrated*	*All white*
Hostile	7	9	7	10
Withdrawal	23	28	24	47
Favorable	66	60	65	39
No prediction	4	3	4	4
Total	100	100	100	100

White soldiers in the United States:

Attitude	*Training division, integrated*	*T/O & E units, all white*	*Training division, all white*	*National Guard, all white*
Hostile	5	10	4	6
Withdrawal	17	27	28	33
Favorable	74	61	67	59
No prediction	4	2	1	2
Total	100	100	100	100

quently as whites in groups IV and V, the categories into which the least capable individuals fall.

Despite the differences between Negroes and whites reflected in Table 8.1, a high proportion of officers reported that they believed integrated units performed as well as white units. Table 8.2 gives the replies of three groups of officers to various questions concerning the behavior in combat of integrated units. The percentage of favorable opinions was highest among officers who had commanded integrated units in combat in Korea and lowest among officers who had never commanded integrated units.

The willingness of white soldiers to accept Negroes assigned to their units was measured by their responses to the following question: "Now suppose the captain announced [to an all-white platoon] that a number of colored replacements will be assigned to the platoon and went on to say, 'We want these men to be good soldiers and a real part of our outfit and I want all of you to go out of your way to help and be nice.' " The distribution of replies from white soldiers in different types of units is given in Table 8.3. About 2,600 soldiers gave answers. About two-thirds of the soldiers reacted favorably to the question. Favorable responses were given most frequently by white soldiers serving in integrated units, indicating that experience of integration tended to lessen prejudices. Commanders of integrated units reported that integration seemed to lessen, rather than increase, racial tensions. A related Army study found that integration on military posts did not cause appreciable resentment among civilians in adjacent towns, including those near bases in the Southern states. Reassured by these studies, the Army went ahead with its integration program.

RESULTS OF INTEGRATION OF THE ARMED FORCES

The desegregation of the Federal military establishment was completed within six years after the issuance of the Truman executive order.

By the middle of 1954, all of the segregated all-Negro components had been disbanded and their personnel either integrated with white units or separated from the service. All on-post segregated facilities were integrated, including those on military bases in the deep South. The armed forces even integrated certain on-base schools for children of military personnel prior to the Supreme Court's school desegregation decisions of 1954. Taking into account the long history of segregation in the military services, it is surprising that such a complete reversal of policy could be made effective within a few years. Among certain groups of Southern whites, there is a long tradition of professional military service; and many persons from these groups serve in the officer corps. They bring with them to their military assignments attitudes toward Negroes traditional among Southern whites. Superior-inferior social relationships and employment of Negroes in none but

menial jobs or in segregated groups have been customary in the
South and were firmly established in the services for many years.
Yet in a relatively short time the armed services made radical
changes in their practices, while Southern customs changed but
slowly.

Employment opportunities open to Negroes in the military
services increased following abolition of racial restrictions and admission of Negroes to service training programs on a competitive
basis.

Their response to these new opportunities is reflected in the
trend of Negro participation in the armed forces over the period
since the issuance of the desegregation order, summarized in Table
8.4. Between 1949 and 1962, the percentage of Negroes among

Table 8.4

NEGRO PERSONNEL AS PERCENTAGE OF TOTAL IN MILITARY SERVICES

	1949	*1954*	*1962*
Army:			
Officers	1.7	2.9	3.2
Enlisted men	9.6	12.3	12.2
Navy:			
Officers	. . . a	0.1	0.3
Enlisted men	4.5	3.6	5.2
Air Force:			
Officers	0.6	1.1	1.2
Enlisted men	5.1	8.6	9.2
Marine Corps:			
Officers	. . . a	0.1	0.2
Enlisted men	2.1	6.5	7.6

Source: U.S. Commission on Civil Rights, *Civil Rights '63: 1963 Report*, p. 221.
   a Less than 0.5 percent.

enlisted personnel increased throughout the military services.
Negro representation more than tripled in the Marine Corps and
nearly doubled in the Air Force, during the twelve-year interval.
In the Army, the percentage increased by approximately one-third.
Even in the Navy, where Negro enlistment fell somewhat between
1949 and 1954, a small but significant net increase was evident by

1962. In the armed forces as a whole, Negroes constituted 9.2 percent of enlisted personnel in 1962, a proportion only slightly below that of Negroes in the total population.

Negro representation among officers also rose in the post-desegregation period, but the percentages were still extremely small in 1962 when compared with the percentages for enlisted personnel and with the over-all Negro population ratio. Moreover, it is unlikely that the Negro contingent among officers will grow at a faster rate in the near future, since very few Negroes attend the service academies. Only forty-six Negroes, or 0.36 percent of 12,755 cadets, entered the three service academies in the classes of 1961 through 1965.[10] Negroes are also underrepresented in the student bodies of the colleges that sponsor Reserve Officer Training Corps programs. Enlistment in the ranks and participation in a service-sponsored training program for enlisted officer candidates probably represents the most likely path for Negroes who wish to become military officers. Only a small fraction of total officer personnel, however, is obtained through such programs.

Prior to 1948, Negro enlisted personnel were concentrated in service units engaged in relatively unskilled work or in segregated combat units. There were few opportunities for Negro enlisted men and women to serve in military occupations that require training in a technical specialty, because such occupations were seldom found in segregated service units. When segregation and racial quotas were abandoned, Negroes began to enter a wider range of military occupations. Negro participation in various broad groupings of military occupations in 1962 is shown in Table 8.5.

Negroes are still overrepresented in the relatively unskilled and semiskilled military occupations that form the greater part of the services and ground combat occupational areas. They are, however, also slightly overrepresented in administrative and clerical occupa-

---

[10] Department of Defense, Public Information Division, *Negro Cadets Entering Service Academies, Classes of 1961 through 1965* (news release dated January 19, 1961).

tions. In the craft and "other technical" occupations, Negro representation is only slightly less than average. The only categories in which Negroes are seriously underrepresented are electronics and mechanics and repairmen.

The meaning of the data is obvious. Negroes have made much greater occupational progress in the armed forces than in civilian

Table 8.5

ENLISTED PERSONNEL OF U.S. ARMED FORCES BY MILITARY OCCUPATIONAL AREAS, AUGUST 31, 1962

Occupational areas	Total	Negro	Negro percentage of total
Ground combat	284,891	40,798	14.3
Electronics	254,274	11,992	4.7
Other technical	138,051	11,723	8.5
Administrative and clerical	349,780	37,099	10.6
Mechanics and repairmen	449,592	25,992	5.8
Crafts	116,744	9,783	8.4
Services	210,013	34,894	16.6
Miscellaneous	311,525	21,645	7.0
Total	2,114,870	193,926	9.2

Source: U.S. Commission on Civil Rights, *Civil Rights '63: 1963 Report*, pp. 219-22.

life. The data are too general in nature to warrant the conclusion that all discriminatory employment practices have been eliminated from the armed forces, but the differences in occupational status of Negroes in military and civilian life are so great that equal opportunity must have been fairly well observed in the armed forces in recent years. In the civilian labor force (in 1960) Negroes comprised only 3.7 percent of all clerical and sales workers, whereas in the armed forces (in 1962) they constituted 10.6 percent of the personnel in the administrative and clerical category—a roughly equivalent group of occupations. Similarly, only 4.7 percent of all skilled craft workers in the civilian labor force were Negroes, as contrasted with 8.4 percent in the armed forces. Negroes were less concentrated in the relatively unskilled service occupations in the armed services than in the civilian population—16.6 and 20.2 percent respectively.[11]

Thus it is clear that Negroes have made much greater occupational progress in the armed services under a policy of equal opportunity than they have in civilian life, where discriminatory employment practices are still common.

Negro servicemen employed as skilled technicians, craftsmen, and mechanics re-enlist more frequently than whites employed in the same occupations.[12] This indicates that many Negroes feel they have a better opportunity to advance on merit in the armed forces than in civilian employment.

In sum, abolition of segregated units and facilities and of racial quotas has encouraged Negroes to enter the armed forces and facilitated their use in a wider variety of military occupations through more ready admittance to service training programs on a competitive basis. Manpower utilization practices have improved, and the many wastes inherent in maintenance of racially separate facilities and units have disappeared. Use of Negroes in entry occupations has increased sharply, but use of Negroes as officers and in certain military occupational specialties requiring advanced training has not increased to the same extent. This may be due in some degree to continued covert discrimination; but it is probably mainly attributable to the handicapped educational status of Negroes as a group, which prevents them from competing successfully with whites for the higher-level specialties. Despite these limitations, it is apparent that integration has widened the range of service employment opportunities open to Negroes and that they have responded by participating to an increasing extent in military service. If civilian racial employment practices had changed as sharply as military practices between 1948 and 1962, much of the present occupational disadvantage of Negroes would be a thing of the past.

[11] See Chapter 4, Table 4.5, for roughly comparable civilian occupation groups.

[12] Interviews with various staff officials, Department of Defense.

Utilization of Negroes in Federal Civilian Employment

The history of Negro employment in civilian capacities is not so clear as it is in the military services. In this sphere, no single event had as decisive an effect as did President Truman's order of 1948 desegregating the armed services. Nevertheless, substantial employment opportunities have been opened to Negroes in Federal civilian employment as a result of various efforts to assure equality of opportunity. The more important measures taken to secure these ends, and the results obtained, are summarized below.

PROGRAMS TO ASSURE NONDISCRIMINATORY EMPLOYMENT PRACTICES IN FEDERAL CIVILIAN ESTABLISHMENTS

Discrimination based on race or color in Federal employment was first prohibited by law in a civil service act of 1940, but no administrative machinery was provided to give effect to the prohibition.[13] The Roosevelt Committees on Fair Employment Practice, established during World War II, conducted the earliest formal programs to eliminate discriminatory employment practices in Federal establishments. The committees were authorized to make recommendations to Federal departments and agencies, but were not given power to require that their recommendations be adopted.[14] The committees operated almost exclusively on the basis of complaints when dealing with government employment. Responsibility for complaint investigations was divided between the committees, the U.S. Civil Service Commission, and the various Federal departments and agencies. Committee reports indicate that the committees devoted most of their time to complaints concerning practices in defense industries, not in government establishments.[15]

[13] Ramspeck Act, Title II, 54 Stat. 1211 (1940), superseded by Title I, 5 U.S.C. sec. 631a (1958).
[14] See Executive Order No. 8802, June 25, 1941, and Executive Order No. 9346, May 27, 1943.
[15] Committee on Fair Employment Practice, *First Report, July 1943–December, 1944* (Washington, D.C., 1945), pp. 25, 48, 92, 126.

Between 1946 and 1948, the U.S. Civil Service Commission was responsible for the fair employment program. The Commission's staff investigated complaints of discrimination and prepared recommendations as to their disposition. The Commission could require Federal agencies to take corrective action only when it could be shown that the agencies had violated one of the Commission's regulations. Proof of such violations was so difficult that little was accomplished. In 1948, President Truman established a Fair Employment Board in the Civil Service Commission. The Board had final authority in complaint cases and, at least in theory, could direct the head of a Federal agency to take specific action on complaints. In practice, its directives were frequently ignored by the agencies. The Board devoted itself almost entirely to review of complaints.[16]

The Fair Employment Board was replaced in 1955, when President Eisenhower issued an executive order creating a Committee on Government Employment Policy.[17] The latter was organized as an interdepartmental committee, to which members representative of the public were added. The committee's budget never exceeded $40,000 per year, while its staff totaled three persons, of whom one was a secretary.[18] The committee was given advisory, consultative, fact-finding, and review functions. Federal departments and agencies were made responsible for giving effect to the nondiscriminatory policy stated in President Eisenhower's executive order creating the committee,[19] which reviewed agency action on complaints, conducted surveys of Negro employment in Federal establishments, and sponsored some thirty conferences attended by more than 4,000 officials of Federal agencies. During the conferences, committee members explained the program of the

[16] Interview with a former member of the staff, Fair Employment Board, U.S. Civil Service Commission.

[17] Executive Order No. 10590, January 18, 1955.

[18] U.S. Commission on Civil Rights, Book 3, *Employment*, p. 21, and interview with a former member of the Committee on Government Employment Policy.

[19] Executive Order No. 10590, secs. 2 and 3.

committee, pointed out the responsibilities of local officials, and sought support for the nondiscriminatory employment policy. During the committee's life of about six years, 1,053 complaints were filed. Corrective action was taken in 173 cases, or 16 percent of the total. Only 225 cases came to the committee for review; all other cases were settled by the departments and agencies.[20]

EMPLOYMENT OF NEGROES IN FEDERAL ESTABLISHMENTS

Beginning about 1940, information as to race and religion was gradually eliminated from Federal personnel records.[21] Consequently, it is not possible to obtain comprehensive information on changes in racial employment patterns in Federal establishments between 1940 and 1962. The reports of the Roosevelt Fair Employment Practice Committees indicate that Negro employment gains in Federal civilian employment paralleled roughly similar changes in the economy as a whole during the second World War. Negroes found employment primarily in arsenals, Navy yards, and temporary war agencies in the District of Columbia—i.e., in areas that experienced labor shortages during the war years as was the case in private civilian employment. About 70 percent of the Negroes employed in Federal establishments in 1944 were working in Army and Navy industrial establishments, while the remaining 30 percent were in civil service jobs, 60 percent of the latter group in temporary war agencies. Negroes as a percent of total Federal employment increased from less than 10 percent in 1938 to about 12 percent in 1944.[22] Many of these employment opportunities disappeared with the end of the War.

The 1950 and 1960 Census statistics include figures on employment in Federal nonindustrial civilian establishments, by race, for the country as a whole and for major cities. Table 8.6 shows how the Negro-to-total percentage for Federal establishments changed

20 The President's Committee on Government Employment Policy, *Fourth Report* (Washington, D.C., January 18, 1961), pp. 28–29.
21 *Ibid.*, p. 21.
22 Committee on Fair Employment Practice, *First Report*, pp. 48 and 92.

over the ten-year period in each of ten cities. These percentages
are compared with the Negro-to-total percentages for all employment in the respective cities.

Table 8.6

NEGROES AS PERCENTAGES OF TOTAL AND FEDERAL EMPLOYMENT,
SELECTED STANDARD METROPOLITAN AREAS

	1950		1960	
	Total employ-ment	*Federal employ-ment*	*Total employ-ment*	*Federal employ-ment*
Northern metropolitan areas:				
Chicago	9.6	19.5	11.9	31.5
Detroit	10.6	16.3	12.3	28.3
Los Angeles	5.2	11.1	6.4	15.9
New York	8.8	12.3	11.5	16.5
Border metropolitan areas:				
St. Louis	11.2	13.1	11.8	19.8
Washington, D.C.	24.1	17.6	24.5	21.0
Southern metropolitan areas:				
Atlanta	25.4	12.5	21.4	15.6
Birmingham	34.7	7.5	29.4	11.5
Dallas–Fort Worth	13.7	4.8	12.6	6.0
Mobile	31.8	14.8	28.9	16.4

Source: U.S. Bureau of the Census, *U.S. Census of Population, 1950:* Vol. II,
Characteristics of the Population, Parts 13 (Illinois), 22 (Michigan), 5 (Cali-
fornia), 32 (New York), 25 (Missouri), 9 (District of Columbia), 11 (Georgia),
2 (Alabama), 43 (Texas), Table 83; *1960: Detailed Characteristics,* Final Report
PC(1)–15D (Illinois), 24D (Michigan), 6D (California), 34D (New York), 27D
(Missouri), 10D (District of Columbia), 12D (Georgia), 2D (Alabama), 45D
(Texas), Table 129.

Negroes obtained a growing share of Federal employment in
each of the cities shown in Table 8.6, but there were marked differences between geographic areas. In the four Northern metropolitan areas combined, Negroes constituted nearly twice as large
a percentage of Federal employment as they did of total area employment in 1950 and more than twice as large a percentage in
1960. In the Southern cities the Negro share of Federal employment, though increasing, was still only about one-half as large as
Negro representation in total area employment in 1960. The

Washington and St. Louis metropolitan areas fell between these extremes. Obviously, the policy of nondiscrimination in Federal employment has been made effective to a much greater extent in Northern and Western cities than in Southern cities.

To the outside observer of Federal agency employment, Negroes appear to be concentrated in the lower ranks of the Federal civil service. In 1956, the Committee on Government Employment Policy conducted surveys in five cities to determine the distribution of employees in the classified civil service, by grade and race. The results of the surveys are summarized in Table 8.7. The classified civil service includes employees engaged in clerical, administrative, and other white-collar occupations. About one-half of all Federal civilian employees are in the classified service, in which the lowest pay grade is 1 and the highest 18.

*Table 8.*7

PERCENTAGE DISTRIBUTION OF EMPLOYEES IN CLASSIFIED CIVIL SERVICE
POSITIONS IN FIVE METROPOLITAN AREAS, JUNE, 1956

	GRADES 1–4		GRADES 5–11		GRADES 12–15	
	Negroes	*All others*	*Negroes*	*All others*	*Negroes*	*All others*
Chicago	90.9	46.9	8.9	43.7	0.2	9.4
Los Angeles	93.9	45.4	6.0	46.9	... a	7.7
Mobile	95.8	51.4	4.2	44.4	0.0	4.2
St. Louis	90.4	45.5	9.5	49.0	... a	5.5
Washington	83.3	28.0	16.4	49.8	0.3	22.2
Total	85.5	33.5	14.2	48.6	0.3	17.9

Source: President's Committee on Government Employment Policy, *A Five-City Survey of Negro-American Employees of the Federal Government* (computed from unpublishd data prepared for inclusion as an appendix to the survey: Table IV, "Comparison of Negroes and [all others] in Classification Act positions in Washington, D.C., as of June 30, 1956—for 55 agencies only"; Table V, "Comparison of Negroes and [all others] in Classification Act positions for Chicago, Ill., as of June 30, 1956—for 23 agencies only"; Table VI, "Comparison of Negroes and [all others] in Classification Act positions for Los Angeles, Calif., as of June 30, 1956—for 23 agencies only"; Table VII, "Comparison of Negroes, and [all others] in Classification Act positions for St. Louis, Mo., as of June 30, 1956—for 20 agencies only"; Table VIII, "Comparison of Negroes and [all others] in Classification Act positions for Mobile, Ala., as of June 30, 1956—for 16 agencies only"; Table IX, "Comparison of Negroes and [all others] in Classification Act positions for all [5] cities, as of June 30, 1956").
    a Less than 0.1 percent.

The survey confirmed the general impression that Negroes are concentrated in the lower grades. In each city, except Washington, 90 percent or more of the Negroes employed in Federal civil service classified positions were in the four lowest pay grades. In the five metropolitan areas taken together, only 0.3 percent of the Negro employees were in the four highest pay grades, grades 12 to 15, whereas about 18 percent of all other employees were in these grades. Unfortunately, earlier studies of the distribution of Negro employees by grade cannot be compared with the 1956 study because of statistical difficulties.

The five-city study of 1956 cannot be compared with more recent distributions of Negroes employed in classified civil service positions, because data are not available for metropolitan areas. In both 1961 and 1962, however, the Kennedy committee collected employment data, by race and grade, for the entire Federal civilian establishment.

Though not statistically comparable, the data in Tables 8.7 and 8.8 suggest that Negroes improved their position in the classified civil service between 1956 and 1962. The concentration of Negroes

Table 8.8

PERCENTAGE DISTRIBUTION OF EMPLOYEES IN CLASSIFIED
CIVIL SERVICE POSITIONS

	GRADES 1–4		GRADES 5–11		GRADES 12–18	
	Negroes	*All others*	*Negroes*	*All others*	*Negroes*	*All others*
June, 1961	71.5	31.5	27.3	51.9	1.2	16.6
June, 1962	68.3	30.7	30.2	52.0	1.5	17.3

Source: President's Committee on Equal Employment Opportunity, *Negro and Total Employment by Grade and Salary Groups, June, 1961, and June, 1962* (Washington, D.C., 1963, mimeographed), Table 1, Summary, All Agencies.

in the lowest pay grades was reduced significantly, and there was a small increase in the percentage of Negroes employed in the highest pay grades. Part of the apparent improvement in the occupational status of Negro civil servants was, however, occasioned by an upward shift in the distribution of employees by grade. In 1956, 43 percent of all employees were in grades 5 thru 11; but by 1961, about 50 percent of all employees were in these grades.

It is useful to compare racial employment patterns in two Southern shipyards, one Federally owned and operated, the other privately owned and frequently engaged in work on Federal contracts.[23] In 1960, Negroes formed about one-third of the populations of the areas where the yards were situated. In both yards Negroes constituted some 20 percent of the work force in 1960 and 1961. The private yard employed no Negroes in professional, technical, clerical, or stenographic positions. In the Federal yard there were a number of Negroes employed as professional engineers and clerks, but Negroes were less than 2 percent of yard employment in white-collar occupations. In the private yard about 4 percent of skilled manual employees were Negro. In the Federal yard Negroes constituted about 14 percent of the workers engaged in a number of such occupations. In both yards Negroes were well represented in semiskilled occupations and performed almost all unskilled work. Racial employment practices of the yards were entirely different. Briefly, the private yard practiced segregated employment, while the Federal yard was integrated. In the private yard, skilled Negroes were employed only in a limited number of occupations such as spray-painting, sand-blasting, cement-finishing, rigging, and other occupations traditionally regarded as Negro jobs in that yard. No whites were employed in these occupations. In the Federal yard, Negroes were employed in a much wider variety of skilled occupations, including electronic technician, electrician, bridge crane operator, boilermaker, and others from which they were excluded in the private yard. There was some supervision of whites by Negroes in the Federal yard, but none in the private yard. The Federal yard reported no difficulties resulting from inte-

[23] Federal shipyard: Committee on Equal Employment Opportunity (unpublished survey of employment, by race and occupation, July, 1961). Private shipyard: Committee on Government Contracts (unpublished survey of employment, by race and occupation, 1960).

gration of work crews and elimination of facilities segregated on a racial basis. It is apparent that observance of the policy of equal employment opportunity in the Federal yard had brought significant gains to Negroes employed there, in marked contrast to the private yard, where no attempt was made to effectuate the Federal policy.

In a very general way, the racial employment pattern of the Federal shipyard was duplicated in Federal agencies in Atlanta, Georgia.[24] In Atlanta post offices, for example, about 50 percent of the employees in the spring of 1962 were Negro. Though heavily concentrated in the letter carrier, or "mailman," category, there were a few Negro supervisors, including a few who supervised both whites and Negroes. Negroes and whites did not work in segregated groups in post offices. On-the-job relations between the races were said to be good. There was some employment of Negroes in clerical positions where there was contact with the general public. Negroes, for example, served post-office windows in the principal office in the city. On the other hand, persons active in seeking employment opportunities for Negroes reported, without qualification, that discrimination still existed in subtle forms. They reported, for example, that no Negroes were employed in the nearest regional office of the Post Office Department and stated that local Negroes did not learn of openings in the regional office until after they had been filled by promotion of white employees. The allegations were confirmed when the Post Office Department, in the autumn of 1962, suspended for an indefinite period the promotional authority of the Atlanta Postmaster on the ground that his policies had shown racial discrimination.[25]

In other Federal agencies in Atlanta, Negroes formed a much smaller part of total employment than in the Post Office and were concentrated in the lowest manual job classifications, although a few were employed in clerical and other white-collar jobs and a

[24] See Chapter 2, note 6.
[25] New York *Times,* November 10, 1962, p. 1.

still smaller number supervised racially mixed groups of employees. As was the case in the Post Office, relations on the job between whites and Negroes were said to be good, nor were any difficulties reported between Negro employees of Federal agencies and members of the public. While Negroes have made only modest progress in securing employment in nontraditional jobs in Federal agencies in Atlanta, practices in private employment have changed even more slowly. The local transit system, for example, was reported to employ but four Negro drivers out of a total 750 such employees.[26]

Competitive examinations are frequently used to screen candidates for Federal employment. Generally, Negroes do not score as well on such tests as whites, particularly those from Southern states, where Negroes still complete fewer years of school and receive education of poorer quality than whites. The following examples illustrate the point. Only 8 percent of the graduates of Southern Negro colleges who took the Federal entrance examination given by the U.S. Civil Service Commission in May, 1961, passed. On the other hand, 45 percent of the graduates of white Southern colleges passed. In the 1959 and 1960 examinations for the Foreign Service, all examinees from Southern Negro colleges failed the written examination. A number of Negroes who had attended integrated colleges passed the same examination.

In the Southern Federal shipyard described earlier, there were, in 1961, five Negroes among 264 apprentices and one Negro among 280 "leading men," a foreman category.[27] Written examinations play a part in the selection of apprentices and leading men. A representative of the Navy Department advised us that poor test performance was an important cause of the small number of Negro apprentices and leading men.[28] In the same shipyard, Negroes comprised 72 percent of the persons employed as helpers.[29] Written

---

[26] See Chapter 2, note 6.
[27] See note 24, above.
[28] See note 5, above.
[29] See note 24, above.

examinations are seldom used in screening candidates for appointment to helper occupations.

Conclusions

During the past two decades, Negroes have increased as a proportion of Federal civilian and military personnel. Negro penetration has been particularly noticeable in unskilled and semiskilled jobs, but has been much less apparent in the middle and upper job ranges. Promotion of Negroes in the Federal service seems to have been retarded by their inadequate preparation for work and by the persistence of discriminatory practices. Discrimination on the basis of race in civilian employment became unlawful in 1940. Explicit statements of policy by the President, acting as Commander-in-Chief of the armed forces and as Chief Executive of the civilian establishment, preceded changes in Federal racial employment patterns. The President's authority to fix Federal policy on such matters was accepted by his military and civilian subordinates and did not become the subject of controversy in the Congress.

Only modest administrative measures were taken to assure observance of nondiscriminatory employment practices. Nevertheless, the policies prescribed by the President were made sufficiently effective in practice to attract Negroes in increasing numbers to Federal civilian employment and military service. The hierarchical organization of the armed forces made possible a quite rapid and complete change in their racial practices once the President had acted to establish a new racial policy. In the civilian establishment, changes in practice took place more slowly because policy could be made effective in civilian departments and agencies only through the cooperation of many thousands of individuals whose decisions as to employment or promotion determined the results attained to a greater extent than in the armed services.

Changes in racial employment practices did not cause racial conflict in military units or in civilian establishments. In many in-

stances, Negroes now command integrated units in the armed services and supervise white and Negro civilian employees—a practice
almost unheard of before the President prescribed a policy of
equality of opportunity in Federal employment.

The racial employment patterns of Federal civilian establishments situated in Southern states still tend to reflect traditional local
practices, although less discrimination is apparent than in private
employment. Statements of policy implemented only by little-
known complaint procedures have not had much effect in such
situations. If greater attention could be given to racial employment
patterns in Federal civilian establishments in the South, larger increases might be possible in their use of Negroes.

The available evidence indicates that Negroes have made
greater occupational progress in the armed forces and in Federal
civil service than in private employment. The policy of equal opportunity in Federal civilian employment has been based on law,
and in the armed services, on the President's constitutional powers
as Commander-in-Chief of the armed forces. Progress in these areas
of employment contrasts strikingly with the poor record of Federal
contractors, whose practices were subject to review only by committees established by executive order.

9

ALTERNATIVES TO FAIR EMPLOYMENT
LEGISLATION

In addition to the public FEP programs discussed in the four preceding chapters, there are various other possible ways of combating employment discrimination through governmental means. Some of these approaches are already available; others are still in the proposal stage. Experience under the former, which include actions invoking Federal labor laws and lawsuits in the Federal courts, is reviewed in the first section of this chapter. The second section considers the merits and drawbacks of certain proposals for indirect legal sanctions and governmental subsidies. Finally, the effectiveness of the boycott as a *private* pressure device for obtaining more and better jobs for Negroes is briefly discussed.

Union Racial Practices, Labor Legislation, and the Courts

The state FEP laws apply to all types of enterprise within the particular state, whether the activity is intrastate or interstate in nature. The applicability of the state laws to interstate as well as to intrastate business is well established. In a 1945 case involving an early New York State antidiscrimination law directed solely at unions, the U.S. Supreme Court upheld the right of states to prohibit discriminatory practices by labor organizations operating in interstate industries; [1] and in a recent case the Court ruled that the states can also prohibit discriminatory practices by employers engaged in interstate business.[2]

In the non-FEP-law states—since there is no Federal FEP law

[1] *Railway Mail Association vs. Corsi*, 326 U.S. 88 (1945).
[2] *Colorado Anti-Discrimination Commission vs. Continental Air Lines, Inc.*, 83 S.Ct. 1022 (1963).

—the only available legal approaches to seeking redress from employer or union discrimination are state court actions under the common law and proceedings before administrative agencies under Federal labor relations legislation with subsequent appeal to the Federal courts. Moreover, the possibilities of obtaining meaningful redress are decidedly limited under both these approaches.

THE COMMON-LAW APPROACH

With regard to the first of these, once a person has obtained employment in an establishment covered by a union-management agreement, he may be able to obtain relief from discriminatory treatment through court action under the common law. It is not possible under common law, however, to compel a discriminatory employer to hire Negroes or other minorities nor to compel a discriminatory union to admit them to membership. The traditional common-law doctrine that the courts cannot compel involuntary association of persons is controlling in such cases; and even in the case of persons already employed, there are few precedents for such action. In cases decided in 1945 and 1946, the Supreme Court of California found a basis in the common law for preventing a union from using the closed-shop provisions of a labor agreement to compel the discharge of a Negro employee who was eligible for membership only in a Negro auxiliary local he had refused to join.[3] These cases emphasize the limited nature of the remedies available under the common law. In effect, the California courts merely held that closed-shop agreements could not be used to compel the discharge of an employee who had been relegated to second-class membership in a Negro auxiliary local subordinate to a white local, provided the Negro employee desired to join the white local.

These decisions may have contributed to the decline of Negro auxiliary locals, but they provide no relief to persons who are dis-

[3] *James vs. Marinship Co.*, 25 Cal. 2d 721, 155 P. 2d 329 (1944), and *Williams vs. International Brotherhood*, 27 Cal. 2d 586, 165 P. 2d 903 (1946). These cases are discussed at greater length in Greenberg, *Race Relations and American Law*, pp. 171–73.

criminatorily denied employment or union membership because of race. The key fact in the California cases was that the complainants had secured employment which they would lose if the closed-shop provisions of the labor agreement were enforced when they refused to join the Negro auxiliary. Under these circumstances, the Negro complainants could prove a danger of damage to themselves. Such cases are quite rare. Discriminatory unions and employers are more likely to exclude Negroes from membership or employment or to restrict them to unskilled occupations than they are to seek their discharge once they have been employed. Moreover, in common-law cases complainants must themselves bring action in state courts. The expense and delay involved in such proceedings are sufficient to discourage all but the most hardy litigants. Given these limitations, the common law does not provide adequate relief for persons who encounter discriminatory employment practices.

THE DUTY OF FAIR REPRESENTATION UNDER THE NATIONAL
LABOR RELATIONS AND RAILWAY LABOR ACTS

Three Federal labor statutes afford potential means of redress from discriminatory employer and union practices—the National Labor Relations Act, the Railway Labor Act, and the Labor-Management Reporting and Disclosure Act. The Federal courts have issued a number of significant decisions involving complaints of discriminatory practices by labor unions under these laws.

The Railway Labor Act of 1926 and the original National Labor Relations Act of 1935 established for the first time national ground rules for the conduct of collective bargaining. Both acts were passed at a time when FEP legislation was unheard of and were concerned with other matters. Racial employment practices were not discussed during the hearings and debates that preceded their passage. Consequently, there is nothing in the legislative history of either act to suggest that Congress intended them to be used as substitutes for Federal FEP legislation. Given such a legislative history, the administrative agencies responsible, in the first instance, for interpreting the acts have been extremely reluctant to assert jurisdiction over complaints based on discriminatory racial practices. The National Labor Relations Act sought to redress the inequality of bargaining power between employees and employers by encouraging unionization and collective bargaining. It was a one-sided act in the sense that it prohibited employers from engaging in a number of unfair labor practices but made no mention of labor-union practices. Under the Taft-Hartley Amendments of 1947, labor unions as well as employers were forbidden to engage in unfair labor practices. Discrimination in employment or union membership was not declared to be an unfair labor practice under the original 1935 act nor under the 1947 amendments. Nevertheless, a number of cases in the Federal courts have established a sort of Federal common law which can be used to attack certain discriminatory employment practices. The development of this body of precedents is summarized below.

The Steele Case. Neither the National Labor Relations Act of 1935 nor the Railway Labor Act contains any provisions requiring unions to represent employees or union members fairly. The courts have found the duty to be implicit in the acts by reason of the power given labor unions to act as the exclusive collective bargaining representatives for all employees in appropriate bargaining units. The duty of fair representation was first established in the Steele case.[4] Steele was a Negro fireman employed by the Louisville and Nashville Railroad. When locomotives were fired by coal, the fireman's job was a disagreeable one and was generally considered a "Negro job" on Southern railroads. The advent of diesel locomotives made the fireman's job more attractive to whites, who then sought to displace Negroes. In 1941, the Brotherhood of Locomotive Firemen and twenty-one railroads entered into a labor agreement under which Negro firemen could not exceed 50 percent of the firemen in each class of service in each seniority district.

---

[4] *Steele vs. Louisville and Nashville Railroad Co.*, 323 U.S. 192ff. (1944).

Under the agreement no new jobs could be filled by Negroes until the proportion of Negro firemen had been reduced to 50 percent, and no Negroes could be assigned to jobs they did not already hold. Steele worked as a fireman in the passenger pool of the Louisville and Nashville Railroad with three other Negroes and one white until April, 1941, when the jobs held by the Negroes were declared vacant and filled with four whites, all junior in seniority to the Negroes whom they replaced. Steele was laid off for sixteen days and then assigned to less desirable jobs than the passenger service from which he had been removed. On January 3, 1942, after suit was filed in the Alabama state courts against the Brotherhood of Locomotive Firemen and the railroad, Steele was reassigned to passenger service.

The Negro firemen resorted to the courts only after their protests to the union and the employer had been disregarded. The Alabama Supreme Court ruled that the Negroes' complaint stated no cause of action, on the ground that the union had been elected to represent all of the members of the craft or class of employees and had authority either to create or to destroy the rights of members of the craft or class. The Alabama court apparently felt that the Negro firemen exhausted their legal rights when they were allowed to vote for or against the Brotherhood of Locomotive Firemen. It therefore held that neither the Brotherhood nor the railroad violated any of the Negroes' rights by negotiating the contracts which discriminated against them. The Negro firemen appealed the decision of the Alabama Supreme Court to the Federal courts, and the matter was decided by the United States Supreme Court in 1944. The latter court took the view that the constitutionality of the Railway Labor Act would be open to question if it gave exclusive bargaining rights to employee representatives without imposing a duty to represent all members of the bargaining unit fairly. The Supreme Court stated the problem as follows:

For the representative is clothed with power not unlike that of the legislature which is subject to constitutional limitations on its power to deny, restrict, destroy or discriminate against the rights of those for whom it legislates and which is also under an affirmative constitutional duty equally to protect those rights. If the Railway Labor Act purports to impose on petitioner [Steele] and other Negro members of the craft the legal duty to comply with the terms of the contract whereby the representative has discriminatorily restricted their employment for the benefit and advantage of the Brotherhood's own members, we must decide the constitutional questions which petitioner raises in his pleading.

The Court avoided the question of constitutionality, however, by finding that

Congress, in enacting the Railway Labor Act and authorizing a labor union, chosen by a majority of the craft, to represent the craft, did not intend to confer plenary power upon the union to sacrifice, for the benefit of its members, rights of the minority of the craft, without imposing on it any duty to protect the minority.

We think that the Railway Labor Act imposes upon the statutory representative of a craft at least as exacting a duty to protect equally the interests of the members of the craft as the constitution imposes upon a legislature to give equal protection to the interests of those for whom it legislates. Congress has seen fit to clothe the bargaining representative with powers comparable to those possessed by a legislative body to create and restrict the rights of those whom it represents . . . but it also imposed upon the representative a corresponding duty. We hold the language of the act . . . expresses the aim of Congress to impose on the bargaining representative . . . the duty to exercise fairly the power conferred upon it on behalf of all those for whom it acts, without hostile discrimination against them.

In the same case, the Court pointed out that its decision did not require unions to admit Negroes to membership in order to satisfy the duty of fair representation:

While the statute does not deny to such a bargaining labor organization the right to determine eligibility to its membership, it does require the union, in collective bargaining and in making contracts with the carrier, to represent nonunion or minority union members of the craft without hostile discrimination, fairly, impartially, and in good faith.

The Court's decision in the Steele case is quoted at some length because it established the doctrine that unions have a duty to represent fairly those for whom they bargain and defined, at least by implication, the limits of that duty. To put the matter as simply as possible, the Court held that a union must represent fairly all persons employed in a group of employees for whom it bargains, union members and nonmembers alike. The decision imposed no corresponding duty on employers and permitted unions to continue to exclude persons from membership on the basis of race if they wished to do so. In 1955, the Court extended the duty of fair representation to unions covered by the National Labor Relations Act.[5]

In the Steele case and later cases arising under the Railway Labor Act or the National Labor Relations Act, various Federal courts have held that, under the duty of fair representation implicit in the statutes, unions are acting illegally when they seek the removal of Negroes from their jobs in order to make room for whites,[6] deny equal promotion opportunities to Negroes,[7] fail to protest the discriminatory discharge of Negro workers,[8] block the promotion of Negroes,[9] relegate Negroes to certain kinds of jobs from which they cannot be promoted under departmental or other forms of seniority,[10] eliminate Negroes from employment by requiring that they take tests the failure of which would result in discharge,[11] limit a Negro to only one employer during a period of

[5] *Syres vs. Oil Workers International Union*, 350 U.S. 892, reversing 223 F. 2nd 739 (5th Cir. 1955).

[6] *Steele* case.

[7] *Dillard vs. Chesapeake and Ohio Railroad*, 199 F. 2nd 951; 136 F. Supp. 689; *Race Relations Law Reporter*, I (1956), 389.

[8] *Conley vs. Givson*, 355 U.S. 41, 33 L.C. 71077 (1951).

[9] *Richardson vs. Texas and New Orleans Railway Co.*, 242 F. 2nd 230, and *Haynes vs. Union Pacific Railroad*, 184 F. 2nd 377.

[10] *Syres* case; *Clark vs. Norfolk and Western Railway Co.*, *Race Relations Law Reporter*, III (1958), 988; *Jones vs. Central of Georgia Railroad*, F. 2nd 648; *Race Relations Law Reporter*, I (1956), 558.

[11] *Salvant vs. Louisville and Nashville Railroad Co.*, 83 F. Supp. 391; *Rolax vs. Atlantic Coast Line Railroad*, 186 F. 2nd 478; *Brotherhood of Locomotive Firemen vs. Palmer*, 178 F. 2nd 723.

six months,[12] and discriminate against Negroes in wage rates, hiring, discharge, layoffs, and job assignments.[13] A Federal court has also held that the duty of fair representation imposes upon a union the obligation to use its bargaining power to *remove* discrimination.[14] In the same case the court ruled that employers and unions are jointly liable for damages caused by a union's failure to observe the duty of fair representation.[15] The last of these rulings has not been reviewed by the Supreme Court.

From the preceding enumeration of discriminatory practices found by the Federal courts to be unlawful, one might conclude that a wide range of discriminatory practices could be attacked successfully through proceedings before the National Labor Relations Board (NLRB), the National Mediation Board, or the National Railroad Adjustment Board. If this were indeed true, it would be possible to eliminate many discriminatory practices from firms where unions have been certified as bargaining representatives. Unfortunately, such a conclusion is very far from correct. To understand why this is so, we must review the work of the agencies responsible for administration of Federal labor relations legislation.

THE NATIONAL MEDIATION BOARD AND THE

NATIONAL RAILROAD ADJUSTMENT BOARD

The National Mediation Board and the National Railroad Adjustment Board are responsible for administration of the Railway Labor Act. The Act governs collective bargaining between unions and railroads and airlines engaged in interstate commerce. The Mediation Board attempts to resolve disputes between unions and managements over the terms of new labor agreements, but does not hear grievances arising during the life of the agreements. The

---

[12] *Blue vs. Shaefer, Labor Relations Reporter Manual,* XXXIII, 2852.
[13] Archibald Cox, "The Duty of Fair Representation," *Villanova Law Review* (January, 1957), p. 159.
[14] *Jones* case.
[15] *Ibid.*

Board has seldom, if ever, concerned itself with racial employment problems. The railroad and airline unions are dominated by
whites, with the sole exception of the Brotherhood of Sleeping Car
Porters. The Board deals only with employer and union representatives, not spokesmen for dissident minorities, because the latter are not the representatives of a majority of a craft or class of
employees as defined by the Railway Labor Act. The discriminatory agreement which led to the Steele case was concluded with
the assistance of the Board.

The National Railroad Adjustment Board hears disputes that
arise during the life of agreements, and one might think that the
Adjustment Board would have had occasion to implement the duty
of fair representation formulated by the Supreme Court in the
Steele case. The Board has not done so, however. The Board does
not act on the grievances of railroad employees unless the appropriate railroad union files a complaint on their behalf. Since
railroad unions frequently discriminate against their Negro members or exclude Negroes from membership, it is seldom possible for
Negro railroad workers to use the grievance procedures of the
Board.

In the Steele case, the Supreme Court pointed out that the Adjustment Board had "consistently declined in more than 400 cases
to entertain grievance complaints by individual members of a craft
represented by a labor organization." [16] The Court also pointed out
that, since unions selected the members of the National Railroad
Adjustment Board and prescribed the rules under which it operated, "the Negro firemen would be required to appear before a
group which is in large part chosen by the respondents against
whom their real complaint is made." [17] The Court also pointed out
that unions and carriers are empowered by the Act to select regional boards of adjustment and stated, "We cannot say that a
hearing, if available . . . would constitute an adequate administrative remedy." [18]

[16] *Labor Relations Reporter Manual*, XV, 7141.
[17] *Ibid.*   [18] *Ibid.*

The persistent refusal of the National Railroad Adjustment Board to review racial employment practices has forced Negroes to resort to the Federal courts for relief, with the result that many of the leading cases defining the duty of fair representation have been decided by Federal courts in railroad matters.

THE NATIONAL LABOR RELATIONS BOARD

In 1943, the year before the decision of the Supreme Court in the Steele case, the NLRB stated that a union acting as bargaining representative under the National Labor Relations Act was obligated to represent fairly all persons employed in the bargaining unit.[19] Racial discrimination was not involved in the case. The NLRB's interpretation of the Act was upheld by the U.S. Supreme Court on the same day its decision in the Steele case was issued.[20]

In one of two similar cases decided at about the same time the NLRB defined the duty of fair representation as follows:

This Board has no express authority to remedy undemocratic practices within the structure of union organizations, but we have conceived it to be our duty under the statute to see to it that any organization certified . . . as the bargaining representative acted as a genuine representative of all of the employees in the bargaining unit.[21]

Despite the language of this decision, the NLRB has interpreted its powers narrowly in racial matters and has issued decisions in only a handful of cases which dealt with racial discrimination.[22] The NLRB's reluctance to deal with racial employment practices, which apparently stems from the fact that racial discrimination, as such, is not included in the list of unfair practices prohibited by the Act, has forced aggrieved Negroes to resort to the Federal courts rather than to the NLRB for relief. In the Syres case, for example, Negro employees at the Gulf Oil Corporation's refinery in Port

[19] *Wallace Corporation*, 50 NLRB 138 (1943).
[20] *Wallace Corporation vs. NLRB*, 323 U.S. 248 (1944).
[21] *Larus and Bros. Co.*, 62 NLRB 1095 (1945).
[22] For a detailed discussion of this issue, see Michael I. Sovern, "The National Labor Relations Act and Racial Discrimination," *Columbia Law Review*, LXII (1962), 563–622.

Arthur, Texas, brought suit against Local 23 of the Oil Workers International Union to prevent that organization from entering into a contract restricting Negro employees to the labor division of the refinery.[23] The Negroes brought suit in Federal court because their attorney had been unable to persuade the NLRB to entertain a similar complaint.[24]

EXCLUSION OF NEGROES FROM UNION MEMBERSHIP
PERMITTED UNDER EXISTING FEDERAL LAWS

As matters now stand, it is not possible for a person excluded from membership in a union because of his race to force the union to accept him by proceedings before Federal administrative agencies or before the Federal courts. In the Steele case, the Supreme Court ruled that the Railway Labor Act "does not deny to . . . a bargaining labor organization the right to determine eligibility to its membership." In effect, the Court extended the protection of the doctrine of involuntary association to labor unions. At the time of this decision, the original National Labor Relations Act had not been amended.

The next important case concerning admission to union membership was decided in 1959 in Oliphant vs. Brotherhood of Locomotive Firemen and Enginemen. In the Oliphant case a Federal district court held that Congress, in passing the Railway Labor Act, obviously did not intend to require unions to admit Negroes to membership. The district court put the matter this way:

The court can feel that a situation is unjust and may need some remedial action, but unless upon sound equitable principles relief can be granted, the remedy does not lie with the courts. Certainly voluntary action by the defendant or Congressional legislation present the only corrective where a manifest inequality exists. . . . To compel by judicial mandate membership in voluntary organizations where the Congress has knowingly and expressly permitted the bargaining agent

---

[23] *Syres* case.
[24] Interview with Roberson L. King, attorney for the complainants, Houston, Texas, June 7, 1962.

to prescribe its own qualifications for membership would be usurping the legislative function.[25]

The U.S. Supreme Court denied certiorari on direct appeal of this decision: [26] on appeal, a U.S. Court of Appeals affirmed the district court's decision, and the Supreme Court again denied certiorari in 1959 "in view of the abstract context in which the questions sought to be raised are presented by this record." [27]

While this case was filed under the Railway Labor Act, the same rule would also apply to cases filed under the National Labor Relations Act, though no such case has yet been decided by the Supreme Court. During the fifteen years that intervened between the Court's decisions in the Steele and Oliphant cases the 1947 Taft-Hartley Amendments to the National Labor Relations Act had become law. The language of the amendments and the debate that preceded their passage clarified Congressional intent with respect to exclusion from union membership because of race. During the course of debate on the amendments, Senator Taft said,

Let us take the case of unions which prohibit the admission of Negroes to membership. If they prohibit the admission of Negroes to membership, they may continue to do so; but representatives of the union cannot go to the employer and say, "You have got to fire this man because he is not a member of our union." [28]

Congressional intent on this point was made explicit in Section 8(b)(1) of the revised National Labor Relations Act, which reads, in part, "Provided that this paragraph shall not impair the right of a labor organization to prescribe its own rules with respect to the acquisition or retention of membership therein."

Even before passage of the Taft-Hartley Amendments, the NLRB consistently refused to require unions to admit Negroes to membership, on the ground that the Act did not give it power to

[25] *Oliphant vs. Brotherhood of Locomotive Firemen*, 156 F. Supp. 89; *Race Relations Law Reporter*, II (1957), 1128.

[26] 355 U.S. 892.

[27] 79 S.Ct. 648.

[28] Remarks of Senator Robert Taft, *Congressional Record*, XCIII (1947), 4193.

do so. In 1945, the NLRB stated its policy with respect to exclusion from membership as follows:

Neither exclusion from membership nor segregated membership per se represents evasion on the part of a labor organization of its statutory duty to afford "equal representation." But in each case where the issue is presented the Board will scrutinize the contract and conduct of a representative organization and withhold or withdraw certification if it finds that the organization has discriminated against employees in the bargaining units through its membership restrictions or otherwise.[29]

CURRENT STATUS OF NLRB POLICY CONCERNING
DISCRIMINATORY UNION PRACTICES

Between 1945 and 1962, no important change in NLRB policy on the issue of racial discrimination could be discerned in its decisions. In no single case during these years did the NLRB withhold or withdraw certification as bargaining agent because of racial bars to union membership.

In a recent case, however, the NLRB refused to recognize an existing discriminatory contract between a union and an employer as a bar to a representation election requested by a rival union. In the same case the NLRB also stated that discriminatory contracts "warrant revocation of [a union's] certification" as bargaining representative of employees, although revocation of certification was not an issue in the case.[30] In a second recent proceeding, a trial examiner of the NLRB found that the maintenance of racially segregated unions in a single bargaining unit was a "practice . . . basically incompatible with a bargaining agent's duty of fair representation of all employees in the unit." He also recommended that the certification of any union as a bargaining agent be revoked if it persisted in such practices.[31] At this writing (July, 1963), the NLRB has not acted on its trial examiner's recommendations, nor

[29] National Labor Relations Board, *Tenth Annual Report* (1945).
[30] *Pioneer Bus Company*, 140 NLRB 18 (1963).
[31] *Independent Metal Workers Union, Locals Nos. 1 and 2, United Steelworkers of America, and Hughes Tool Company*, NLRB, Division of Trial Examiners, Case No. 23-CB-429 and Case No. 23-RC-1758 (1963), *passim.*

has the earlier decision of the NLRB been reviewed by the Federal courts.

The policies stated in these cases may indicate a significant change in the Board's concept of the duty of fair representation. For example, the maintenance of segregated unions and of discriminatory seniority and promotion provisions in union contracts could be successfully attacked under such policies. Even under these policies, however, proceedings before the NLRB would be of no avail in a large proportion of discriminatory union situations. Many unions—both craft and industrial—are not dependent on the NLRB election and certification procedure for maintenance of their bargaining representative status. And Negro workers excluded from membership in craft unions that control access to jobs would still be unable to utilize the NLRB's procedure to obtain redress.

THE LABOR-MANAGEMENT REPORTING AND DISCLOSURE ACT OF 1959

This act, usually referred to as the Landrum-Griffin Act after its authors, is the most recent addition to the growing body of Federal labor legislation. The Act seeks to protect members of labor organizations from unfair treatment by their own unions. Title I of the Act protects, among other things, the right of union members to nominate candidates for union office, vote in union elections, participate in union meetings, and freely express their views. During debate on the Act in 1959, an attempt by Congressman Powell to amend Title I of the Act to provide "except that no labor organization shall . . . refuse membership, segregate, or expel a person on the grounds of race, religion, color, sex, or national origin" [32] was defeated. Congressman Landrum, co-author of the Act, opposed the Powell amendment, declaring: "We do not seek in this legislation, in no way, no shape, no guise to tell the labor unions of this country whom they shall admit to their unions." [33]

[32] Remarks of Congressman Adam C. Powell, *Congressional Record*, CV (1959), 15721.
[33] Remarks of Congressman Landrum, *Congressional Record*, CV (1959), 15724.

Given such a legislative history, it is evident that the Landrum-Griffin Act affords no protection to persons denied membership in labor unions because of race. It is possible, however, that the Act may make it somewhat easier for Negroes to secure equal treatment within a union once they have been accepted as members. The rights of members of labor organizations are specified in Title I of the Act. Persons who believe that the rights secured by Title I have been infringed must bring civil suits in the Federal courts to secure redress of their grievances. Such actions are both slow and costly and probably do not constitute practical remedies for Negro union members who experience discriminatory treatment by their unions. If the provisions of any of the remaining titles are violated, the Secretary of Labor can bring an action for relief in the Federal courts. The expense of such proceedings is borne by the Federal government rather than by the complainant. The legislative history of the Act suggests that Congress prescribed suits by individuals rather than the Secretary of Labor as the means for attacking violations of Title I in order to avoid giving to the Secretary any jurisdiction over labor union racial practices.[34]

SUMMARY OF EXPERIENCE UNDER FEDERAL LABOR LEGISLATION

The possibilities and limitations of utilizing Federal labor relations laws as instruments to combat racial discrimination in employment can be summed up as follows. The duty of fair representation enunciated by the Supreme Court is of decidedly limited value as a means of obtaining redress from discriminatory treatment by employers or unions. An employer's refusal to *hire* Negroes cannot be attacked through proceedings under any Federal statute. Moreover, unions are free to exclude Negroes from mem-

[34] Senator Johnston of South Carolina denounced the original version of Title I, under which the Secretary of Labor could bring suits for aggrieved union members, as "the first step to a broad Federal FEPC program." The Senator said it would give the Secretary "power to force integration of thousands of union locals and certainly would set an example or a pattern for the Attorney General to follow in school cases throughout the nation." Benjamin Aaron, "The Labor-Management Reporting and Disclosure Act of 1959," *Harvard Law Review*, LXXIII (1960), 858–59.

bership under both acts; and since, as noted in Chapter 3, in many exclusionist craft-union situations exclusion from membership is equivalent to debarment from employment, this constitutes a serious limitation on the usefulness of the legislation to the Negro group. Furthermore, even in situations where Negroes *are* employed, and the duty of fair representation is therefore operative, it is unlikely to be of much help if the union excludes them from membership. Since they have no voice in union affairs and hence no power to influence the union leaders, the latter are not likely to observe the duty of fair representation in practice. The victimized Negro workers' only recourse in such cases is a costly lawsuit, which very few are financially able to undertake.

Other Public FEP Measures and Approaches

To round out the discussion of possible substitutes for FEP legislation, it is necessary to give consideration to two other types of public measures—indirect sanctions and subsidies. Included under the first head are certain existing Federal and state programs. For the most part, however, the measures discussed are still in the proposal stage.

INDIRECT SANCTIONS

Included in this category are cancellation and withholding of procurement contracts by public agencies at all levels of government, cancellation and withholding of Federal grants and other financial aids to state and local governments, and revocation of licenses and franchises issued by Federal, state, and municipal authorities. The communications and interstate transportation industries operate under Federal franchises; state and local licensing arrangements cover such enterprises as restaurants and taverns, plumbing and electrical contractors, private employment agencies, and local transit concerns.

Cancellation and withholding of procurement contracts have

been potentially available to the Presidential FEP committees that have functioned successively over the past two decades, but have never been utilized by them. The experience of these agencies is dealt with in detail in Chapter 7. A number of state governments have also attempted to promote fair employment practices through inclusion of nondiscrimination clauses in procurement and construction contracts, with cancellation as a potential enforcement weapon. The authors of a recent study of these and other civil rights measures promulgated by the executive branch of state governments concluded that "despite large annual state disbursements for construction of roads, schools, hospitals and public works, the contractual obligations are practically meaningless today for lack of policing and affirmative enforcement." [35] New York City announced a similar program in 1962, but up to the time of writing it had not been in operation sufficiently long to permit an evaluation of its effectiveness.[36]

If provision were made for cancellation and withholding of contracts in enforceable FEP laws, the device might be useful as a supplement to the regular enforcement procedures provided for in the laws. As noted in Chapter 7, however, government procurement agencies tend to give greater weight to cost, quality, and delivery than to employment practices when awarding contracts; and cancellation of contracts already begun is frequently impracticable or even impossible. Similarly, cancellation or withholding of Federal grants-in-aid may often be impracticable, since it may mean depriving the people of the particular state or locality—including its minority-group citizens—of hospitals, urban-renewal projects, or other much-needed public facilities or improvements.

Revocation of licenses and franchises as an antidiscrimination compliance sanction has never been seriously attempted; hence, it is difficult to assess its potentialities. It would, however, require either that licensing agencies undertake responsibility for conduct-

[35] Silard and Galloway, *State Executive Authority*, p. 21.
[36] New York *Times*, February 25, 1962.

ing antidiscrimination compliance and enforcement activities in the firms under their jurisdiction or, alternatively, that they establish close administrative relationships with a specialized FEP agency. The difficulties attending both of these alternatives are fairly obvious. It is possible, also, that in the absence of legislation authorizing such action, the courts would hold revocation of licenses and franchises as an antidiscrimination sanction to be an improper use of executive power.

Whatever the merits of these indirect sanctions may be, it seems clear that the problem of employment discrimination can be dealt with more directly and efficiently by a specialized FEP agency, utilizing the techniques of conciliation, public hearings, and enforceable cease-and-desist orders than through such roundabout devices as cancellation of procurement contracts or revocation of licenses.

SUBSIDIES AS INCENTIVES TO FAIR EMPLOYMENT

While FEP laws emphasize voluntary compliance, the underlying incentives are basically negative, since they provide for penalties for persistent noncompliance. There is no positive inducement for employers to employ more Negroes or to give them access to traditionally "white" jobs.

Proposals for utilizing positive incentives as means of reducing employment discrimination include subsidies to defray the cost of special training programs and subsidies to facilitate the establishment of plants in areas having large Negro populations.

A program of skill improvement, supported in part by payments to employers who undertake specified training responsibilities on their own or in conjunction with local school systems, might be feasible. Such a program should have as its primary objective improving the skills of the uneducated and under-utilized segments of the labor force without regard to race. Because Negroes are a disproportionate part of these segments of the labor force, they would benefit from such a program more than other groups. Negroes who participated in special employer-sponsored training programs would be in a better position to compete on equal terms with whites in the labor market. Such a program would entail serious administrative difficulties, however; and it would therefore probably be more efficient to utilize public educational and retraining programs to improve the skills of marginal elements in the labor force instead of approaching the problem through employers. The recently enacted Federal Manpower Development and Retraining Act is a notable step in this direction.

Subsidies might also be used to induce employers to establish plants in areas of high Negro concentration, especially in the South. On the local community or state level, subsidies might be used to facilitate voluntary movement of Negroes out of the South to Northern communities where they are small fractions of the population. Of the two, the subsidization of outmigration is potentially the more desirable from the viewpoint of the general public interest. A reduction of the concentration of Negroes in the South might well decrease the resistance of Southern whites to measures intended to improve the status of Negroes remaining in the South.

Despite the heavy emigration of Southern Negroes in recent decades, they still represent a much larger fraction of the population of the South than of any other region.[37] A redistribution of the nation's Negro population on a scale sufficient to equalize the proportions of Negroes living in the South and the North would require movement from the South of about 6 million Negroes, or somewhat more than one-half of the South's present Negro population. Migration on such a large scale is obviously out of the question as a short-run solution to Negro employment problems. The employment problems of Southern Negroes can be attacked more readily by means of FEP laws than by measures intended to result in a radical redistribution of the nation's Negro population.

None of the incentives sketched above could be utilized on a sufficiently large scale to improve Negro employment opportuni-

[37] See Chapter 4.

ties without additional legislation. As a practical matter, passage of such legislation would involve almost as many difficulties as enactment of enforceable Federal FEP legislation. For this reason and because of the administrative difficulties presented by such programs, we conclude that employment incentives are not realistic alternatives to FEP legislation.

Boycotts and Job Discrimination

Over the past several years Negro groups in a number of Northern and Southern cities have sought to obtain more and better jobs for members of their race through boycotts, picketing, and other types of collective action. The largest and best-organized of these actions was a boycott program launched early in 1960 by the ministers of about 400 Negro churches in Philadelphia. During the ensuing year, a committee of the Negro ministers met successively with managements of various baking, soft drink, gasoline, and other consumer goods concerns and demanded that they hire specified numbers of Negroes for office work, trucking, and other traditionally all-white jobs. The ministers backed up their demands by threatening to call boycotts against the respective companies' products. Boycotts were actually instituted against several companies which resisted the demands and were so effective that the demurring managements soon capitulated. In the remaining instances, the issue was settled through conference and compromise, with the employers offering concessions which the ministers agreed to accept without invoking the boycott weapon.[38] Similar programs have been instituted more recently in several other Northern cities. Job-demand boycotts have also been conducted in various communities in the South—usually against department stores or other retail establishments.[39]

[38] Hannah Lees, "The Not-Buying Power of Philadelphia's Negroes," *The Reporter*, May 11, 1963, pp. 33–35.
[39] *Wall Street Journal*, January 7, 1963, p. 1.

Despite the effectiveness of the Philadelphia program, it is highly unlikely that use of the boycott could ever lead to any significant aggregate improvement in the Negro group's occupational status. The device can be effectively utilized only against makers of locally produced consumer goods readily identifiable by their brand names and against retail and service establishments patronized largely by Negroes. It would obviously be unworkable in such industries as steel, chemicals, or textiles, or even—unless nationally organized—against producers of automobiles or other durable consumer products. Moreover, to bring about an appreciable aggregative upgrading of Negro status, even within the limited sphere of branded consumables and local retail enterprises, would require an extended series of successive boycott actions conducted over a period of several years. The degree of mass discipline shown by the Philadelphia Negroes has seldom been demonstrated in any other Negro community; and it is highly doubtful that such discipline could be sustained over an extended period of years, either in Philadelphia or elsewhere. It is even more doubtful that an effective Negro boycott could be organized and sustained on a national scale. In short, the boycott, even at its most effective, can hardly be considered more than a localized, limited-coverage, and highly uncertain partial substitute for enforceable FEP legislation.

10

IMPLICATIONS OF
FAIR EMPLOYMENT EXPERIENCE FOR
FUTURE POLICY AND PRACTICE

In the preceding five chapters we have presented and analyzed in some detail the results of the intensive inquiry into the various types of governmental antidiscrimination measures and agencies which constituted the central subject area of the study. In the present chapter the major findings emerging from the detailed analysis of the several types of local, state, and Federal programs and agencies are summarized and arranged in a logical sequence. This coordinated summary of findings has a twofold purpose: to provide a brief but comprehensive overview, in appropriate perspective, of the entire array of experience under all existing and past governmental FEP measures and to establish a suitable basis for examining the implications of the study findings for improving existing FEP laws and developing more effective approaches to the employment discrimination problem. The chapter concludes with a brief discussion of the prospects, in terms of political feasibility, of extending FEP legislation to additional states and cities and of obtaining passage of a comprehensive Federal FEP law.

Implications of Previous Experience

NON-ENFORCEABLE FEP LAWS AND VOLUNTARY PROGRAMS

Neither non-enforceable FEP laws nor voluntary FEP programs have had any appreciable effect in reducing employment discrimination. The City of Baltimore experimented for a time with an ordinance that did not contain enforcement provisions. It was replaced with an enforceable ordinance when it became apparent that little progress could be made on a voluntary basis. When the Commission lacked enforcement powers, its negotiations with Baltimore banks were fruitless. The banks sent representatives to a meeting sponsored by the Commission; but the representatives refused to make any commitments, and the banks continued their past practice of excluding Negroes from clerical jobs.[1] The Baltimore FEP Commission also conducted negotiations with retail establishments to no avail when it lacked enforcement powers. In one particularly difficult case, the Commission scheduled a public hearing; but the employer refused to attend, and the Commission was powerless to enforce its decision in the case. Shortly after the ordinance was amended to provide penalties for violation, the Commission was able to require the employer who was the respondent in this case to eliminate his discriminatory practices.[2] At about the same time, the Commission also succeeded in persuading several banks to begin to employ Negroes in clerical positions.

Experience under a non-enforceable Kansas FEP act from 1953 to 1960 was much the same as that in Baltimore. Only eighty-nine complaints were filed with the Kansas commission over a period of eight years. Only twenty of these complaints could be adjusted satisfactorily. Respondents would not cooperate with the commission in twenty-four cases.[3] The Indiana Civil Rights Commission, which has administered a non-enforceable law since 1945, concluded its 1963 report with a recommendation that an enforceable civil rights law be enacted by the state. The commission noted that "the one public hearing held by the commission . . . resulted in a unanimous finding of discrimination. The hearing and its find-

[1] Baltimore Equal Employment Opportunity Commission, *1960 Annual Report* (Baltimore, 1961), p. 2.

[2] Baltimore Equal Employment Opportunity Commission, *1959 Annual Report* (Baltimore, 1960), p. 8.

[3] Kansas Anti-Discrimination Commission, *1961 Report of Progress* (Topeka, 1961), p. 11.

ings were completely ignored by the respondent who realized the law was without enforcement provisions." [4]

The City of Cleveland experimented for a time with a completely voluntary FEP program before adopting an ordinance forbidding discrimination. This program, called the Cooperative Employment Practices Plan, was established in 1949. The Cleveland Chamber of Commerce suggested such an approach as a substitute for a proposed local FEP ordinance. After about a year of experience, it was generally conceded that the Plan had failed to effect a significant change in the practices of many employers, labor unions, and employment agencies. Cleveland adopted an enforceable ordinance in 1950 with the support of the local Chamber of Commerce.[5] The episode indicates that voluntary programs are unlikely to attain their objectives.

In the states that have enforceable FEP laws, there has been little overt opposition to commission actions. In cases where resistance has been encountered, enforcement proceedings have usually led to compliance. We conclude that enforceability is the first prerequisite to an effective FEP law.

FEDERAL FAIR EMPLOYMENT PROGRAMS

The need for enforceable FEP statutes, administered in such a way as to encourage and facilitate employment of Negroes in nontraditional jobs, is shown by developments in the use of Negroes in the armed forces, in Federal civilian establishments, and in Federal contractor plants.

In the case of the Federal civil service, there has been a statutory provision prohibiting discrimination in employment on the basis of race since 1940. The President, as constitutional Com-

[4] Indiana Civil Rights Commission, *Toward Equal Opportunity, 1963 Report* (Indianapolis, 1963), p. 12.

[5] Morroe Berger, *Racial Equality and the Law—The Role of Law in the Reduction of Discrimination in the United States* (Paris, United Nations Educational Scientific and Cultural Organization, 1954), pp. 63–64.

mander-in-Chief of the armed forces, was free to impose a non-discriminatory manpower policy on the military services. In both the armed forces and the civil service, Negroes were able to secure a larger number of employment opportunities when discriminatory practices were forbidden and efforts were made, albeit on a modest scale, to enforce the prohibition.

In the case of the armed forces, overt discrimination and segregation ended within a few years after the issuance in 1948 of President Truman's executive order banning discrimination, but little was done to assure observance of equal opportunity. The armed forces acted on the assumption that abolition of segregated military units, racial quotas, and separate facilities was a sufficient response to the President's statement of policy. No positive efforts were made to increase participation of Negroes in the armed forces.

Despite the absence of any affirmative program for implementing the President's policy, however, racial employment patterns in the armed forces have changed sharply since the Truman order was issued. Subordinate Federal military officers realized that overt opposition to the President's policy might lead to unpleasant consequences. When formal discriminatory practices were abandoned by the armed forces, Negroes were able to advance on their merits, largely because informal arrangements that frequently support discriminatory racial employment patterns are less feasible in the military services than in private life. Negroes came into the military services in increasing numbers when equal opportunity became government policy. Negro military personnel are still concentrated to some extent in low-level military occupations, but a substantial number are employed in skilled craft and technical occupations.

In the civil service, complaint procedures were established, but their very existence was unknown to many Negro applicants for employment or promotion. Only modest efforts were made to monitor Federal agency employment patterns by race and occupation. Surveys of Negro employment were conducted in five cities by Eisenhower's Committee on Government Employment Policy.

Although the results indicated that Negroes were concentrated in the lowest ranks of the Federal civil services, no systematic efforts were made to review agency recruitment, hiring, training, and promotion practices. Nevertheless, Negroes have obtained an increasing share of civil service jobs, both quantitatively and qualitatively, in recent years. Data from the decennial Censuses of population show that, while total Federal employment increased by about 25 percent between 1950 and 1960, Negro employment increased by well over 50 percent. While the increase was less marked in the South than in the North and West, Negroes made considerable job progress in Federal civilian establishments located in the Southern states. It seems clear that the proscription of racial discrimination in the Civil Service Act, coupled with a system of executive authority stemming directly from the President, has been the main impetus behind the improvement.

Racial integration on the job in Federal civilian establishments and military units has not been followed by any of the increases in racial conflict commonly predicted by opponents of changes in racial employment practices. In recent years, Negroes have begun to move up into supervisory positions where they direct the activities of integrated work crews and military units. There is no evidence of overt racial conflict in such situations. All in all, the developments in the Federal services support the view that a Federal FEP law could be effective in reducing discrimination in employment and that it could be enforced without undue difficulty, even in the South.

In the plants of Federal contractors, matters were quite different than they were in the armed forces and the civil service. Between 1941 and 1961, FEP committees appointed by the President were unable to effect a significant improvement in the racial practices of Federal contractors or of labor unions that represented their employees. The prohibition of discriminatory employment practices contained in Federal procurement contracts could not be made effective, because suitable enforcement techniques were not available to the presidential contract committees. Contract cancellation and debarment are awkward and clumsy means of enforcing a fair employment policy and conflict with other government objectives, such as timely and inexpensive procurement of supplies and services. In practice these difficulties have proven so formidable that the Federal government has never canceled a contract with one of its suppliers for violation of the nondiscrimination clause contained in all procurement contracts.

During the Eisenhower administration, the Federal contract committee apparently suffered from a failure of will. It frequently took refuge in technicalities as a means of avoiding its responsibilities. Enforcement of the nondiscrimination clause in Federal contracts was not attempted in any meaningful way during Eisenhower's years in office. The Kennedy committee has given greater attention to enforcement problems than its predecessor, but its experience is too brief to permit evaluation.

There is little reason to expect that further attempts to change the racial practices of private employers or of labor unions via enforcement of a clause in Federal procurement contracts will be more successful than those of the past. An executive order is a poor substitute for a statute in the area of private employment when the subject matter of the order is as controversial as racial employment practices. In the private sphere, in contrast to the course followed in the Federal services, Presidents have been unwilling, or unable, to enforce effectively fair employment practices prescribed in their executive orders. A Federal FEP statute, applicable to interstate commerce, would provide remedies not available under executive orders.

STATE AND MUNICIPAL FEP LAWS

The FEP laws in effect in most Northern and Western states and in several major Nothern cities have up to now resulted in only a very modest and spotty decrease in discriminatory employment practices. Nevertheless, the analysis of experience under these laws demonstrates that enforceable FEP legislation, if properly designed and wisely administered, can be an effective means of combating racial discrimination in employment.

Most existing FEP laws specify only one approach to enforcement, namely, through the filing of complaints by aggrieved individuals. The administering commissions, it is true, do possess the potential power to deal with general discriminatory practices when investigation of individual complaints reveals their existence. The commissions are required to give individuals' grievances first priority, however; and since the great majority of commissions operate on very limited budgets, they are forced to devote most of their resources to processing and adjusting complaints.

Manifestly, if the administering agencies could focus their efforts on discriminatory employment policies and general practices rather than on individual complaints, they would be able to perform their compliance function far more efficiently. A few commissions, notably those in New York State, New Jersey, and Philadelphia, have given increasing attention to this "pattern-centered" approach. In their earlier years even these agencies did little more than adjust complaints, but it soon became apparent that no more than token progress was possible under a complaint-centered approach. As their budgets and staffs were augmented, these agencies began to direct more efforts toward eliminating discriminatory employment practices and patterns.

The New York State Commission, in particular, has devoted a substantial proportion of its efforts to pattern-centered compliance activities. In dealing with individual complaints, it has frequently insisted that noncomplying employers agree to revise their over-all policies and practices and has conducted periodic follow-up surveys to assure observance of these commitments. The New York Commission has also, in many instances, dealt directly with discriminatory employment patterns through informal investigations and surveys—sometimes on its own initiative, though more usually at the behest of private civil rights organizations. While it does not have enforceable jurisdiction in informal investigation cases, the Commission has nonetheless succeeded in opening up many new employment opportunities to Negroes and other minorities through the use of this device.

The Philadelphia Commission on Human Relations, the New Jersey Division Against Discrimination, and, to a lesser extent, several other relatively long-established FEP agencies have also placed increasing emphasis on pattern-centered compliance efforts in recent years. The Philadelphia Commission, unlike most of its city and state counterparts, is empowered by its statute to institute enforceable compliance action on its own initiative—a feature that has proved definitely advantageous, since it has enabled the Commission to direct its major efforts toward industries and occupations characterized by especially pervasive discriminatory practices.

In negotiating compliance settlements on a pattern basis, several of the longer-established commissions have adopted the policy of seeking commitments from noncomplying employers that they will go beyond the bare statutory requirements and make affirmative efforts to employ Negroes in nontraditional jobs. Even in states where the policy is not actually being implemented, most commission officials agree that this "affirmative action" approach is essential to the achievement of any substantial progress toward real equality of employment opportunity.

Discriminatory practices by employment agencies and by certain types of labor unions have posed particularly difficult compliance problems for state and local FEP commissions, and their record of accomplishment in these two areas is far from impressive. The widespread exclusion of Negroes from membership by unions in a number of skilled crafts and the equally prevalent discrimination in job referrals by unions in other crafts have proved especially troublesome, primarily because these practices are often strongly supported by the rank-and-file members of these unions. As a result, the commissions have seldom made any positive efforts to bring these unions into compliance. Even the New York State Commission has made only token progress in this area.

Despite this meager achievement in dealing with noncomplying unions, however, the New York Commission, through its pattern-centered compliance activities, has undoubtedly brought about a substantial aggregate reduction in employment discrimination over the period since its establishment. This conclusion is supported by the marked improvement in the occupational status of Negroes in the state during the past decade and a half. The efficacy of the pattern-centered approach is further attested by the more modest but none the less noteworthy occupational progress of Negroes in New Jersey and Philadelphia over the same period. While labor market conditions, improved education of Negro youth, and other circumstances have no doubt also played a part, the evidence is strong that the efforts of the commissions have been the major contributing factor.

In sum, there are good grounds for believing that FEP legislation can be a potent instrumentality for insuring fair treatment of minorities in the job market and the work place, provided the administering agencies are given sufficiently broad and flexible powers and supplied with adequate funds to function efficiently and provided they follow sound policies and tested procedures in securing compliance. Proposals for improving existing and future FEP laws and their administration, based on our analysis of experience under FEP measures at all three levels of government, are outlined in the two concluding chapters of this volume.

The Need for Federal Legislation

A Federal FEP law, designed to give primary attention to employment patterns, would be an effective means of reducing job discrimination over the nation as a whole. As matters stand at present, while discriminatory employment practices are unlawful in most Northern states, legal remedies are almost nonexistent in the South. More than half the nation's Negro citizens have no effective means of securing relief from discrimination in employment. The President's Committee on Equal Employment Opportunity—the only existing fair employment agency whose jurisdiction includes the South—is confined to dealing with Federal contract employment situations and even within this limited sphere lacks practicable enforcement powers. Moreover, while enactment of FEP laws may soon be politically feasible in several major municipalities in the South, there is little likelihood that this change will occur in Southern cities generally nor that any Southern states will adopt such legislation in the near future.

A Federal FEP law would fill the major portion of the existing lack in the South, although there would still be a need for state laws to deal with purely intrastate situations. Indeed, with respect to most interstate employment, Federal legislation would undoubtedly be more effective than either state or municipal laws. Large business enterprise is organized predominantly on national and multiregional lines, with final decision-making authority vested in top management. Hence, fair employment compliance negotiations involving such enterprises could be best conducted by a Federal agency, dealing with managements at the national level. A Federal agency would also be more effective than state or municipal agencies in dealing with the widespread problem of discrimination in the operation of state public employment offices, since these offices are supported entirely by Federal funds.

This is not intended to mean that Federal FEP legislation should pre-empt or replace existing state and municipal laws. On the contrary, through appropriate provision for Federal-state and Federal-municipal agreements for sharing of jurisdiction and cooperation in compliance activities, the Federal law could serve to reinforce and facilitate the compliance efforts of the state and local FEP agencies. The salient provisions of a proposed Federal FEP law, including a suggested arrangement for Federal-state and Federal-municipal cooperation, are outlined in Chapter 11.

The Outlook for Further FEP Legislation

In the absence of a Federal FEP statute, state laws and municipal ordinances can be used to deal with problems raised by discriminatory employment practices. Since virtually all Northern and Western states having any serious employment discrimination problems have already adopted enforceable FEP laws, the question of whether further extension of such legislation is feasible—at any level of government—focuses chiefly on the South. Over the period 1945–63 twenty-two states, all in the North and West except Delaware, adopted enforceable FEP laws. On the other hand, no FEP laws or agencies operated in the South during this period. Nor—except in a few rare instances—has FEP legislation been seriously proposed in Southern states or cities. Over the same period, numerous proposals for Federal FEP legislation have been introduced in Congress, but none has been enacted into law and only one—a weak advisory bill passed by the House of Representatives in 1952—has been approved by even one branch of the national legislature.

In a number of Northern states, FEP laws were enacted following a substantial increase in the number of Negro voters. In the Midwestern states of Illinois, Michigan, and Ohio, for example, FEP laws were adopted when the Negro population increased to about 10 percent of the total state population. Major increases in the Negro populations of a number of cities, notably Baltimore, Cleveland, Philadelphia, and Pittsburgh, were also followed by passage of municipal FEP ordinances.

It is thus apparent that the likelihood of FEP legislation being established anywhere in the South depends largely on whether the Negro vote can be increased sufficiently to bring about its enactment. In appraising the prospects in this regard, it will be useful to review the recent trend and current developments in Negro voting registration in Southern states and cities.

Up to 1944, fewer than 150,000 Negroes were registered for voting in the entire South. The invalidation of the white primary by the Supreme Court in that year removed a major barrier to

Table 10.1

PERCENTAGE OF NEGROES IN TOTAL VOTING-AGE POPULATION
AND IN TOTAL VOTING REGISTRATION

	NEGRO AS PERCENTAGE OF TOTAL VOTING-AGE POPULATION		NEGRO AS PERCENTAGE OF TOTAL VOTING REGISTRATION	
	1947	*1961*	*1947*	*1961*
Alabama	30	26	1	7
Arkansas	21	19	7	12
Florida	20	14	5	9
Georgia	28	25	11	13
Louisiana	30	29	1	14
Mississippi	41	36	1	5
North Carolina	24	22	6	14[a]
South Carolina	34	29	8	11
Tennessee	16	15	6	13
Texas	12	12	3	9
Virginia	21	19	4	10[a]

Sources: Florence B. Irving, "The Future of the Negro Voter in the South," *Journal of Negro Education*, XXV (1957), 390–407 (estimates of Negro registration by the Southern Regional Council, based on county surveys); U.S. Commission on Civil Rights, *1961 Report:* Book I, *Voting;* U.S. Bureau of the Census, *Census of Population, 1940, 1950, 1960.*

[a] Estimated from data on voting and registration of whites and nonwhites in the U.S. Commission on Civil Rights 1961 Report on Voting. The recorded figures yield a Negro percentage for North Carolina of 10.3 percent and for Tennessee 11 percent. Both percentages substantially understate the actual Negro voting strength, however, owing to the heavy "padding" of white registration rolls with voters who have died or moved out of the state.

Negro voting. By 1947, Negro registration in the South as a whole had more than quadrupled. By 1961, the number of Southern Negro registrants had tripled again, to a total of nearly 1,500,000. Such a total by itself, however, is of little help in judging whether the Negro's ballot-box power increased over this period. A more meaningful picture can be obtained by observing how Negro registration as a percentage of total registration changed over the fourteen-year interval. This is shown, for each of the eleven states comprising the "South proper" in Table 10.1.

Negro voting registration percentages increased markedly in all eleven states between 1947 and 1961. While the 1961 registration percentages still fell considerably short of the potential percentages, in five of the states (Arkansas, Georgia, Louisiana, North Carolina, and Tennessee) they ranged from 12 to 14 percent—a voting strength magnitude approaching balance-of-power proportions with respect to many issues in the South.

In all likelihood, FEP legislation will become politically feasible at the municipal level sooner than at the state level, since present Negro voting strength is concentrated largely in certain major cities, mainly in the upper South. Thus, for example, in 1961 Negro voters constituted 31 percent of the total registration in Memphis, 25 percent in Atlanta, 22 percent in Durham, 23 percent in Richmond, and 17 percent in New Orleans. When one considers that approval of enforceable FEP legislation was obtained in Baltimore when the Negro voting ratio in that city reached 27 percent, it is apparent that serious efforts to enact such legislation will soon be feasible in these cities, as well as in several others where Negroes have attained comparable voting strength. Indeed, the first results of such efforts are already in evidence. Within the past year two Southern cities—Richmond and El Paso—have enacted ordinances prohibiting racial discrimination in municipal employment.

The growing strength of the Negro vote has as yet had little practical effect at the state level. Many Southern state legislatures are dominated by sparsely populated rural counties, where the Negro vote is weakest. This situation may, however, undergo a radical change in the not-too-distant future, as a result of the U.S. Supreme Court's "reapportionment decision" of March 26, 1962. In effect, this decision requires states with rurally dominated legislatures to revise their legislative districts to give fairer representation to urban areas. As this is being written, four Southern states—Alabama, Georgia, Mississippi, and Tennessee—are either in process of redistricting or have been ordered to do so by Federal courts. The other states may follow suit when their legislatures convene again. The effect of such redistricting will be to make the Negro vote more potent at the state level and thus hasten the day when state FEP legislation can be seriously proposed in the South.

The growing Southern Negro vote will also, in due course, enhance the prospects for enactment of Federal FEP legislation.[6] Three main circumstances in the current Congressional situation prevent the passage of a national FEP statute: (1) incumbent Senators representing the Southern states are committed to resist such legislation, (2) a Senate rule requires a two-thirds majority of attending senators to terminate debate on legislative proposals under consideration, and (3) Senators from Northern states with negligible Negro populations frequently support Southern Senators in their opposition to cloture of debate.

Since the term of Senators is six years, it will be some time before the recent and prospective increases in Southern Negro voting strength can exert sufficient influence on the political situation in the Southern states to bring about either a shift to candidates more sympathetic to FEP legislation or a change in attitude on the part of incumbent Senators. Such a shift may be expected to occur within the foreseeable future, however, at least in the five or six

[6] Proposals for Federal FEP legislation have been introduced in nearly every session of Congress since the early 1940s, but none has had any real chance of being enacted into law. A weak bill, providing for "advisory" strictures against job discrimination, passed the House of Representatives in 1949, but was killed by a filibuster in the Senate. A civil rights "package" bill, including a proposal for enforceable FEP legislation, was reported out by the House Judiciary Committee in October, 1963; and was passed by the House on February 10, 1964. As this is written (March, 1964), the leaders of the Southern contingent in the Senate are, however, preparing to launch an all-out filibuster aimed at defeating it, and the prospects that it will pass that body are decidedly less favorable.

states where Negro voting strength already approaches balance-of-power magnitude. In this event, the present seemingly insurmountable barrier to the enactment of Federal FEP legislation would be removed, for it is highly unlikely that the Senators from the remaining Southern states could conduct a successful filibuster against such legislation.

There has been relatively little employer opposition to enactment of FEP laws. Many employers have cited state and local laws as a justification for opening a wider range of occupations to Negroes. National and state labor organizations have advocated the passage of Federal and state legislation. Such labor organizations have referred to FEP laws when advocating liberalization of local union racial practices. These considerations suggest that increasing Negro political power can be utilized to secure passage of enforceable FEP legislation without serious opposition from spokesmen for management and labor.

PART THREE

A Program for
Public Fair Employment Policy
and Action

11

PROPOSALS FOR FAIR EMPLOYMENT
PRACTICE LEGISLATION

The account of recent and prospective gains in Negro political power in the preceding chapter indicates that extension of enforceable FEP legislation beyond its present confines in the North and West will soon become a practicable possibility in several large Southern cities, in certain states in the upper South, and at the Federal government level. This assessment lends added significance to our earlier conclusion that legislation is necessary in order to deal effectively with the problem of racial discrimination in employment, since it indicates that application of such legislation to all areas of prevalent employment discrimination is an attainable goal.

As the concluding phase of the project, therefore, we have developed proposals for legislation and governmental action based on the findings of the study. The proposals are presented under the following three headings—the first two in the present chapter and the third in Chapter 12: proposals for strengthening and standardizing state and municipal FEP laws, proposed provisions for a Federal FEP law, and guide lines for improving administration of FEP laws. In developing these proposals, we have not intended to attribute superior merit to Federal action over state or municipal action—or vice versa. The purpose has been, rather, to translate the findings and conclusions of the study in terms and in a form that will aid legislative and administrative leaders at all levels of government in formulating programs to resolve major problems of employment discrimination.

These proposed programs, as will be shown, are mutually consistent. Formulation and enactment of municipal, state, and Federal legislation could proceed simultaneously without any resultant conflict of public policy or serious duplication of coverage—although it is more likely that legislative action at the three levels will occur successively. Moreover, the proposed Federal legislative program would not conflict with existing state and municipal laws.

Strengthening and Standardizing State and Municipal FEP Laws

This section comprises a series of suggested amendments to existing enforceable state and municipal FEP laws—which would also be applicable to any such laws enacted in the future. The need for these amendments derives in part from the need for improving the effectiveness of commissions in states and cities already possessing enforceable laws and in part from the necessity of dealing with discrimination problems which are peculiar to the South. From a somewhat different viewpoint, the study indicates a need to amend existing state and municipal laws in two ways: to incorporate certain advantageous legislative and administrative features now found in one or a few of the laws into all existing and future state and municipal laws and to incorporate in these laws certain additional features not now found in any state or municipal statute. In delineating and discussing the proposed amendments, we take as our basis of reference the summary of the salient provisions of existing laws in Chapter 5.

While most of the existing laws are basically similar, there are many variations in detail among them, with respect both to substantive content and to administrative procedures and practices. Upon analysis, however, it appears both practicable and desirable to draft a single prototype law, uniform for all jurisdictions with respect to all major substantive and procedural provisions except the number of commissioners and the size of administrative budgets and staffs.

A proposal outlining the essential provisions of such a prototype law is set forth below, including proposed revisions and amendments to the existing laws, as well as the provisions which it is proposed to retain in their present form. In line with the division and arrangement of subject matter in most of the state and local statutes, the model law is outlined and discussed under six headings, as follows: (1) declaration of unlawful discriminatory practices, (2) composition and functions of the commission, (3) staffing and compensation, (4) powers of the commission, (5) procedures in invoking the law and obtaining voluntary compliance, (6) procedures for enforcement.

DECLARATION OF UNLAWFUL DISCRIMINATORY PRACTICES

As noted in Chapter 5, most of the existing laws follow closely the declaration of unlawful practices in the New York State law. This declaration explicitly identifies only the more common unfair practices—e.g., discriminatory hiring and discharge by employers, discriminatory exclusion and expulsion from membership by unions, and discriminatory advertising and employment application questions by employers and employment agencies—the less common practices being forbidden only by inference or implication. While the New York State and some of the other commissions operating under this declaration have interpreted it to include a broader range of discriminatory employment practices, there is none the less considerable doubt as to whether certain obviously unfair practices are covered. A more explicit identification of these practices is needed to assure comprehensive protection against employment discrimination. A proposed prototype identification of unlawful discriminatory practices is set forth below in summary terms. Since it is obviously not possible to list all discriminatory practices that might be devised, a provision should be added stating that the practices which are prohibited under the act are not limited to those listed. For the sake of brevity, the term "race, etc."

is substituted for "race, color, religion, national origin, or ancestry" in each of the proposed identification items.

It should be declared unlawful:

1. For an employer to refuse to hire any individual or to discharge, segregate, or otherwise discriminate against any employee on grounds of race, etc.

2. For a labor union to exclude or expel any individual from membership or to segregate or classify its membership in any way on the basis of race, etc.

3. For an employer, union, or union-employer apprenticeship committee to debar any individual from an apprentice or other training program on grounds of race, etc.

4. For an employment agency or a labor union performing employment agency functions to refuse to refer any individual for employment because of his race, etc., or to refer any individual for employment on the basis of his race, etc.

5. For an employer, union or employment agency to issue advertisements indicating any preference in applicants based on race, etc.; to keep records of the race, etc., of applicants; to announce any policy of denying employment or admission on grounds of race, etc.; or to discriminate against any person for filing charges under the Act.

6. For an employer and a union to make any agreement requiring or permitting any unlawful act listed in the foregoing items.

COMPOSITION AND FUNCTIONS OF THE COMMISSION

The New York State Commission on Human Rights is unique among FEP commissions with respect to several important features of composition, organization, and manner of functioning. In the first place, it is the only commission with as many as seven members, all serving on a full-time basis. Second, it is the only commission in which the salary paid to commission members ($19,500 per year) is reasonably adequate to attract persons with the requisite qualifications in terms of knowledge, experience, and judgment to deal successfully with difficult minority group employment discrimination problems—a fact which largely explains why the average caliber of Commissioners has been and still is considerably higher in New York than in any other state. Third, it is one of only four states in which the individual Commissioners personally conduct conciliation-compliance efforts; and among these it is the only one in which the Commissioners, in their capacity as conciliators, are provided with sufficient professional staff assistance (field representatives) to assure adequate prior investigations of complainants' allegations and minority-group employment patterns and to make periodic post-settlement surveys to ascertain the extent of compliance.

The analysis of nonwhite employment trends in Chapter 6 indicates that there is a close relationship between the New York Commission's approach to the conciliation-compliance function and the notably greater occupational progress achieved by Negroes in New York State than elsewhere. There is, therefore, a strong case for taking the New York State Commission as a model in drafting the provisions in the prototype law defining the composition, organization, and functioning of the administering commission. The one necessary departure from this is that the number of full-time commissioners needed to assure adequate administration of FEP laws will vary from state to state and will depend primarily on the magnitude of the employment discrimination problem in the particular state. This in turn will depend chiefly on the size of the state's population, the proportion of Negroes and other minority groups in the population, the extent to which the state's economy is industrialized and commercialized, and the occupational status of Negroes and other minority groups existing at the time the law becomes effective. Thus, if New York's present complement of seven full-time commissioners is regarded as reasonably adequate to cope with that state's employment discrimination problem, other highly industrialized states such as Illinois and Ohio, with smaller populations but with Negro populations comparable to New York's, would probably need four or five full-time commissioners each. On the other hand, such states as Iowa and Kansas, with relatively little industry and small Negro populations, would probably need only a single full-time commissioner.

It is proposed that existing state and municipal FEP laws be amended and future laws formulated:

1. To provide that the commissioners comprising the administering commission shall serve on a full-time basis.

2. To provide that the commission shall consist of a specified number of commissioners (and size of supporting staff) proportioned to the magnitude of the state's or municipality's employment discrimination problem. (Suggested range of number of commissioners: from a single commissioner in jurisdictions with relatively small work loads to seven commissioners in those with the largest work loads.)

3. To retain the method of appointing commissioners and commission chairmen provided for in most existing FEP laws, namely, nomination by the governor or mayor, as the case may be, and approval by the appropriate legislative body.

4. To define the principal functions of the commission, along the following lines:

(a) Acting as a plenary body, the commission should be given responsibility for setting commission policies, for promulgating operating rules and regulations, and for making final decisions on questions of cease-and-desist order action in cases not settled through conciliation.

(b) The handling of all compliance cases through the investigation and conciliation stages should be made the responsibility of individual commissioners, and the chairman should be made responsible for assigning commissioners to compliance cases.

(c) Responsibility for conducting public hearings in cases not settled through conciliation should be assigned to hearing panels composed of two or three commissioners (or to a single commissioner, in states with small commissions) to be designated by the chairman.

STAFFING AND COMPENSATION

It is proposed that existing state and municipal FEP laws (where necessary) be amended and future laws formulated:

1. To provide for the appointment by the commission chairman, in accordance with the relevant civil service laws and regulations, of adequate professional, administrative, and clerical staffs to enable the commission to carry out the purposes of the act in an effective manner.

2. To provide (in states having large and geographically dispersed FEP work loads) for appropriate regional offices.

3. To provide that the commission chairman shall be responsible for the administrative operations of the commission.

4. To specify a salary for commissioners commensurate with the qualifications required for effective performance in carrying out the purposes of the law. (Suggested salary for commissioners: $20,000 a year; somewhat higher for commission chairmen, with a range of increments proportionate to the administrative responsibilities involved.)

The actual amounts of money provided for paying salaries and other operating expenses are seldom specified in the formal text of FEP laws. Customarily these funds are determined through annual or biennial appropriations by the respective state or municipal legislative bodies. Guide lines for municipal, state, and national legislatures in appropriating funds for the operation of FEP commissions are set forth in Chapter 12.

POWERS OF THE COMMISSION

Nearly all state and municipal FEP laws have certain provisions in common which endow the respective commissions with specifically defined "operating" powers. These powers are clearly necessary to the effective functioning of the commissions. Accordingly, it is recommended that they be retained without change in the prototype law.

The essential substance of these powers may be summarized as follows:

1. To receive, investigate, and act upon complaints filed by individuals in which the complainants allege that they have been discriminated against, in violation of the act, by employers, labor unions, employment agencies, or joint union-employer apprenticeship councils.

2. To hold hearings, subpoena witnesses and compel their attendance, take the testimony of witnesses under oath, and in connection therewith require the production of any books or papers relating to any matter under investigation or in question before the commission. Persons failing to obey commission subpoenas are subject to contempt action, usually by the appropriate county court.

3. To make such technical studies as are needed to effectuate the purposes of the law, and in its discretion to make the results of such studies available to other government agencies or to the general public.

As the first provision indicates, under most of the state and municipal FEP laws the commissions are empowered to deal only with complaints filed by individuals alleging discrimination against themselves. In only two states (Ohio and Rhode Island) and one city (Philadelphia) are the commissions empowered to deal with complaints filed by individuals or organizations on behalf of *other* individuals or groups that are victims of employment discrimination. Thus only these three commissions have explicit "enforceable jurisdiction" over complaints concerning discriminatory *patterns* of employment or concerning pervasive discrimination by unions or employment agencies as distinct from discrimination against single individuals. Yet our study of commission experience has shown that commissions can achieve far greater results by emphasizing pattern-centered compliance activities than by concentrating on the adjustment of individual complaints. And it is hardly necessary to point out that the NAACP, the Urban League, and other organizations primarily concerned with combatting discrimination and fostering civil rights are far better informed concerning the existence of discriminatory employment pattern situations than any individual job seeker or employee and are also in a better position to initiate and follow through on complaint actions in such situations.

Provisions empowering the commission itself to initiate complaints are likewise found in only a few FEP laws. Three state laws which limit the commissions to handling "individual" complaints have such provisions, as do also the aforementioned Ohio, Rhode Island, and Philadelphia laws, which as noted also empower the commissions to handle "pattern" complaints. In all the remaining states with FEP laws, however, the commissions are without power to initiate complaints. Yet on this score, also, it is clear that commissions can be more effective if they are given wide discretion in selecting areas of emphasis in their compliance activities.

In sum, the analysis of study findings shows that fair employment commissions can achieve the greatest aggregate results if they possess the power to receive and act upon complaints filed by organizations and to institute complaint actions on their own initiative, and if both of these powers apply to complaints involving discriminatory employment patterns—embracing entire plants, companies, local union organizations, etc.—as well as to complaints alleging discrimination against individual persons.

It is proposed that existing FEP laws be amended (and future laws formulated) to give commissions the following powers, in addition to the already widely-established powers outlined above.

4. The power to receive, investigate, and act upon complaints concerning discriminatory employment practices filed by organizations on behalf of aggrieved individuals or groups of persons.

5. The power to initiate complaints on behalf of aggrieved individuals or aggregations of persons or with respect to generally applicable unlawful policies and practices of employers, labor unions, and employment agencies.

PROCEDURES IN INVOKING AND OBTAINING VOLUNTARY
COMPLIANCE WITH FEP LAWS

As noted earlier, the essential steps of the complaint-processing procedure outlined in the statutes are substantially the same in most of the state laws, although there are significant differences in the details of procedure among the commissions. These basic steps— and also the major procedural details, as exemplified in the New York State Commission's practice—are described in Chapter 5.

Since some variations in the detailed investigation-conciliation procedures of different states will be necessary, even under a uniform prototype law, the section of the law itself dealing with this procedure should be confined to a statement of the essential steps, leaving the details of procedure to be dealt with in the administrative regulations or to the discretion of the commission. The following proposal outlining the salient features of a prototype procedural provision represents a combination of the provisions in the Ohio, Rhode Island, and New York laws. The Ohio and Rhode Island provisions were selected because they extend the commissions' compliance-enforcement powers to include complaints initiated by organizations and by the commission itself, as proposed in the preceding section. Also incorporated in the proposed provision is the procedural stipulation in the New York law which directs the commission chairman to assign each compliance case to an individual commissioner and makes the latter responsible for handling the case through the conciliation stage.

It is proposed that the procedural provisions relating to the investigation-conciliation stage in existing FEP laws be amended (and future laws formulated) to embody the following essential features:

1. Charges alleging that employers, labor organizations, or employment agencies are engaging in unlawful employment practices may be brought by organizations, or upon the commission's own initiative as well as by aggrieved individuals.

2. Whenever such a charge is made, the chairman of the commission shall designate one of the commissioners to assume responsibility for handling the matter to the point of completion of the conciliation effort.

3. The designated commissioner, with the assistance of the commission's staff, shall conduct a preliminary investigation into the charge.

4. (a) If the commissioner determines after such an investigation that no probable cause exists for crediting the charge, he shall notify the complainant that he has so determined and that the commission will not take further action in the matter.

   (b) If the commissioner determines after such an investigation that probable cause exists for crediting the charge, he shall endeavor, through conference and conciliation, to persuade the respondent to eliminate the unlawful practices. Nothing said or done during such endeavors may be used as evidence in any subsequent proceeding.

5. If, upon conducting such conciliation efforts, the commissioner is satisfied that the unlawful employment practices of the respondent will be eliminated, he may treat the complaint as satisfactorily adjusted and make entry of such disposition in the commission's records.

ENFORCEMENT PROCEDURES

The procedures for enforcing state and municipal FEP laws when efforts to obtain voluntary compliance fail provide, in most of the statutes, for two distinct procedural stages: the hearing stage and the judicial review stage. The former lays down rules for the conduct of public hearings by the commission itself and (when the outcome of the hearing warrants it) for the issuance of cease-and-desist orders. The latter provides for referral of commission orders to the state courts for enforcement and for appeals for court review of commission orders by respondents and complainants and provides the procedures to be followed by the courts in conducting such enforcement proceedings and reviews.

Hearing Stage. The procedures prescribed for the hearing stage in the various FEP laws are considerably more formalized and are spelled out in greater detail than the investigation-conciliation procedures. The obvious reason for this is that, since the hearing stage is utilized only in cases where noncompliance persists after conciliation has failed, formal sanctions are needed to bring about compliance with the law. The procedural provisions relating to the conduct of hearings and the issuance of cease-and-desist orders are closely similar in the great majority of the state and municipal laws.

In a recent proposal for Federal FEP legislation sponsored by the Committee on Education and Labor of the House of Representatives (H.R. 10,144, Eighty-Seventh Congress, second session) the hearing procedure is omitted. Instead the commission is empowered, in cases where conciliation has failed, to bring civil action against respondents in the Federal courts for the purpose of obtaining injunctive relief. The Committee, in its report accompanying the proposal, justifies this departure from the procedure prescribed in most state FEP laws on two grounds, that the proposed procedure is "in line with a longstanding position of the American Bar Association" and "more in keeping with basic principles of American jurisprudence [than the hearing procedure]" and that in practice the state commissions have seldom found it necessary to carry proceedings through the hearing stage.

As has been shown, however, the principal value of the hearing provision lies not in the actual holding of hearings, but in the judicious reference by commissioner-conciliators to the commission's power to order a hearing, with consequent unfavorable publicity for respondent employers and unions as an aid in expediting the conciliation process and obtaining voluntary compliance. It is unlikely that the prospect of a civil court action would have a comparable compliance-inducing effect, since such actions would usually be subject to long delays before being brought to trial and would tend to be overshadowed by other, more dramatic, events in the judicial sphere.

Moreover, while commissions seldom take formal enforcement action against respondents, such action is necessary in some instances. Most such cases involve complex questions of hiring standards and procedures, job performance requirements, etc. Established FEP commissions, owing to the specialized training and experience of their members, are better equipped to deal with these questions than the courts and consequently are better able to determine whether respondents in such situations are engaging in discriminatory employment practices as defined in the law.

Still another advantage of the hearing procedure is that, in cases where the procedure is invoked, the hearing affords a further opportunity for obtaining voluntary compliance through conciliation. On such occasions, the prospects of a negotiated settlement are enhanced by the fact that the conciliation talents and experience of several commissioners are brought to bear on the situation. The New York State Commission, in particular, has obtained voluntary settlement of a number of difficult pattern cases during the hearing proceedings.

We conclude, therefore, that the hearings and order-issuance procedure incorporated in most of the existing state and municipal

FEP laws should be continued and should be incorporated (in somewhat amended form) in future laws. The abbreviated procedural provision set forth below embodies the essential features of the hearings procedure prescribed in the New York State law (on which most of the later laws have been modeled) supplemented by certain amendatory clauses contained in the Ohio law which serve to make the provision clearer and more explicit.

It is proposed that, in line with most existing state FEP laws, the procedural provision relating to the hearing stage in future laws be formulated to include the following essential features:

1. If the designated commissioner fails in his efforts to eliminate the unlawful employment practices through conciliation, he shall issue on the respondent a written complaint stating the charges and requiring the respondent to answer the charges at a hearing before the commission, to be held at a specified time and place.

2. The case in support of the complaint shall be presented by one of the commission's attorneys. The commissioner issuing the complaint shall not participate in the hearing (except as a witness) nor in the deliberations of the commission. The above-mentioned conciliation efforts shall not be received in evidence. In the discretion of the commission, the complainant may be allowed to intervene and present testimony.

3. The commission shall not be bound by the strict rules of evidence prevailing in courts of law or equity. The testimony taken at the hearing shall be under oath and shall be transcribed.

4. If upon all the evidence at the hearing the commission finds that the respondent has engaged in any unlawful employment practices, whether against the complainant or others, the commission shall issue on the respondent an order requiring him to cease and desist from the unlawful practices and to take such affirmative action as in the judgment of the commission will effectuate the purposes of the Act, including a requirement for reports of the manner of compliance. Upon submission of such reports, the commission,

if it finds that the respondent is in affirmative compliance, may issue a declaratory order stating that he has ceased to engage in the unlawful practices.

5. If upon all the evidence at the hearing the commission finds that the respondent has not engaged in any unlawful practices against the complainant or others, it shall issue on the complainant an order dismissing the complaint.

6. A case may be ended at any time during the hearing, or thereafter up to the time the hearing record has been filed in a court, upon agreement between the commission and the respondent for elimination of the unlawful employment practices charged.

Judicial Review Stage. All the enforceable state laws that provide for public hearings and the issuance of cease-and-desist orders also empower the respective commissions to seek court enforcement of their orders. There is a strong consensus among FEP officials that this power further strengthens the hand of commissioners in conducting their conciliation efforts. Moreover, most of the state laws also provide that the complainant or the respondent may petition for review of a commission cease-and-desist order by the courts. Although in practice these provisions are rarely invoked, it is clearly desirable, in the interests of equitable treatment, to extend to both respondents and complainants the right to appeal from commission orders. Accordingly, we conclude that the power of commissions to seek enforcement of their orders in the courts and the right of complainants and respondents to petition for court review of commission orders should be retained in existing state and municipal FEP laws and that these provisions should be incorporated in FEP laws enacted in the future. The following abbreviated provision embraces the main procedural features of the judicial review provision in the New York State law, which has been closely followed in the great majority of subsequently enacted FEP statutes.

It is proposed that, in line with most existing state laws, the judicial review provision in future FEP laws be formulated to include the following procedural features:

1. The commission may petition for enforcement of any of its cease-and-desist orders; and any complainant or respondent claiming to be aggrieved by a cease-and-desist order of the commission may petition for judicial review thereof. Such proceedings shall be brought in the [appropriate state] court in the county where the unlawful practice occurred.

2. Upon filing of a petition in court for enforcement or review of an order of the commission, the commission shall submit to the Court a transcript of the hearing in the case. The Court may grant a request for admission of additional evidence when satisfied that such evidence is newly discovered. The findings of the commission as to the facts shall be conclusive if supported by substantial evidence on the record considered as a whole.

3. Upon consideration of the record and such additional evidence as it has admitted, the Court may issue an order enforcing, modifying, and enforcing as modified, or setting aside the order of the commission. Such order of the Court shall be final, subject to appellate review. Violation of the Court's order shall be punishable as contempt.

Proposed Provisions for a Federal FEP Law

As noted earlier, our purpose in these final chapters is to furnish practical guides to lawmakers and administrators in dealing with the problem of employment discrimination. The foregoing attempt to furnish such a guide at the state and local levels, in terms of a model state FEP law, was based on two conclusions drawn from our analysis of the study findings: that there is a need for improving existing laws and their administration in all of the states possessing such laws, and that there is no less a need for enacting FEP legislation—of the most effective kind that can be devised—in the non-FEP-law areas of the country, and particularly in the Southern states. We concluded further, however, that only through national FEP legislation will it be possible to achieve racial employment equality in *all* states and localities—Southern, Border, and Northern —within the calculable future. While it may soon be possible to obtain passage of FEP laws in several Southern cities, there is little prospect of any such development in the South at large in the reasonably near future. Yet the need for governmental action to promote employment equality is, if anything, more urgent in the South than elsewhere, since employment discrimination is more prevalent and deep-rooted there and since, moreover, the Southern Negro's occupational status has actually deteriorated in recent years and will likely deteriorate further in the years ahead. Finally, as shown in the preceding chapter, Federal FEP legislation would undoubtedly be more effective than state laws, even if all states enacted such statutes. The following proposal for Federal FEP legislation is outlined under the same six sequential headings utilized in the proposal on state and municipal legislation.

DECLARATION OF UNLAWFUL DISCRIMINATORY PRACTICES

The types of discriminatory employer, union, and employment agency practices declared unlawful would of course be the same in the proposed Federal law as in a state FEP law, since the basic purpose and substantive scope of the legislation would be the same in both cases. Hence, the comprehensive list of discriminatory practices proposed for inclusion in the prototype state-municipal law, outlined previously, would be equally appropriate for the proposed Federal law. It would also be necessary to include a "catch-all" clause stating that the practices which are unlawful under the statute are not limited to those listed in the itemized provision.

In addition to explicitly proscribing discriminatory practices in the Federal FEP statute, it would be necessary to bring existing Federal labor laws into conformity with the FEP law. As shown in Chapter 9, the Federal courts have ruled that railroad unions may legally exclude Negroes from membership under the Railway

Labor Act, and the same ruling is applicable to unions covered by the Taft-Hartley Act—which means virtually all other unions. The legislative history of the Landrum-Griffin Act shows that it, too, leaves unions free to exclude Negroes and other minorities. In order to assure that these statutes conformed with the proposed Federal FEP act, it would be necessary to include in the latter a provision stating that anything in the substantive content, legislative history, or subsequent judicial or administrative interpretation of any other law that conflicts with the FEP law is without force or effect.

COMPOSITION AND FUNCTIONS OF FEDERAL FEP COMMISSION

In the proposal on state legislation it is recommended that the prototype law provide for establishment of a commission composed (in the larger states) of from three to seven full-time commissioners appointed by the governor, with a designated salary of at least $20,000 a year and with each commission member participating directly and individually in securing compliance with the law. The vital importance of conciliation in the compliance process leads us to conclude that the agency created to administer the Federal FEP law should also have this structural form and that the individual commission members should participate directly as conciliators in promoting compliance. The independent commission form of regulatory agency, as exemplified by the National Labor Relations Board, the Federal Trade Commission, and other existing administrative bodies, lends itself well to the appointment and development of such a group of "working" fair employment commissioners. The term of office is relatively long—usually five years and in some instances longer; and the salary—$20,000 in most commissions—is adequate to attract public-spirited individuals with the knowledge, experience, and judgment required for effective performance in conducting compliance negotiations. Commission members are appointed directly by the President, which in the case of fair employment commissioners would provide the prestige needed to command respect from employers and union officials. Finally, since the political affiliation of independent commissions is "mixed," with no more than a bare majority of the members affiliated with the same party, as bodies they are generally regarded as being relatively free from political bias.

Accordingly, the proposed Federal FEP law should provide for the establishment of an independent Federal Fair Employment Practices Commission (to be referred to hereafter as the "Federal FEPC") which should be invested with the necessary authority to administer and—with the aid of the Federal courts—to enforce the law. The provisions concerning the makeup of the FEPC should include the following: seven full-time members, to be appointed by the President with the consent of the Senate, no more than four to be of the same political party; seven-year appointments, with staggered beginning dates of the respective members' terms so that one member will be appointed each year; the President to designate one member as Chairman and one member as Vice Chairman.

A provision should also be included outlining the general functions of the FEPC. The functions outlined previously for state and municipal commissions would be equally appropriate for the proposed Federal FEPC.

STAFFING AND COMPENSATION

The problem of the staffing and the compensation of the proposed Federal FEPC parallels that of the commissions in the major FEP-law states, despite the differences in scope and diversity of the operations; accordingly the general provisions relating to staffing suggested previously for the prototype state law would also be applicable to the proposed Federal law. The Federal FEPC would, of course, require a substantially larger and more diversified staff and a larger number of regional offices than any individual state agency, owing to the greater volume and diversity of its compliance workload. On the other hand, the Federal FEPC would be able to utilize the expert personnel and facilities of existing Federal fact-gathering and law-enforcement agencies, and consequently its staffing requirements would be commensurately reduced. The provision of adequate funds for commission and staff salaries and other operating expenses would be a matter for Congressional determination through annual appropriations, and accordingly this question is dealt with separately in Chapter 12.

POWERS OF FEDERAL FEPC

In order to function effectively, the Federal FEPC would need to possess all the powers proposed for the prototype state commission, as outlined in the preceding section. It would also be necessary to provide for certain additional powers to enable the Federal FEPC to negotiate and cooperate with existing state and municipal FEP commissions.

We have noted that in several states with long-established FEP laws, significant reductions in employment discrimination have been achieved through the compliance activities of the respective commissions. It is not contemplated that the proposed Federal law would supplant the existing state and municipal laws nor that it would reduce the scope or range of the respective commissions' activities in administering them. To the contrary, with appropriate cooperative arrangements between the Federal FEPC and state and city commissions, the compliance activities of the existing state and municipal commissions could be made more effective. We do not believe, however, that the Federal FEPC should simply cede all jurisdiction within a particular state or city to the state or municipal agency, as the case may be. In our view, a greater over-all result could be achieved if the jurisdiction were divided between the Federal FEPC, on the one hand, and the existing state and municipal agencies, on the other, in a manner that would permit both to function as effectively as possible. A close approximation to such a division could be achieved through agreements between the Federal FEPC and the respective state and municipal agencies, whereby the former would handle all pattern-compliance cases and other compliance problems involving large multiphase companies with major employing operations in a number of states, leaving to the state and municipal commissions all cases and problems involving employers (or unions or employment agencies) operating wholly within the particular state or locality. For obvious reasons, no state or local agency has been able to deal effectively with pattern compliance problems involving all establishments of multi-establishment companies or indeed any such establishment outside its own jurisdiction. A number of these agencies have testified that they would welcome such a division of jurisdiction with a Federal FEPC.

The Federal FEP law should therefore provide:

1. That its enactment does not preempt or in any way reduce the force and effect of any existing state or municipal law, *except* laws that *require* discrimination and/or segregation in employment.

2. That, where enforceable state or municipal FEP legislation is in effect and where the Federal FEPC has determined that the state or municipal enforcement agency is effectively enforcing this legislation, the Federal FEPC is empowered to seek a written agreement with the state or municipal agency whereby each agency will be responsible for handling such types of noncompliance cases and situations (involving the particular state or city) as may be agreed upon. It is further empowered to consummate arrangements with a state or municipal agency enabling the FEPC to utilize the services of the agency and of its employees in conducting compliance activities remaining under the FEPC's jurisdiction.

PROCEDURES IN INVOKING AND OBTAINING VOLUNTARY COMPLIANCE
WITH FEDERAL FEP LAW

While the Federal FEPC would be chiefly concerned with multistate and other wide-scope employment discrimination situations, it would also be required, in states without FEP laws, to deal with smaller-scale problems and even, to some extent, with complaints filed by individuals. Hence, the range of its compliance activities would be comparable to, though wider than, that of the larger state commissions. Moreover, as has been noted, it is essential to successful administration both at the Federal and state levels that the individual commissioners be responsible for and engage directly in conciliation efforts in all cases involving substantial aggregations of employees. It is apparent, therefore, that the proposal outlining the five salient features of a procedural provision for the conciliation stage in a prototype state-municipal FEP law described previously would be equally suitable for the proposed Federal law.

ENFORCEMENT PROCEDURES FOR FEDERAL FEP LAW

From the outset, under the state and municipal FEP laws, the great bulk of employment discrimination problems dealt with by the commissions have been settled and compliance effected through conciliation, leaving only a small fraction of cases in which formal enforcement action has been necessary. There is every reason to expect that this would also be true under the proposed Federal law. The provisions for formal enforcement powers in the state and municipal laws have, however, proved essential—as *potential* sanctions—in supporting and expediting the commissions' conciliation efforts. It would obviously also be necessary to provide for such powers and for appropriate concomitant procedures in the proposed Federal law.

The question of whether the widely established hearing procedure, with commission orders enforceable in the courts, should be retained, or whether direct civil court actions by commissions would be preferable has already been discussed in the preceding section. The considerations there adduced with respect to state and municipal laws apply with equal cogency to the problem of administering a Federal statute. We therefore conclude that the power of the FEPC to order and conduct public hearings, to issue cease-and-desist orders, and to have them enforced by the courts, should be incorporated in the proposed Federal law, together with appropriate procedures for exercising these powers. Substantially the same procedures as those proposed for the model state-municipal law previously described would be called for in a Federal statute. In the interests of expeditious enforcement, the judicial review procedure should provide that the Federal Commission, in seeking judicial enforcement of cease-and-desist orders, may bypass the Federal District Courts and petition directly to the Courts of Appeal.

12

GUIDE LINES FOR IMPROVING ADMINISTRATION OF FAIR EMPLOYMENT LAWS

The comparative analysis of experience under long-established FEP laws in Chapter 6 showed that the notably better record of progress against discrimination in New York State, New Jersey, and Philadelphia than elsewhere was attributable, not to any differences in statutory provisions, but rather to certain distinctive enforcement policies and practices followed by the FEP agencies in these jurisdictions. In this final chapter, the significance of these policies and practices for FEP commission procedures generally is reviewed, and the resulting conclusions are presented as a series of suggestions for better planning and carrying out of compliance efforts by commissions of all governmental levels.

Employer-Related Compliance Activities

In the earlier proposals, suggesting improvements in the substantive content of antidiscrimination laws, it is recommended that FEP commissions be empowered to process complaints filed by organizations and to initiate complaints on their own motion, in order to facilitate dealing with pervasive discriminatory practices of employers, unions, and employment agencies as distinguished from discriminatory acts against individuals. Arming commissions with these powers, however, merely opens the way for compliance action based on employment patterns. In order to bring about any significant abatement of employment discrimination and expansion of employment opportunities for racial minorities, the commissions must, as a conscious and continuing administrative policy, direct their compliance efforts toward eliminating establishment-wide and organization-wide discriminatory practices.

It would be especially desirable that the proposed Federal FEPC pursue such a policy, since it would be the only agency capable of handling problem situations that are inherently interstate in scope and consequently can be effectively dealt with only through conciliation efforts at a national or regional level. Under the proposed Federal law, it would be feasible for the Federal FEPC to devote most (though probably not all) of its attention to problems involving discriminatory employment patterns, by consummating agreements with state (and on occasion with municipal) commissions of proved effectiveness, whereby these agencies would handle individual-grievance complaints arising within their respective jurisdictions. Moreover, as noted earlier, with such agreements it would also be possible to allocate to the state commissions responsibility for dealing with pattern compliance problems essentially concerned with intrastate or intralocal labor markets, thus enabling the Federal FEPC to give more of its attention to problems inherently interstate in scope—for example, those involving the several units of large national or regional multiplant concerns—and to areas lacking any state or municipal legislation.

To plan and carry out its over-all compliance task as effectively and expeditiously as possible, it would first be necessary for the Federal FEPC to institute a comprehensive survey for assessing the extent and distribution of racial employment discrimination throughout the nation. The survey (which might well be designed and carried out for the FEPC by the Department of Labor) would be conducted in a representative sample of all private and public employing establishments and would elicit information on current employment by race (white versus nonwhite) and by racially significant occupational categories. Correlative information on unemployment by race and occupational categories would be obtainable from the Census Bureau's periodic sample surveys of households. This comprehensive body of racial employment and unemployment data, properly analyzed in terms of significant geographic, industrial, and occupational subdivisions, would enable the Federal FEPC to plan and program its compliance effort over an extended period such as three to five years. It would also facilitate the consummation of jurisdiction-sharing agreements between the Federal FEPC and the several state commissions and would aid the latter in programing their pattern-based compliance activities.

In formulating the Federal FEPC program, the establishment of time priorities for instituting action in the various problem areas would need to be based on the relative pervasiveness of employment discrimination, the existence or absence of effective compliance efforts by established state (or municipal) FEP agencies, and the prospects for early tangible results of compliance efforts in terms of jobs—or better jobs—for members of racial minorities. In situations where the survey revealed that pervasive discrimination existed in all or most firms within a particular industry and geographic area, the compliance effort might well be planned on an industry-wide basis, through joint conciliation conferences with representatives of all firms and labor organizations involved.

In pursuing the broad objective of eliminating over-all patterns of discrimination, commissions at all levels should give primary attention to obtaining affirmative compliance with the FEP mandate. We noted in Chapter 6 that certain of the long-established commissions, in negotiating with noncomplying employers, have for some years insisted as a matter of policy that the resultant conciliation agreements include "affirmative action" provisions, whereby the employers agree to go beyond the mere literal observance of the statutory requirements and make an affirmative effort to employ Negroes in jobs above the menial-unskilled level. This approach is justified on the ground that, under conventional hiring standards, Negro applicants are likely to be less well qualified than whites for such jobs, owing to their lower educational attainments, and on the further ground that the educational standards established for these jobs are often unnecessarily high. The commissions do not suggest that employers hire Negroes who are less well qualified than white applicants, but rather that they broaden their recruitment efforts or that they modify the formal educational requirements. Despite the fact that experience with this approach has been limited, there is little doubt that it constitutes a potent means by which FEP agencies can promote real, as contrasted with mere nominal equality of employment opportunity.

The analysis of commission experience has also shown that the effectiveness of pattern-based compliance efforts by FEP commissions can be further enhanced by conducting periodic follow-up surveys of employment patterns in erstwhile noncomplying establishments for the purpose of assessing the extent and manner of compliance. The experience of the few commissions that have consistently pursued this practice over a period of years indicates that there is a definite positive relationship between the practice and the rather impressive record of results achieved by these commissions. While the resolution of discriminatory-practice problems through conciliation is essentially a voluntary process, a skilled conciliator can and does use the potential power of the commission to invoke legal sanctions as a stimulus to expedite the consummation of conciliation agreements with reluctant noncomplying managements. Similarly, the follow-up survey constitutes a catalyst in the *compliance process*, spurring the respondent management to make a positive effort to employ Negroes and other minorities in desirable jobs and to demonstrate "affirmative compliance." Thus, there are good grounds for concluding that FEP commissions at all levels—Federal, state, and municipal—should adopt the practice of conducting periodic follow-up surveys following the consummation of conciliation agreements involving discriminatory employment patterns.

The most difficult policy problem that commissions have to face in conducting follow-up surveys is whether to permit the identification of employees by race after they have been hired. (It is generally agreed that racial identification on pre-employment application records should be prohibited, and most existing FEP laws so provide.) Some civil rights organizations oppose permitting racial identification on post-employment records, on the ground that it conduces to discrimination in promotions, transfers, layoffs, etc. Many FEP commissions, however, favor permitting such identification in order to facilitate compliance investigations and follow-up reviews, which must otherwise be conducted through "head counts" or other cumbersome and time-consuming devices. It seems clear that the advantages of identifying employees by race on post-employment records considerably outweigh the dangers of abuse. In our view, therefore, the commissions, in negotiating conciliation agreements with noncomplying employers, should include provisions for keeping racial identification records on personnel subsequent to hiring.

One administrative weakness observable in virtually all existing commissions is the tendency, in dealing with exceptionally resistant noncompliers, to prolong conciliation efforts over unduly long periods, in preference to invoking the public hearing and cease-and-desist order procedures. The commissions have exhibited this tendency most frequently in cases involving noncomplying unions, but it has also been much in evidence in employer-related compliance cases. The reluctance of the commissions to invoke the mandatory and legal-sanction features of the FEP laws appears to stem from a desire to create and preserve a public image of the governmental antidiscrimination effort as primarily a persuasive process, by keeping the evidences of coercion at a minimum level. It seems apparent, however, that the net effect of this propensity to stretch out the conciliation process is to reduce the commissions' over-all effectiveness, mainly because it encourages determined noncompliers to continue flouting the law, but also because it consumes a disproportionate amount of the commissions' time and resources.

The obvious way to correct this pervasive weakness is to reverse the present emphasis. In dealing with highly resistant non-complying employers, unions, or employment agencies, commissions should discontinue their conciliation efforts as soon as determined resistance becomes manifest and proceed to invoke the public hearing procedure, followed—where the evidence adduced so warrants—by the issuance of cease-and-desist orders.

The Employment Agency Problem

The persistence of discriminatory referrals of workers by employment agencies in FEP-law states (as well as in states without such laws) poses a troublesome problem for FEP commissions. While the practice continues both in private and public employment offices, its occurrence in the latter is conspicuously incongruous, since the public employment offices and the FEP commissions are integral parts of the same state administrative entities and since the employment offices are financed entirely by Federal funds. As shown in Chapter 6, the basic causes of the continued widespread noncompliance in the public employment office system stem primarily from weaknesses in Federal policies and rules—more especially the failure of the USES to establish an explicit mandatory policy prohibiting discrimination in the operation of public employment offices and the USES's practice of allocating Federal funds to these offices on the basis of their past record of workers placed in jobs, which encourages the acceptance and honoring of discriminatory employer requests for workers. A further contributing factor is the state employment services' refusal, in all FEP-law states except two, to cooperate with the FEP commissions by reporting discriminatory employer job orders to the commissions. This problem likewise stems in part from weakness on the part of the policy-setting Federal agency, the USES, which has failed to authorize such cooperation by the state services.

The USES, first, should establish a clear policy, mandatory on all state employment services, unequivocally prohibiting discrimination in the structure, staffing, and operation of public employment offices and stipulating as a penalty for violation the forfeiture of Federal operating grants. Second, the USES should discard its present formula for allocating Federal funds to local public employment offices and adopt in its place a formula that will encourage referrals on a nondiscriminatory basis. Third, the USES should explicitly authorize the state employment services in FEP-law states to cooperate fully with the respective FEP commissions by reporting all discriminatory job orders received by their constituent local employment offices to the commissions; and the state employment services and FEP commissions should promptly establish such cooperative arrangements. Finally, the FEP commissions should launch vigorous efforts to bring discriminatory employers uncovered through these reporting arrangements into compliance, utilizing the public hearing and court-enforcement procedures when conciliation efforts fail to bring prompt agreement to comply.

Union-Related Compliance Activities

The problem of racial discrimination by labor unions, while relatively narrow in industrial and occupational scope, is perhaps the most difficult problem area confronting FEP commissions. Largely for this reason, it is also the area in which they have made the least progress toward eliminating discriminatory practices. The two most widespread discriminatory union practices are exclusion of Negroes from membership by local unions in the plumbing, electrical, sheet-metal, and other high-skill construction crafts and racial discrimination in allocating job opportunities to members by local unions in various lower-skill craft and noncraft occupations.

Exclusionist craft unions pose an unusually difficult compliance problem for FEP commissions, for three closely related reasons:

first, admission to these unions is decided by vote of the incumbent membership; second, there is a strong sentiment against admitting Negroes and other minorities in most high-skill craft unions; and third, the commissions cannot deal directly with large aggregations of union members, but must confine their conciliation efforts to the union leaders. Since the leaders are elected officials, they are seldom willing to go counter to the views of their constituents. Thus, the conciliation approach is ill-suited for dealing with the problem of racial exclusionism in craft unions.

These same factors are also present to some extent in local union situations involving discrimination in the operation of union job-referral systems. In addition, when such unions are approached by FEP agencies, they frequently deny any intent to discriminate and insist they are merely complying with the express requests of employers that only white workers be referred to them. Hence, the commissions are faced with the added problem of determining which party is the actual discriminator. Owing largely to these circumstances, most commissions have been reluctant to institute compliance programs aimed at discriminatory unions; and even where they have done so, they have seldom succeeded in obtaining more than token compliance.

The foregoing considerations lead to several suggestions as to how FEP commissions can make their union-oriented compliance activities more effective and bring more discriminatory unions into compliance. In the first place, it is essential that the commissions direct their main efforts toward eliminating over-all discriminatory practices of unions rather than seeking redress for aggrieved individuals. This is as clearly essential to meaningful accomplishment in the union area as it is in dealing with employer practices.

Second, with regard to exclusionist craft unions, it is highly unlikely that the widely followed practice of "stretching out" conciliation efforts will prove fruitful in such cases, owing to the strong rank-and-file opposition to admitting Negroes that exists in many craft unions. In seeking compliance by strongly exclusionist craft unions, commissions would be well advised to discontinue their conciliation efforts whenever it becomes evident that resistance will be prolonged and promptly thereafter invoke the public hearings procedure. It may be expected that the mere prospect of a public hearing, with its attendant adverse publicity, will induce some craft unions to revise their admission practices. In other instances, where recalcitrance is more persistent, the actual holding of the hearing and subsequent issuance of a cease-and-desist order may well have the desired effect. The commissions should, however, allow no more than a reasonably adequate period for compliance with such orders before seeking enforcement by the courts. In those instances where referral to the courts proves necessary, the issuance of a confirming order by the court, with contingent substantial fines for continued nonobservance, should be sufficient to make the most die-hard exclusionist unions open their membership rolls.

Again with regard to exclusionist local unions, the commissions should give special attention to obtaining removal of racial barriers to apprentice training and should seek commitments from the respondent unions that they will make affirmative efforts to place Negro youths in their apprentice programs. When admission to apprentice programs is decided jointly by the union and the employers, the conciliation efforts should of course be conducted jointly with both parties.

In dealing with local unions that discriminate against Negro members in the functioning of union job referral offices, it may not always be necessary to short-cut the conciliation procedure, since union leaders usually control the operation of these offices without close supervision by the membership. On the other hand, union leaders in such situations, when confronted with charges of discrimination in distributing job opportunities among the membership, have often sought to attribute the blame to discriminatory employers. Hence, in union job-referral cases commissions should, whenever possible, conduct conciliation negotiations jointly with union and employer representatives.

Guides for Legislators in Appropriating
Operational Funds for Commissions

More effective administration and enforcement of FEP laws— the objective of the three preceding series of recommendations— can be achieved only if the administering agencies are adequately manned, in terms of caliber of commissioners and size and competence of supporting staffs, to carry out the suggested improvements in planning and conducting the compliance effort. This objective, in turn, can be realized only if the commissions are provided with sufficient funds to afford salaries that will attract commissioners possessing the requisite qualifications and that will attract competent professional staff personnel in the required numbers. In short, the provision of adequate appropriations by the respective legislative bodies is without doubt the most important single requirement for the effective functioning of FEP agencies.

In the chapters dealing with state and municipal FEP agencies, it was pointed out that the New York State Commission has perennially had the largest annual budget of any state FEP agency and concomitantly has been—and still is—well in the lead among agencies in terms of adequacy of manpower. It was also shown that the New York State Commission, through its compliance efforts, has achieved a larger aggregate reduction in employment discrimination than any other state FEP agency; and it was concluded that this record of achievement is attributable in substantial part to the Commission's relatively favorable budget and manpower situation. More specifically, it was noted that, in comparison with the New York Commission's 1960 budget (and with due allowance for that state's larger compliance work load) the budgets of the commissions in five other major FEP-law states were only fractionally adequate—less than one-third in the case of California, Michigan, and Ohio and somewhat more than one-third in the case of New Jersey and Pennsylvania.

While it is not possible to state with any precision the magnitude of the appropriations that are needed in particular states to permit adequate enforcement of the FEP laws, certain rough guide lines can be outlined on the basis of the foregoing summary of study findings. Thus, in view of the evidence of substantial accomplishment in New York State, its expenditure for FEP-law administration may be taken as a rough criterion of minimum adequacy. The New York Commission's budget for the current (1963) fiscal year is $1,537,000. The New York Commission, however, unlike most other FEP agencies, has jurisdiction over discrimination in housing and public accommodations as well as in employment; consequently, the New York figure must be scaled down in proportion to the volume of housing and public accommodations compliance activity in order to make it a valid criterion for judging the adequacy of the budgets in the other FEP-law states. When this allowance is made, the current New York budget figure to be used as a standard of minimum adequacy becomes approximately $1,100,000.

Even when compared with this scaled-down figure, however, the current and recent budgets of the five above-named states, from $150,000 to $250,000 a year, are obviously grossly inadequate. On the basis of the New York State standard of adequacy and with proper allowance for its moderately larger compliance workload, the appropriations for the commissions in these five states would need to range between $600,000 and $900,000—more than triple the current and recent budget amounts in each instance. Comparable increases in appropriations would be required in most of the remaining FEP-law states. And if and when FEP laws are enacted in Southern states, the commissions created to administer them would undoubtedly also require appropriations of this order of magnitude, owing to the large Negro populations and consequent heavy compliance work load in most of these states.

Any estimate of the appropriations that would be needed for the proposed Federal FEPC must of necessity be even more imprecise, since the extent to which such a commission would supplant or complement existing state and municipal commissions cannot be predicted. It is possible, however, to indicate, in very approximate terms, the upper and lower limits of commission budget amounts that would be required. Thus, if the adjusted New York State budget of $1,100,000 is translated into national terms, on the basis of the respective state and national totals of nonwhite population, the resultant figure is approximately $15 million. This may be taken as a rough estimate of the annual cost of operating a Federal FEPC, on the assumption that it would largely supplant existing state and local commissions. If we assume that the Federal FEPC would operate only in states having no FEP laws, the figure is approximately $9 million. The proposed Federal program, however, envisions cooperative arrangements between the Federal FEPC and the various existing state and municipal agencies; accordingly, the Federal FEPC budget requirement would probably fall somewhere between these limits. It is worth noting that these estimated budgets compare favorably with the actual budgets of existing Federal regulatory agencies, which in recent years have ranged from approximately $8 million for the Federal Power Commission to $20 million for the Interstate Commerce Commission. The NLRB, the regulatory body whose functions and procedures most closely resemble those of the proposed Federal FEPC, had a budget in 1961 of $17,300,000.

Expenditures on the scale of these estimates are small in comparison with the outlays that would be necessary to alleviate the Negro's disadvantaged status in other areas of daily living, such as education, housing, and health. For example, it has been estimated that additional expenditures of at least $50 million a year would be necessary to bring the educational level of Negro children in New

York City up to parity with the city's white children. Applied on a national scale, the annual cost of such a program would amount to nearly 1 billion dollars. Thus, it is evident that the outlay needed for effective administration of FEP legislation on a national scale is only a small fraction of the expenditure that would be required to provide equality of educational opportunity for the nation's Negro group.

Concluding Observations

To place the program outlined above in somewhat broader perspective, we may well conclude with a brief estimate of what FEP legislation, if properly designed and effectively administered, can be expected to accomplish. The short-run limitations on its potentialities are readily apparent. Even a comprehensive Federal law, and even the most effective implementation of such a law, could bring about only a rather modest improvement in the Negro's occupational status in the near future. Significant further progress could be anticipated in the semiskilled job categories in which Negroes already have substantial representation; and sizable gains could also be expected in the skilled crafts, in clerical and sales occupations, and in various supervisory capacities.

In most managerial and professional occupations, however, little improvement would be possible, since only a small fraction of the Negroes now in the labor force are educationally qualified to hold even entry jobs in these categories. Manifestly, the nation's Negro minority cannot aspire to full occupational parity with whites until effective public measures are instituted that will assure equal educational opportunities. Even then full parity cannot be realized until a younger generation of Negroes has had time to avail itself of the full sequence of the improved opportunities.

The admittedly modest improvement that effective FEP legislation alone could bring about would nevertheless be an essential and important first step toward eventual full job and income equality for the Negro group. Occupational upgrading of a substantial proportion of present-generation Negro breadwinners would make additional years of education for their offspring financially possible. Equally important, the visible evidence of Negro adults in representative numbers holding skilled, respect-commanding jobs would provide a stimulant for younger Negroes to aspire to and prepare for still better jobs—a source of motivation that is sadly lacking as long as their elders are confined to menial and unskilled work. The aim of this study will be accomplished if the proposed program, by pointing the way to wider and more effective application of fair employment legislation, can aid Negroes and other disadvantaged minorities in taking this first major step toward full equality.

BIBLIOGRAPHY

Allport, Gordon W. The Nature of Prejudice. Cambridge, Mass., Addison-Wesley, 1954.

Babow, Irving, and Edward Howden. A Civil Rights Inventory of San Francisco. Council for Civic Unity of San Francisco, 1958.

Becker, Gary S. The Economics of Discrimination. Chicago, University of Chicago Press, 1957.

Berger, Morroe. Effects of Fair Employment Legislation in States and Municipalities. Staff Report, U.S. Senate, Eighty-Second Congress, Second Session. Washington, D.C., Government Printing Office, 1952.

———. Equality by Statute: Legal Controls over Group Discrimination. New York, Columbia University Press, 1952.

Bullock, Paul. Merit Employment: Nondiscrimination in Industry. Los Angeles, Institute of Industrial Relations, University of California, 1960.

Dewey, Donald. Four Studies of Negro Employment in the Upper South. Washington, D.C., National Planning Association, 1953.

Frazier, E. Franklin. The Negro in the United States. New York, MacMillan, 1949.

Gallaher, Art, Jr. The Negro and Employment Opportunities in the South—Houston. Atlanta, Southern Regional Council, 1962.

Ginzberg, Eli. The Negro Potential. New York, Columbia University Press, 1956.

Glazer, Nathan, and Daniel Moynihan. Beyond the Melting Pot. Cambridge, Mass., Technology Press, 1963.

Greenberg, Jack. Race Relations and American Law. New York, Columbia University Press, 1959.

Hawley, Langston T. Negro Employment in the Birmingham Metropolitan Area. Washington, D.C., National Planning Association, 1954.

Henderson, Vivian W. The Economic Status of Negroes: In the Nation and in the South. Atlanta, Southern Regional Council, 1963.

Hope, John, II. Equality of Opportunity: A Union Approach to Fair Employment. Washington, D.C., Public Affairs Press, 1956.

——. Three Southern Plants of International Harvester Company. Washington, D.C., National Planning Association, 1953.

Javits, Jacob K. Discrimination—U.S.A. Rev. ed. New York, Washington Square Press, 1962.

Jones, Major J. The Negro and Employment Opportunities in the South—Chattanooga. Atlanta, Southern Regional Council, 1962.

Kesselman, Louis C. The Social Politics of FEPC. Chapel Hill, N.C., University of North Carolina Press, 1948.

King, Martin Luther. Stride Toward Freedom: The Montgomery Story. New York, Harper, 1958.

Konvitz, Milton R. A Century of Civil Rights. With a Study of State Law Against Discrimination by Theodore Leskes. New York, Columbia University Press, 1961.

Marrow, Alfred J. Changing Patterns of Prejudice. New York, Chilton, 1963.

——. Living Without Hate. New York, Harper, 1951.

Myrdal, Gunnar. An American Dilemma: The Negro Problem and Modern Democracy. 2 vols. New York, Harper, 1944.

Nicholls, William H. Southern Tradition and Regional Progress. Chapel Hill, N.C., University of North Carolina Press, 1960.

Nichols, Lee. Breakthrough on the Color Front. New York, Random House, 1954.

Norgren, P. H., A. N. Webster, R. D. Borgeson, and M. B. Patten. Employing the Negro in American Industry. New York, Industrial Relations Counselors, 1959.

Northrup, Herbert R. Organized Labor and the Negro. New York, Harper, 1944.

Rose, Arnold. The Negro in America. New York, Harper, 1948.

—— and Caroline Rose. America Divided: Minority Group Relations in the United States. New York, Knopf, 1948.

Ross, Malcolm. All Manner of Men. New York, Reynal and Hitchcock, 1948.

Ruchames, Louis. Race, Jobs, and Politics: The Story of FEPC. New York, Columbia University Press, 1953.

Seidenberg, Jacob. Negroes in the Work Group. Ithaca, N.Y., New York State School of Industrial and Labor Relations, Cornell University, 1950.

Silard, John, and Harold Galloway. State Executive Authority to Promote Civil Rights. Washington, D.C., The Potomac Institute, 1963.

Sterner, Richard. The Negro's Share. New York, Harper, 1943.

UNESCO. Race and Science: The Race Question in Modern Science. New York, Columbia University Press, 1961.

U.S. Commission on Civil Rights. Civil Rights '63: 1963 Report. Washington, D.C., U.S. Government Printing Office, 1963.

——. The 50 States Report. Washington, D.C., U.S. Government Printing Office, 1961.

——. 1961 Report: Book I, Voting. Washington, D.C., U.S. Government Printing Office, 1961.

——. 1961 Report: Book III, Employment. Washington, D.C., U.S. Government Printing Office, 1961.

Weaver, Robert C. Negro Labor: A National Problem. New York, Harcourt, Brace, 1946.

INDEX

Aaron, Benjamin, 218n
Administration: FEP laws, 96, 266–79; of employment by Federal civilian establishments, 193–95, 202; Railway Labor Act, 211–13; NLRB, 213–14
Advertising, prohibition of discriminatory, 245, 246
Air Force, see Armed forces
Airline Pilots Union, discrimination by, 41
Alabama: Negro voting registration in, 236; redistricting in, 238
Alaska: FEP law, 93n, 96; budget and staff of FEP commission, 101
Amalgamated Clothing Workers: Southern locals, 50; fair practices program, 52
Amalgamated Meat Cutters: Southern locals, 50
American Federation of Musicians, 141, 142; segregation by, 44
Amendments, suggested, to FEP laws, 244–58
Apprenticeship, discrimination in: by unions, 22, 48–49, 142; FEP laws and, 95–96; prohibition, 246, 274
Arizona, FEP law of, 93n
Arkansas, Negro voting strength in, 236, 237
Armed forces: segregation in, 180, 183; integration of, 182–92, 202, 203; employment opportunities for Negroes, 189–92, 203, 227–29; occupations of Negroes in, 190–92, 203
Army, see Armed forces
Army General Classification Test (AGCT), white and Negro performance on, 186
Atlanta: employment discrimination in, 24–27, 170, 200, 201; Federal employment in, 196, 200; Negro voting strength in, 237

Atomic Workers' union, Southern locals, 50
Automobile Workers' union (UAW), fair practice programs, 52–55
Automotive industry, Negro employment in, 24–25, 170

Baltimore: FEP commission, 94n; discrimination by employment agencies, 131; industrial employment in, 170; FEP law, 225, 226, 237
Bamberger, Michael A., 102n
Banking, Negro employment in, 27, 226; FEP commissions and, 119–21, 124, 144
Berger, Morroe, 227n
Birmingham, Federal employment in, 196
Boilermakers Union, discrimination by, 41
Boycotts, job discrimination and, 10, 11, 223, 224
Bricklayers' union, and FEP commission action, 140
Brotherhood of Locomotive Firemen and Enginemen, 41, 207, 208, 214, 215
Brotherhood of Railroad Trainmen, 46, 139
Brotherhood of Railway and Steamship Clerks, 41, 44, 46, 141, 142
Budgets: FEP commissions, 99–102, 145, 147, 231, 275, 276; Presidential FEP commissions, 155, 156, 176; Committee on Government Employment Policy, 194; proposed appropriations, 275–78; proposed Federal FEP commission, 277, 278
Building trades, see Construction industry
Bureau of Labor and Management Reports (U.S. Department of Labor), 43
Byers, Jean, 182n